The Builder's Guide to the Tech Galaxy

Martin Schilling, Thomas Klugkist

The Builder's Guide to the Tech Galaxy

99 Practices to Scale Startups into Unicorn Companies

Registered office
John Wiley & Sons Ltd, The Atrium, Southern Gate, Chichester, West Sussex, PO19 8SQ, United Kingdom

Editorial Office
John Wiley & Sons Ltd, The Atrium, Southern Gate, Chichester, West Sussex, PO19 8SQ, United Kingdom

For details of our global editorial offices, customer services, and more information about Wiley products visit us at www.wiley.com.

Wiley also publishes its books in a variety of electronic formats and by print-on-demand. Some content that appears in standard print versions of this book may not be available in other formats.

Library of Congress Cataloging-in-Publication Data

Names: Schilling, Martin, author. | Klugkist, Thomas, author.
Title: The builder's guide to the tech galaxy : 99 practices to scale startups into unicorn companies / Martin Schilling, Thomas Klugkist.
Description: Hoboken, NJ : John Wiley & Sons, Inc., 2022. | Includes bibliographical references.
Identifiers: LCCN 2021062935 (print) | LCCN 2021062936 (ebook) | ISBN 9781119890423 (cloth) | ISBN 9781119892069 (adobe pdf) | ISBN 9781119891598 (epub)
Subjects: LCSH: High-technology industries—Management. | Internet industry—Management. | New business enterprises—Management. | Small business—Growth.
Classification: LCC HD62.37 .S35 2022 (print) | LCC HD62.37 (ebook) | DDC 658—dc23/eng/20220114
LC record available at https://lccn.loc.gov/2021062935
LC ebook record available at https://lccn.loc.gov/2021062936

Cover Design: Wiley
Cover Image: © AlexanderTrou/Shutterstock (modified by Wiley)

8/2/22BB

Printed in Great Britain by Bell and Bain Ltd, Glasgow

For Susanne and Mercedes
and the many entrepreneurs who take personal risks every day,
create millions of new jobs and are working on technological
solutions to tackle the most pressing issues of our time.

The Builder's Guide Partners

We would like to thank the following partners for their invaluable support and help. Without them taking the time to share their knowledge and work on this book, *The Builder's Guide* would not have been possible.

Partners of The Builder's Guide

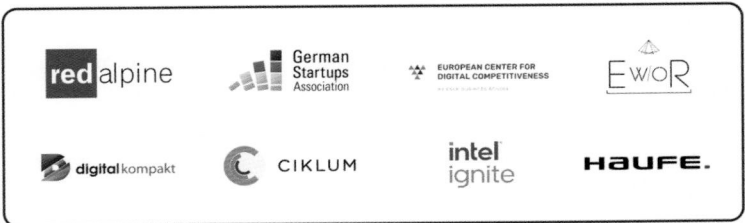

Chapter co-authors

Johannes Lenhard, Hannah Leach – *Environmental, Social and Governance (ESG)*

Constanze Buchheim, Manjuri Sinha, Chris Bell – *People (HR) Excellence*

Johnny Quach, Sven Grajetzki – *Product Management Excellence*

Dr. Christoph Richter – *Technology Excellence*

Kelly Ford – *B2C Marketing Excellence*

Karan Korpal Sharma – *B2B Sales Excellence*

Dr. Nikolas Glusac – *Service Operations Excellence*

Matthias Wilrich – *Supply Chain Excellence*

Vanessa Pinter – *Finding Growth Capital*

Experts

Oliver Ahlberg	Jane Kennedy	Lauriane Requena
Patrick Alberts	Nate Kupp	Marcus Rex
Michael Anspach	Robert Lacher	Dr. Wolf Richter
Jan Bartels	Samantha Lee-Kroll	Christoph Richter
Chris Bell	James Lennon	Jeremy Richter
Gavin Bell	Joshua Levy	Mark Roberge
Neil Berrie	Oliver Löffler	Martin Rode
Gilles BianRosa	Andriy Lysyuk	Lars Rysell
Constanze	Stephan Mansfield	Mika Salmi
Buchheim	Christian Miele	Joachim Schreiner
Ramon Abalo Costa	Léa Miggiano	Stephan Schulze
Filip Dames	Paul Murphy	Dominik Schwarz
Dr. Daniel Holle	Christian Nagel	Thilo Semmelbauer
Gero Decker	Johann Jakob Napp	Birte Sewing
Matt Dixon	Peter Niederhauser	Mahdi Shariff
Tamer El-Hawari	Joern Nikolay	Bogdan Shestakov
Jan Engelhardt	Ciaràn O'Leary	Alexander
Kelly Ford	Christian Osterland	Shevchenko
Florian Furthmüller	Pierre Dominique	Eusden Shing
Eva Glanzer	Ostrowski	Manjuri Sinha
Sven Grajetzki	Anna Ott	Daniel Stammler
Edward Hartman	Christian Poensgen	Jacco van der Kooij
Johannis Hatt	Marc Pohl	Frauke von Polier
Florian Heinemann	Johnny Quach	Christian von Trotha
Christian Hertlein	Ramzi Rafih	Fabian Wesner
Chad Jennings	Madhavan Ramanujam	Felix Würtenberger
Stephanie Kaiser	Scott Raymond	Nils Wolfram
Audrys Kažukauskas	Christian Rebernik	

The Builder's Guide Team

Dünya Baradari
Lead Analyst, Editor

Helene Jung
Lead Analyst

Lyndsey Walsh
Lead Editor

Lucero Barrueto
Lead Analyst

Isabel Kovacevic
Lead Designer

Akeli Mieland
Editor

Ferdinand Dabitz
Lead Analyst

Hugo Schlesinger
Lead Analyst

John Mulford
Analyst, Editor

Nadim Hammoud
*Lead Analyst
& Designer*

Johannes Lenhard
Academic Advisor

Adrian Lehmann
Video Editor

Grant Price
Lead Editor

Nina Gründing
Editor

Harriatte Tran
Designer

Tobias August Ilg
Chief Editor

For more details on our contributors and additional resources visit
www.buildersguide.org.

Table of Contents

Forewords

Building the Third Way

Europe is in danger of becoming the biggest open-air museum in the world. When it comes to the digitization race, our record is truly abysmal. Unicorn companies are rare in general, but the European variety is scarcer than the rest. While Europe is now home to an encouraging 33% of all VC-backed startups, only 14% of unicorns have found their start on this continent. Another damning figure is that only 2 of the 20 most valuable unicorn companies in the world are European. In short, we fail to scale. Everyone needs to do better: the founders, the financiers and also the state, in which I mean governments, legislation and administrations.

This is not a minor matter. It is an existential threat to our economy, our society and our way of life. At the time of writing, only Apple, the largest of the five FAANG companies (Facebook, Amazon, Netflix and Alphabet (Google)), is worth as much as all 90 companies in the DAX and MDAX combined. Tech hypergrowth has made history in the liberal United States. Meanwhile, China is further accelerating its state-controlled technological progress. We are in urgent need of a "third way": a European strategy that can be pursued independently from these dominant players. Otherwise, Europe will undoubtedly become less and less relevant economically and politically. We simply will not get a second chance to regain our digital and political sovereignty – something that the United States, our partner on the global stage, would much prefer for us to have, too.

To establish this third way, we as politicians have a crucial duty to improve European regulatory frameworks in a number of ways. Here, the dominance of the tech giants is the single most important issue we need to tackle, and we need to do this swiftly and rigorously. Google is abusing smaller businesses that are dependent on it by acting as a gatekeeper to online services while taking the lion's share of their profits. Amazon is progressively turning into a "customs office," which no retailer can avoid. Lastly, WhatsApp is now the de facto communication tool for people in the digital era, with few alternatives available.

To break up these monopolistic situations, we need to regain control over our most valuable resource: our data. We need to put regulation in place that makes market-dominating enterprises like Google and Amazon share the data they collect from European users with all competitors to create a level playing field. Furthermore, we are in need of regulations that facilitate genuine connectivity when using messenger services like WhatsApp (i.e., people should be able to communicate with users from other platforms like Threema or Signal with no issues). This competition will be of benefit to both users and, perhaps more importantly, to all competitors.

However, as we currently have no tech giants in Europe imposing their own technological standards and regulations regarding connectivity, interoperability will only be effective if Europe starts setting its own digital standards. We should mandate organizations like CEN/Ceneleg and ETSI to develop shared open standards. This will pave the way for more interoperability and lead to a greater sense of efficiency with lower costs for government agencies and companies. The result: a keen competitive advantage for the European tech industry on the global stage.

Moreover, the state itself needs to get better and faster (and better faster). Without digital and modern public administrative processes, the private markets will simply not be able to flourish. Additionally, we need more capital. Europe is lacking financial sovereignty, especially in terms of later-stage venture capital and SPACs. We should be creating more incentives by building up a state pension fund along the lines of Norway or Sweden, by exempting VC funds from value-added tax, pushing the exit prospects of startups through equity investments by the European Investment Bank and publicly promoting startup funds for broad, low-risk participation by all employees.

Finally, we need more expertise. Once European governments have established a functional framework, the playing field will be open for ambitious startup builders who are constantly faced with managing the unknown in a dynamic and complex tech ecosystem. This is where *The Builder's Guide* comes in. The expertise needed to transform a small startup with a team of fewer than a hundred people into a scale-up company with more than a thousand employees is both rare and intangible.

You cannot "create" this knowledge through legislation or policy, and there is a minimal chance of encountering these skills and insights in an academic setting. The audacious goal of *The Builder's Guide* is to gather the secrets of company-building, structure them in a digestible format and make them accessible to a wide audience.

In Europe, we need more projects like *The Builder's Guide*: created by builders for builders, enriched by the collective experiences of seasoned scale-up leaders and equipped with the potential to accelerate Europe's efforts to catch up with the United States and China. I hope and believe that the future founders of the next "European Facebook" will be inspired and guided by the many actionable and well-grounded insights offered by this handbook. When this happens, *The Builder's Guide* will have succeeded in its ambitious mission.

Thomas Heilmann, *Member of the German Parliament*

Strengthening Europe's Position in Times of Digital Transformation

Modern technology has changed our lives in countless ways and it continues to revolutionize how we communicate, work and live. It has also had a significant impact on education, health and wellbeing, as well as on our productivity.

In line with this trend, the European technology sector offers attractive investment opportunities with promising valuations and excellent growth prospects for many companies. However, as the European ecosystem matures, it has become even clearer that a robust European support system to promote, challenge and foster local innovators from their very early stages to the public markets is still missing. And the technology that we use in our daily lives is missing European values and ideas.

If Europe wants to fund a thriving tech scene and foster digital sovereignty, it needs a thriving financial scene as well. Currently, European tech companies do not have the same access to capital as companies in the United States or Asia. There is a considerable need for action in Europe to provide young innovative companies – especially in the growth phase – with the necessary capital. Capital ultimately decides whether young start-ups become unicorns and global pioneers or not.

We have founded Lakestar to contribute to solving this issue: to identify, fund and grow European technology companies that are capable of re-shaping our modern life. By being deeply embedded in Europe's growth-stage and pre-IPO ecosystem, we know what is needed. As a VC, you have to support European technology entrepreneurs along the entire growth journey. On the one hand, you have to offer both angel invest-ing and strategic seed investments in order to nurture the technology ecosystem from the very early stages. On the other hand, you have to provide an efficient route to transition from private to public markets – like how technology-focused SPACs (Special Purpose Acquisition Com-panies) can. However, the broadened investment scope provides for not only entrepreneurs. Investors also benefit from working with a partner who covers the entire commercial lifecycle and who has the latest inno-vation, capital markets development and exit environment at the front of their mind.

I am convinced that Europe needs to create its own digital sovereignty to reduce dependency on foreign funds and to strengthen the control over its tech innovation. Listings via SPACs can help us close the gaps that we in Europe traditionally have when it comes to equipping our companies with sufficient capital. The biggest needs involve companies that require 200 to 300 million euros in capital to continue growing. Therefore, we aim to invest in European companies that otherwise would have needed to raise capital from US markets. This is the only way we can prevent a structural sell-off of European companies to the United States. We want to play our part in making this happen.

Our aim is to invest in companies to help develop them into European tech champions that are capable of creating European independ-ence. *The Builder's Guide* makes an indispensable contribution toward strengthening Europe's position in the long term during these times of digital transformation.

Dr. Klaus Hommels, *CEO of Lakestar*

Scale-ups as the Future of Our Economy

Startups and scale-ups are the keys to our future economy. They create new jobs, pave the way for sustainable prosperity and ensure our technological sovereignty. They are also of critical importance if we in Europe are to meet the major global challenges of the future and make the world a healthy, more prosperous place for everyone.

For that to happen, startup founders themselves need a vibrant startup ecosystem. In particular, we need to give startups in Europe the tools with which to better attract world-class talent. It is also essential to nurture existing skills within our startup ecosystem. Furthermore, talent has to be fostered at all ages and for all genders, without discrimination.

We must eliminate the talent bottleneck, or we risk squandering the incredible momentum that European tech companies have built up in recent years. The next Google, Amazon, Facebook or Netflix could very well come from Europe, but for that to happen, we need to take the regulation for employee ownership to the next level – amongst other things.

At the German Startups Association, our mission is to stand by founders and startup builders, to pass on knowledge critical to startups and to make Europe a continent of openness and innovation. *The Builder's Guide* is poised to play a key role in this, and the knowledge compiled in this manual will give invaluable support to startup entrepreneurs as they scale their ventures and build talented workforces.

Above all, *The Builder's Guide* answers the essential questions: How can a startup set its direction? How can employers attract the best possible team? How can startup leaders build functional excellence in key departments? What is the best way to acquire growth capital?

The answers to these questions matter – both now and in the future. I am delighted to see these core lessons written down. I am sure *The Builder's Guide* will inspire many future unicorn builders to achieve success.

Christian Miele, *President of the German Startups Association*

Partnerships as a Driving Force for a Strong European Tech Ecosystem

The European startup ecosystem is quietly emerging from the dominant shadows cast by its counterparts from both the East and West and shows a promise of maturity and unicorn potential. Investment in European startups tracked at $21.4 billion in the first quarter of 2021, with funding at every stage showing an uptick.

In truth, startup ecosystems are – in part – defined by the size of their unicorn herds. And though we're growing, we are drastically falling short. While Europe generates 36% of all formally funded startups, it creates just 14% of the world's unicorns. The question is: Where is this disproportion coming from?

While the size and diversity of our region engenders a breeding ground for startups, it is also our Achilles' heel. With no single epicenter to act as a beacon of guidance, our startups often lose their way, their drive and the fight. That's why there's a clear and urgent call right now for all stakeholders who can lend a hand to nurture growth and help unite the European community.

The Builder's Guide is an important step forward in developing this center of experiences and mentorship while providing guidance that will help founders shorten the learning curves and ensure the region can buck the challenges of disparity seen across the global startup ecosystem.

The vision of building a strong European ecosystem is what sits at the heart of what we do at Ciklum. JustEat and eToro are just two examples of fast-growth startups that we have supported in their mission to redefine the way things are done and place a permanent mark on the future landscape for the better. I remember these and many other companies having only a dozen employees when Ciklum joined them on their journey, and we remained with them by helping them grow from those early stages right through to unicorn status.

I envisage a market where more founders from within the European ecosystem will aim and successfully grow companies with the same international dominance of their American West Coast counterparts, building meaningful multi-product platform businesses that stand shoulder to shoulder with the likes of Google, Amazon, Facebook, Tencent, etc.

What I've learned from working with some of the most inspirational and successful European startup leaders, as well as my own unconventional journey, is the importance of partnership. I've also seen how vital it is to forge your own path – think the Gordian knot – after all, how can you truly innovate if you are treading well-worn paths?

Part of their innovation and success comes down to finding the right talent. There will be bumps in the road, and your response rate will be determined by the resilience and strength of your team – whether that's internal or outsourced, leading product engineering practices or ongoing product discovery. It's about building capabilities that can continuously evolve in a perpetually shifting marketplace. You don't want to be locked into a technology that in two years' time will leave you stuck in the past.

Look at eToro, they democratized traditionally privileged trading opportunities, or JustEat, which has brought regional restaurant-quality food to the masses in times of lockdown. They forged their own paths, partnered with the right people to leverage their potential and scale up and lastly, never stood still.

Now, we are at the beginning of a bigger journey: one where a region-wide pool of leaders, thinkers, and operators will come together to establish a vital nerve center that will shape the next generation of unicorns. For those lucky enough to have businesses that have grown from Europe, there is a responsibility to take accountability and channel back this momentum into the system and pay it forward.

The Builder's Guide is going to be essential for founders who are on their journey of fast scale. The actionable takeaways that follow will help push the next generation of startups to meet global ambitions and establish a practice of perpetual discovery that will keep you at the front of the field today, and more crucially, tomorrow.

Kulraj Smagh, *CEO at Ciklum*

Boosting the Likelihood of More European Unicorns

Launching an investor-funded startup has always been a business where the outlier is king. Even before they part with their cash, a venture capitalist knows there will likely be one or two overly successful outliers that will make the fund really successful. However, the majority of startups will either deliver an average performance or fail altogether. It is down to the billion-dollar companies, or "unicorns," as they are known, to compensate for the losers. Unicorns are then linked to major economies of scale and all the economic factors – jobs, social impact, satellite start-ups, etc. – that go with it.

With this in mind, it comes as no surprise that investors are optimizing their activities to identify outlier candidates as accurately as possible. Then, once the outlier is in their cross-hairs, they ramp up their support. In other words, the market for startup financing is geared primarily toward increasing the return on investing in possible outlier companies and betting on their success, rather than getting behind average startup projects.

When it comes to startup creation, recent history shows that Europe has a strong footprint but fails to keep pace at all in creating unicorns or decacorns (companies with a ten-billion valuation). Any framework that could help to improve the ratio of startups to unicorns is essential to the scene.

The Builder's Guide makes this contribution by translating the experiences of successful founders into an in-depth, yet accessible framework. Other companies can use the lessons, KPIs and best practices in *The Builder's Guide* to increase their chances of securing the coveted unicorn status. While factors such as luck and timing cannot be controlled, all the operational elements of the journey can be – as *The Builder's Guide* makes abundantly clear. In an otherwise GAFA (Google, Apple, Facebook and Amazon)-dominated landscape, where software startups are enabling strong economies of scale like never before, this kind of tool kit is immensely important. This is especially true as entrepreneurship should not, as it is claimed in Europe, be about growth as an end in itself. Instead, it is about genuine value and sustainability. Increasing that likelihood is a core element of this book. In the best case, it will generate not only imitators but more discourse about the valuable content within.

Joel Kaczmarek, *Managing Director at digital kompakt*

Forewords

Preparing Europe for maturity

We live in unprecedented times that are not only full of uncertainty but also tremendous opportunities and ground-breaking technological advancements. Covid-19 has accelerated digital transformation by years and highlighted even more the importance of technological innovation in our times. We are closer than ever to making space tourism a norm and drone deliveries ubiquitous. Political and regulatory measures are changing consumer behavior and pushing companies to tackle global warming with evermore sustainable solutions. As a society, we have better tools than ever before to connect, work and communicate virtually.

It is therefore an absolute privilege to be at the forefront of this innovation revolution as a venture capital investor, and in particular thrilling to be one in Europe. The European tech industry has been experiencing extraordinary growth. Over the past decade investments in start-ups have gone up 14.5 times reaching $116bn in 2021. There are more European Unicorns than ever before and growth stage investment has more than tripled in 2021 compared to the previous year. The "State of Europe's tech sector" report shows that returns from European venture capital investments have exceeded those from similar investments in the US over the past 25 years. We see an unprecedented number of American funds set up shop in Europe to participate in this upside.

The above comes as no surprise, Europe has some of the biggest talent pools with world class academic institutions creating the breeding ground for the next generation of entrepreneurs and inventors. Due to Europe's fragmented nature and diversity, entrepreneurs know how to navigate complex legal frameworks, cultural and linguistic subtleties across borders to grow their business. Europe is home to more software developers than the US and arguably the cost of employment is still lower than in the very competitive Silicon Valley.

As a former founder and early employee of a, now, unicorn, I have, however, noticed some opportunities for further improvement. Europe could adopt more entrepreneur-friendly laws. Investors are still largely conservative and more driven by metrics than vision, leaving the more ambitious founders with no other choice but to reach to US funds. Culturally, Europe is more reserved in its sales technique and could do with more confident marketing of its superstars to the outside world. The open nature of Silicon Valley Investors means that access to them seems easier there than in Europe.

At Redalpine, we have been witnessing the exhilarating metamorphosis of the European tech industry over the last 15+ years. As former entrepreneurs and founders ourselves, we take pride in learning from our more experienced counterparts on the West Coast whilst leveraging the many positives that the European start-up ecosystem has to offer and elevating our local talent. We focus our investments on future superstars early on, with Seed and Series-A stage deals to help them take the leap to the next level of growth and scale. With the change in the market dynamics we have also recognized the need to offer follow on and growth funding. This means that we can guide our portfolio companies through every stage of their development up until their exit.

We are at an inflection point in European tech and venture capital and it is essential that we, the investors, politicians and academics nurture the wonderful diversity and inventiveness that Europe has to offer. We are still able to impact and shape the industry into what we believe will make it the most competitive on the global tech scene. *The Builder's Guide* is a fantastic aid to all entrepreneurs, current and aspiring, to take their unique innovations to the next level and not be afraid to think big. Europe has all the necessary ingredients to stay competitive on the international stage and *The Builder's Guide* gives practical advice on how to make the most of this opportunity.

Aleksandra Laska, Partner Redalpine Venture Partners

Introduction

On a cloudless summer night in 1971, a slightly drunk young man lay in a wheat field near Innsbruck, Austria, and looked up at the sky. Beside him lay a stolen copy of *The Hitchhiker's Guide to Europe*. While gazing at the stars, the man decided that someone should write a "Hitchhiker's Guide to the Galaxy" – a book offering answers to "life, the universe and everything." The name of that man was Douglas Adams and his best-selling novel appeared in 1979. Today, it has been translated into over 30 languages.

The guide you have in your hands does not quite cover that scope. But for those with aspirations to scale a technology startup, it offers a starting point to build "unicorns" – companies that are valued with more than USD 1 billion and often employ thousands of people.

As the authors of *The Builder's Guide to the Tech Galaxy*, we have co-scaled a variety of technology startups over the years, including the FinTech N26, the Internet provider Planet Internet and the eCommerce enterprise Vivere, along with several cultural platforms and various ventures for McKinsey & Company. During our time working on these projects, we have realized one thing: when scaling a startup, teams had to reinvent the wheel over and over again. And while much has been written about how to find a product-market fit (such as *The Lean Startup* by Eric Ries) and business model innovation (like Reid Hofmann's *Blitzscaling*), there are few practical handbooks that focus on how to organizationally scale a tech startup.

Those who start looking for the knowledge to scale tech companies can quickly become lost in a maze of topics: setting the company's direction, building a talent acquisition machine, building a tech platform that is both reliable and enables developer productivity, firing up a marketing machine and establishing a functional supply chain. And those are just to name a few, the technical literature is full of such microcosms, from which one cannot find one's way out at some point. Most startup leaders simply do not have the time to read over 100 books and 100 blogs and listen to 100 podcasts to find answers and shorten their learning curves.

That's why we did it instead.

Not only that, but we have also drawn on our 40 years of combined experience in building companies and interviewed close to 100 top scale-up experts from successful technology companies around the world, including Airbnb, Pinterest, N26, Zalando, Salesforce, SoundCloud, Wayfair, AWS, GetYourGuide, Klarna and HubSpot. Together, we have created *The Builder's Guide to the Tech Galaxy*, a handbook for startup employees, leaders and (future) founders, investors and anyone interested in scaling a technology company within months rather than years. It is the book we would have liked to have read when we were scaling up our companies. These insights are especially relevant for technology companies, including those focused on software as a service, eCommerce, FinTech and healthcare.

This book is a guide in the best sense of the word. It is not a collection of eternal truths and not the answer to life, the universe, and everything, but a starting point from which to explore your own path when building and scaling a technology company. The content is intended to serve primarily as inspiration when building scale-ups rather than a strict blueprint.

Who this guide is and is not for: we neither focus on how to create a startup, nor do we tackle taking a unicorn to an IPO. Instead, our focus is on the critical scale-up stage in the middle – upgrading a close-knit pirate ship team into a large spaceship crew. This transition is not about gradually turning a startup into an old-fashioned corporation. Instead, it is about keeping the typical start-up virtues, such as bias to action, ability to quickly change direction and a willingness to fail often and learn fast, while enriching them with the minimum level of structures and processes necessary to be able to scale fast. At the most essential level, there are four key elements to this:

1. A clear *North Star,* an *AAA Team, Functional Excellence* and *Growth Capital.*
2. The *North Star* is necessary for aligning the company's direction, which will in turn attract an *AAA team.*
3. The colleagues will build *Functional Excellence* in deeply specialized teams, which will help to attract *Growth Capital* by delivering exceptional business performance (see Figure 1).

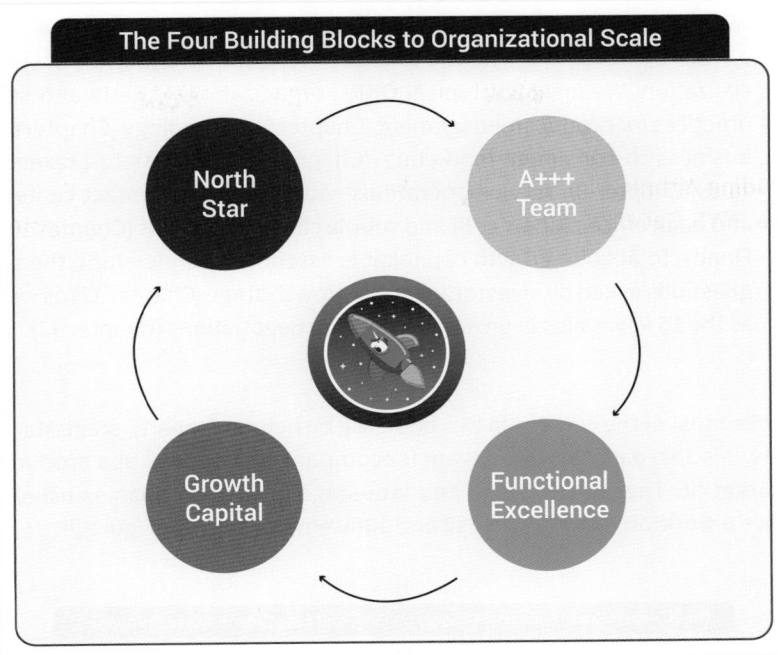

Figure 1: The Four Building Blocks to Organizational Scale

4. Being able to draw on sufficient capital then paves the way for a scale-up to aim for even more ambitious goals.

We cover all four elements in this book in the following order:
- First, there is the task of finding your North Star: the direction in which the company is heading, including purpose, business ambition, values, the company value proposition, the corresponding objectives and key results (Chapter 1). This is also the initial moment to establish sound Environmental, Social and Governance ("ESG") practices, which will make an aspiring unicorn company stand out even more to both future employees and customers (Chapter 2).
- Second, attracting an AAA team with the right mindset is key. To achieve this, a "people team" needs to build a talent acquisition machine and power a superior employee experience (Chapter 3). Instilling a mindset geared around customer obsession, "learn-it-all beats know-it-all" thinking and autonomy can help to build bridges between organizational silos before they arise (Chapter 4).

- While in the early startup phase intelligent generalists are of essence, a scale-up needs experts who take each function on a journey of specialization. We highlight typical OKRs, organizational charts and key practices for product management (Chapter 5), technology (Chapter 6), business-to-consumer marketing (Chapter 7), business-to-business sales (Chapter 8), service operations with a focus on contact centers and back offices (Chapter 9) and supply chain operations (Chapter 10).
- Finally, to acquire growth capital, it is essential to understand the six questions asked by investors at every growth stage (Chapter 11) as well as the 15 key issues in growth term sheet negotiations (Chapter 12).

While most of the content in this book will be helpful for early-stage start-ups, it is also particularly relevant for companies close to or at a product-market fit. These early-stage and late-stage growth companies usually have a workforce of between 50 and 1000 employees (see Figure 2).

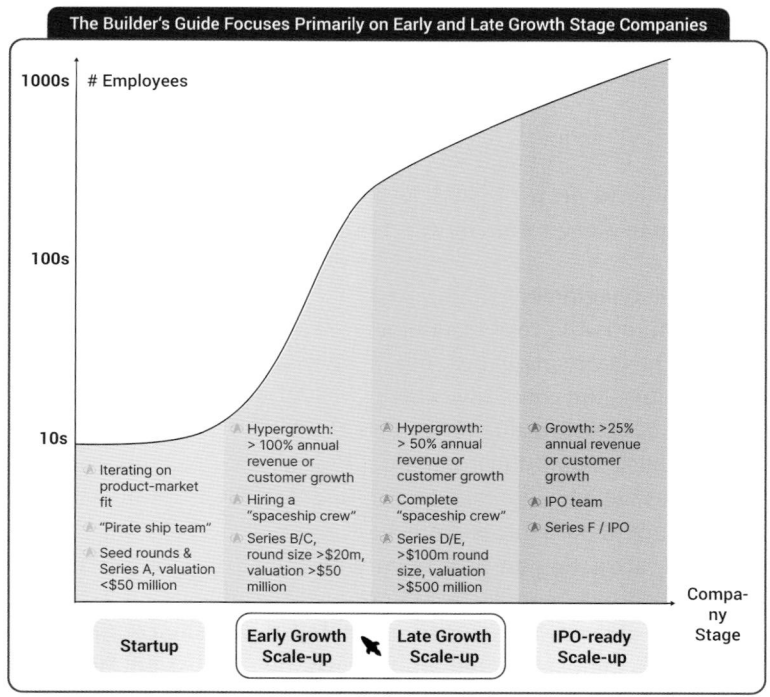

Figure 2: The Builder's Guide Focuses Primarily on Early and Late Growth Stage Companies

There are two ways to use this book: The first is to read it from cover to cover, gain inspiration from its pages and get a feel for the links between the individual chapters and recurring structures. Ideally, the manual will then pave the way for a deeper understanding of the workings of various very different departments and instil the ability to take a broader overall view. The second is to read the book with an all-embracing or more pin-point focus. We have designed each chapter to be self-contained (which is why information earlier in the book may appear again later on). This makes it easier to find specific knowledge on specific interests – be it marketing, software development, product management, services tools or another area.

A technical note: As proof that the sources are mostly available online, we have made all links "available" over the Internet Archive – at the cost of longer loading times. However, the direct links are easy to find in the current permalinks; in the majority of cases, the sources will still be available.

A technical note: As proof that the sources are mostly available online, we have "published" all links over the Internet Archive – at the cost of longer loading times. However, the direct links are easy to find in the current permalinks; in the majority of cases, the sources are still able to be accessed.

We firmly believe that startup builders are the inventors of the 21st century. They are the driving force behind the creation of millions of future jobs. They are securing the technological sovereignty of their nations, and they are already making lasting contributions to solving humankind's most pressing issues: mitigating the effects of climate change, securing energy and water supply resources, providing equal opportunities for all, ensuring sustained economic growth and safeguarding global health in the face of pandemics. Builders dare to venture into the unknown and explore new frontiers. **They often reach for the spectacular, making the seemingly impossible possible and the seemingly unreal real.** With this book, we want to encourage and inspire anyone who is considering starting a venture or joining a thriving startup. The business world does not always have to be a golden cage gilded by pension schemes, company cars and cushy contracts. When you take your seat on a startup rocket, it may sometimes feel like the G-force is too much to handle and that you are dealing with forces you cannot fully control. However, it is also a once-in-a-lifetime opportunity to fully tap into your hidden talents and potential as you journey to the stars.

On this journey, we ourselves are forever learning. In that spirit, we intend to update this book at regular intervals. If you have feedback or any suggestions about topics we should include in future versions, please contact us at martin@schilling.life or tk@thomasklugkist.de.

Martin & Thomas

NORTH STAR

1   Six Dimensions of Direction

What is the one thing that leaders of a startup often lose sight of when upgrading a startup into a scale-up? An aligned direction. When bogged down by 100 operational emergencies while being relatively clear on direction themselves, they forget to co-create and align the direction of the venture with the teams. In the early startup life, the team is often so small that founders and leaders can interact directly with all employees, but when upgrading a "pirate ship" startup (<100 FTEs) to a "spaceship" scale-up (>1000 FTEs), having a sense of clarity on a direction – a shared North Star – makes the difference.

Why?

- **A clear North Star drives growth and profitability.**
  Organizations that score high on direction and purpose are more than twice as likely to be among top total shareholder return performers as those with low purpose scores. And companies that score high on "organizational health" metrics (e.g., values, culture, alignment) have EBIT margins that are 2x as high as businesses with low metrics.[1]
- **A clear North Star helps to attract investors.**
  In particular, before start-ups can show strong business metrics, many investors use clarity of direction as one proxy to assess the strength of a top team. Many top investors even see a "lack of vision" or "lack of why" as an exclusion criterion when funding start-ups.[2]
- **A clear North Star attracts an AAA team.**
  In particular, millennials demand clarity on purpose and values from employers. For example, companies with a clear purpose report 40% higher levels of workforce retention than their competitors.[3]

There are six mutually reinforcing dimensions for defining a meaningful "North Star," which many unicorns follow at least in part (see Figure 3). Few startups have all of them in place at once, but the more they have, the brighter their North Star will shine.

- **First, start with the "Why."**
  What is your company's purpose beyond profit? Why does your company make the planet a better place? Scale-ups with a clearly articulated purpose are a magnet for attracting top talent and are twice as likely to have above-average shareholder returns.[4]
- **Second, add company values.**
  The clearer the guiding principles are for aligning teams, the less prescriptive one needs to be on the "how" and "what."
- **Third, build a crystal-clear long-term business ambition.**
  This is what investors demand and teams expect. Homing in on the business outcomes that truly matter and defining the 10-year aspirations (e.g., "Give a hundred million people an opportunity to earn income") gives teams something tangible to work with.
- **Fourth, derive a "North Star metric" from the business ambition.**
  If one had to choose a singular metric through which to achieve this business outcome, which one would it be?

- **Five, ensure the customer value proposition is crystal clear** in order to achieve the business ambition.
  What are the 1–2 unmet customer needs that your company solves uniquely well? This is the driver of growth.
- **Finally, use quarterly and annual OKRs** as a vehicle to jointly shape the company's direction and align teams on a way to move forward.

Airbnb is a great example of a company that has all these dimensions in place (see Figure 3).

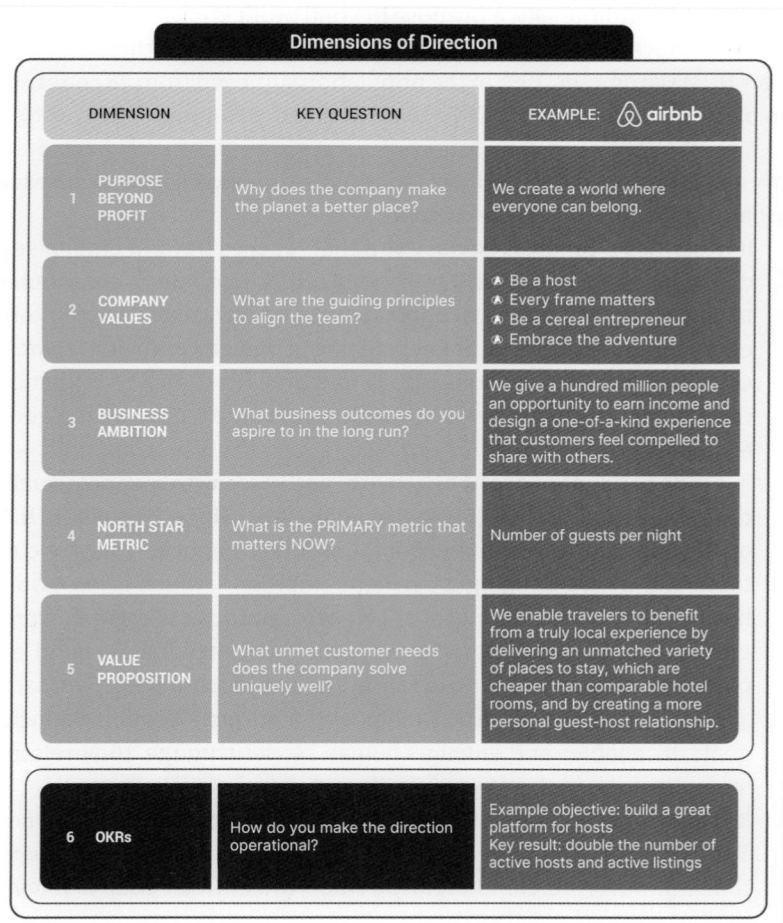

Figure 3: Dimensions of Direction (with example Airbnb)

Purpose beyond profit

Practice 1: A company that makes the planet a better place

All Airbnb offices feature a large sign in dark red letters that reads "Belong anywhere." This is the purpose, or the "Why," put in place by founders Brian Chesky, Joe Gebbia and Nathan Blecharczy. They do this for one reason: scale-ups with a clearly articulated purpose are twice as likely to have above-average shareholder returns (see an excellent <u>analysis</u> by BCG). Additionally, a purpose beyond profit is just as essential for many employees and can be necessary to retain them. In the 2018 Edelman Trust Barometer, 79% of the population surveyed from 28 countries on all continents expected CEOs to personify the company's purpose.[5]

When do you know that you have found a good purpose? A good purpose usually fulfils three characteristics:
* It describes a **timeless social good** that reaches beyond employees, customers and investors. For example, if the company contributes to climate neutrality, equal opportunities, universal access to knowledge, combating food waste or unleashing human creativity, it reaches out to society as a whole, ideally for humanity. Google's "Organize the world's information and make it universally accessible" is a good example here.
* It is **independent of profit or growth**, and therefore it cannot usually describe a quantitative (business) goal. When FinTechs such as N26 or Revolut aim to reach millions of monthly financially active customers, they are defining a business ambition – which is necessary but cannot replace the purpose. Monzo's purpose is a great example: as "make money work foreveryone" and they have a good explanation of how they arrived there. The deeptech startup Synthara. ai from Zurich also aligns its team with a purpose beyond financial goals. It "enables and enriches human senses through body-related smart devices, such as hearing aids and virtual voice assistants".
* It is **never completely attainable**. Its time horizon is infinite. When Spotify talks about unlocking the potential of human creativity, that will never be completed. Or when the FinTech Wise is aiming for "money without borders – instant, convenient, transparent and

eventually free," or Nike for "bringing inspiration and innovation to every athlete* in the world (*if you have a body, you are an athlete)" this will never be fully achieved either. Google is a prime example: "Organize the world's information and make it universally accessible and useful". Nike is another: "Bring inspiration and innovation to every athlete* in the world (*If you have a body, you are an athlete)". Steve Jobs at Apple encapsulated another: "Make a contribution to the world by making tools for the mind that advance humankind."

How do you sharpen the purpose of a company?

As a good first step, the leaders can run the "startup raider thought experiment." Imagine an investor offers to buy the company at a multiple of the given market value. All founders and shareholders are happy, and all employees will receive fulfilling jobs at equal or better pay. However, all services and products will be terminated, and the brand erased. Why would you reject the offer? That answer leads to the theme of the company's purpose, such as carbon neutrality, access to knowledge or healthcare.

In the next steps, it is often helpful to write a one-page manifesto around this theme – ideally delivering an authentic rationale why the founders or the leadership team care about the purpose. An off-site leadership presence that is far away from the office is often a great place to do this. An external author, consultant or agency might also help here.

Finally, you can refine the purpose with your employees by giving them the opportunity to comment on the manifesto. Running the "granny test" with your employees is a good way to check if they feel ownership: What story about why they work for the startup can a front-office employee tell that will excite their grandmother during a Sunday afternoon coffee? If your purpose is compelling, they will be able to tell in simple words why it is valuable to get up every morning to work for your company.

It is essential for startups to walk these steps as soon as they surpass 30–40 employees and start hiring more senior leaders (usually no later than Series A) as a clear purpose helps them set direction for their teams.

One note on purpose for B2B companies is that making the planet a better place is usually more difficult for companies that serve other businesses. There is even a B2B "purpose paradox." According to the US Association for National Advertisers, 86% of B2B companies believe purpose is important, but only 24% of them have this purpose embedded in their business operations.[6] The US B2B payment provider Square is one company which has nailed it: "Empower everyone to participate and thrive in the economy." They are "empowering the electrician to send invoices, helping the clothing boutique pay its employees and giving the coffee chain capital for a second, third and fourth location."[7] The German B2B software company SAP is also built on a strong purpose: "Making sustainability profitable and profitability sustainable." SAP is an outspoken supporter of the 17 United Nations Sustainable Development Goals and is committed to achieving carbon neutrality by the end of 2023. Another B2B company that exemplifies how to put purpose into action is Salesforce. They are committed to the idea of "stakeholder capitalism," or "a system in which corporate purpose is based on a fundamental commitment to all stakeholders – customers, employees, partners, communities, the planet and society – rather than just shareholders."[8] They follow through on this promise with initiatives like the 1-1-1 model, which commits 1% of their equity, technology and employees' time to improving education, equality and the environment. Salesforce also encourages its customers and partners to do the same. To date, more than 12,000 companies have joined this "Pledge 1%" movement.

Company values

Practice 2: Guiding principles for aligning the crew

"Don't fuck up the culture." This is the advice that Peter Thiel gave to the founders of Airbnb after having invested USD 150 million in the company.[9] Why? Because he knew that company values are a strong driver of business success. According to a McKinsey study, companies that score high on "organizational health" metrics (e.g., values, culture, alignment) have EBIT margins that are twice as high as businesses with low metrics.[10] The clearer the company's values and the more that they are lived day by day, the fewer control mechanisms need to be in place. The following three principles are useful for many young tech companies when defining their company values:

- **Create company values that are relatable and unique**
  Shouldn't everyone be honest and strive for excellence? Ideally, startups should be able to formulate values with their team in their own language to set their company apart and codify a personal relationship with those values. One example is Airbnb's "Be a cereal entrepreneur," which is a reference to when the founders sold breakfast cereal called "Obamas-O" and "Cap'n McCain's" at a time when they were in huge debt in its early days. Another is "Draw the owl" from the US cloud communication company Twilio, which serves as a reminder to all employees that they are empowered and are expected to find their own answer to uncommon problems.

- **Design an inclusive process**
  Values cannot be a top-down process: both the executive team and a representative number of employees should work together to shape them. Twilio, for example, assembled a diverse group of 12 employees from its key functions that drafted its first version and then collected 100+ ideas using a survey. Finally, the founder and the executive team boiled these ideas down to nine company values. The Oxygen test ("Which of these values couldn't you live without?") helped them to eliminate nonessential values.[11]

- **Perform a value gap analysis**
  Another structured way to compile a company value is to let employees and top management choose from a set of ~100 possible values. The elements of the Barrett Culture Value Assessment (see Figure 4) are a useful starting point. Three questions are relevant here: "What are the 10 values which best represent who you are?" (personal values); "Which 10 values best reflect our current company culture?" (current company values); and "Which 10 values are most important to you to achieve the true potential of our team?" (desired company values). The results highlight the gaps in the company's desired values and can serve as a starting point to further refine them.

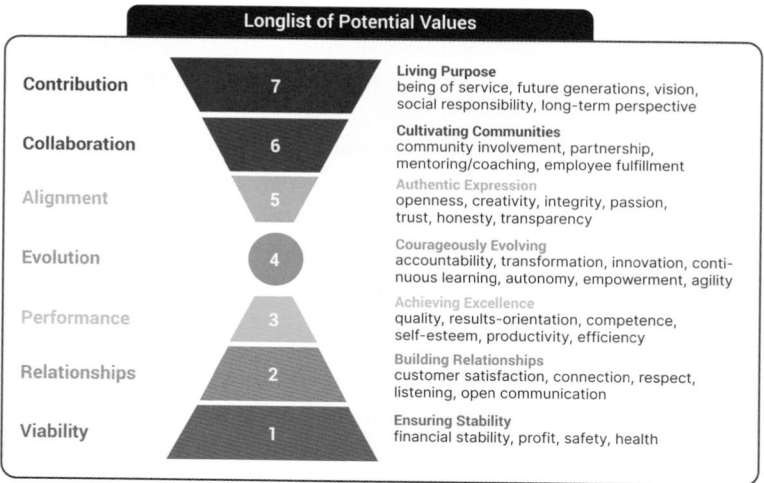

Figure 4: Longlist of Potential Values
Source: Barrett Values Center[12]

Business ambition

Practice 3: Business outcomes to aspire to in the long run

A startup without business ambition is like a rocket with no destination. Once again, Airbnb is a fantastic example of this. Its business ambition is: "Give a hundred million people an opportunity to earn income and design an experience that customers would tell every single person they've ever encountered about." Here, Airbnb uses the Net Promoter Score for guests and income earned for hosts as its underlying KPIs. Netflix's early business ambition is another good example: "Every single household with cable or satellite in every market where people have broadband or TV will have a Netflix subscription." In this case, the subscription rate is the key business outcome. To obtain a clear ambition like this, it helps to zoom in on 1–2 measurable business outcomes that matter the most, which usually focus on growth, financial goals and/or customer experience, as well as envisaging the best-case scenario for the company in 5–10 years. Contrary to the purpose, the business ambition should be achievable within a finite time horizon.

North Star metric

Practice 4: The PRIMARY metric that matters NOW

Many successful startups condense their business ambition into a single "North Star metric." This is the one metric that a team needs to know by heart. As startup investor Sean Ellis put it, this metric should capture the core values that the product best delivers to the customers. Many successful scale-ups have defined it clearly in their early days (see Figure 5).

COMPANY	NORTH STAR METRIC	WHY?
facebook	Daily active users	Drives advertising revenue
Linked in	Total sign-ups	Attracts paying recruiters
ebay	Number of items listed	Draws more transaction value to the platform
Medium	Number of minutes spent reading	Encourages user conversion to the premium service
zoom	Weekly hosted meetings	Promotes traffic and establishes Zoom as the go-to videoconferencing platform
slack	Messages sent within an organization	Speeds up adoption and conversion to paid upgrades
solvemate	Customer requests per day	Encourages swift resolution

Figure 5: North Star Metric

A proper North Star metric needs to do three things: facilitate revenue generation, reflect customer value and be easily trackable. It is best to stay clear of vanity metrics, such as page views, new sign-ups or total registered users, as they usually do not drive long-term business value. Each time leaders are faced with a key decision, the question should be: Will it improve the North Star metric?

Value proposition

Practice 5: Unmet customer needs that you solve uniquely well

To deliver on a startup's business ambition and the North Star metric, the value proposition needs to be crystal clear, as it conveys the main reasons a customer should buy from them. This is the promise to solve a customer's **1–2 key unmet needs** uniquely well. One way to define the value proposition is to complete the following sentence (Figure 6):

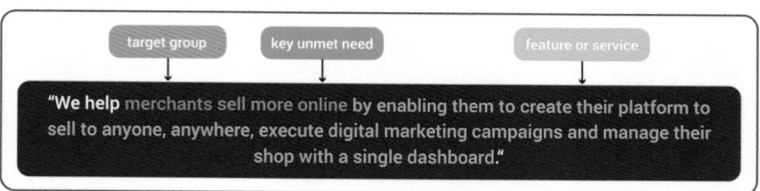

Figure 6: Our Formula for a Value Proposition (example of Shopify)

This sentence captures the value proposition of Shopify (more details are available on Steve Blank's blog). While a company may solve many of their customers' unmet needs, they need to be as plain as possible about the 1–2 KEY ones that they solve uniquely well. The value proposition is then condensed into a headline, with a sub-headline for the 1–2 key unmet needs and 3–5 supporting bullets for the most important features and services. Evernote provides a good example of this in practice (see Figure 7).

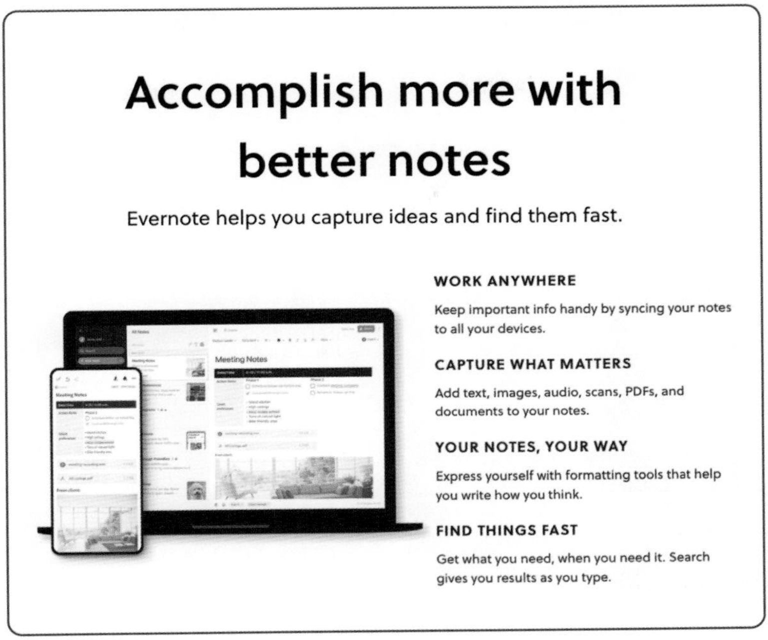

Figure 7: Evernote's "Accomplish more with better notes"[13]

The KEY unmet needs are typically phrased as an "I want. . ." statement from the customer's perspective and are **always linked to a positive outcome** for them. The key unmet needs for B2B and B2C startups usually fall into one of the categories below in Figure 8.

Note: The value proposition is not a slogan like "Nike – Just do it" or "Adidas – Impossible is nothing." It is nice to have one, but it does not replace the value proposition.

The key unmet needs for B2B companies typically revolve around saving costs, time and hassle, while increasing revenue, improving customer experience and reducing business risks. For B2C companies, homing in on key unmet needs is often more complicated. Consumers' needs can often be categorized into four types: "functional" needs, such as saving money, time or hassle; emotional needs, like social connection, feeling good or having fun; life-changing needs, such as being desirable to others or achieving a personal goal; and finally, social impact goals, such as realizing zero carbon emissions (see Figures 8 and 9).[14]

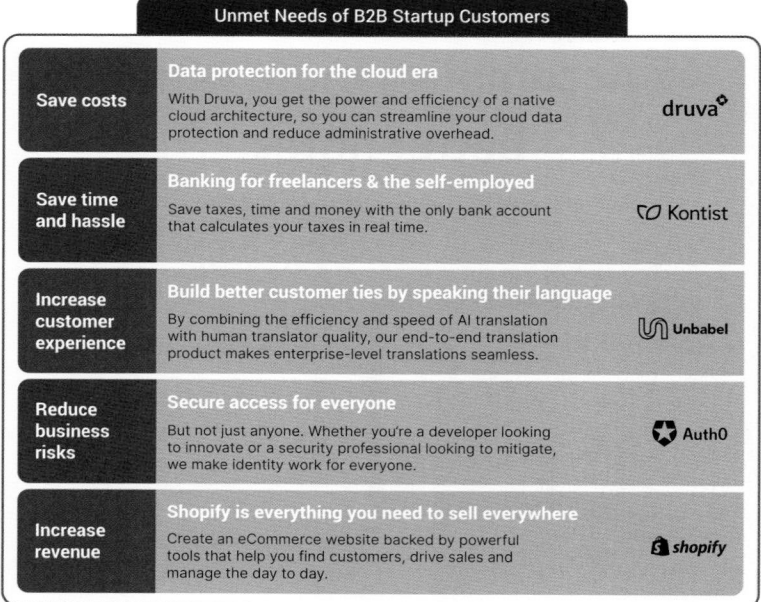

Figure 8: Unmet Needs of B2B Startup Customers

Unmet Needs of B2C Startup Customers

Save money	**Dailies made affordable** We started Hubble so you don't have to chose between your health and your wallet. Our contacts are barely a dollar a day, so you can finally afford to wear fresh lenses as much as you like.	HUBBLE
Save time and hassle	**Accomplish more with better notes** Evernote helps you capture ideas and find them fast.	EVERNOTE
Reduce personal risk	**Get care anytime, anywhere for $0** Our care is "right-size-fits-you", never "one-size-fits-all".	oscar
Choose from a wide range of options	**Soundtrack your life** Let Spotify bring you the right music for every mood and moment. The perfect songs for your workout, your night in or your journey to work.	Spotify
Socially connect and belong	**Bringing you closer to the people and things you love** We're committed to fostering a safe, supportive community for everyone.	Instagram
Have fun	**The ultimate football platform** We offer everything that makes a football fan's heart beat faster. Scores, news, transfer rumors, live streaming, match highlights, video features and much more. We provide the new generation of "mobile-first" football fans with everything they need to stay up to date with the beautiful game 24/7.	7.
Feel good	**Discover the power of breathing. Calm mind. Better sleep.** We provide insomniacs with drug-free and validated sleep solutions to relieve stress & anxiety, resulting in better and deeper sleep.	somnox
Taste, see, hear something great	**Experience a new kind of meal kit** Inspired recipes, curated ingredients, smart preparation: what's not to love?	MARLEY SPOON
Show an exclusive status or aspiration	**Endless access to luxury** Buy, sell and exchange the most coveted designer handbags and accessories.	REBAG
Be desirable for others	**Mermaid + Me stands for naturally beautiful hair** Inspired by the secrets of the oceans and tropical superfoods, our natural and vegan hair care gives you the magical mermaid effect. It's time for your #mermazinghair.	MERMAID + ME
Achieve a personal goal or improve	**A WHOOP membership brings you closer to unlocking your human potential** Get daily personalized fitness, sleep and recovery data delivered to you in real time with WHOOP. Join today for as low as $30.	WHOOP
Contribute to a social need	**Let's plant some trees!** Make Ecosia your new search engine and plant trees with your searches – for free!	ECOSIA

Figure 9: Unmet Needs of B2C Startup Customers

OKRs

Practice 6: Making direction operational

When your startup is growing fast, the execution challenges can grow even faster. Suddenly, you lose direction, responsibilities blur and teams build silos. You're stuck in a Gordian knot of execution. One way to break through? OKRs (Objectives and Key Results). This framework for company goal setting is championed by some of the world's most success fultech companies from LinkedIn to Zynga to Google. And OKRs are standard at some of Europeantech's most sophisticated companies including N26 (where Martin was COO).

These objectives refer to the "what" – ambitious, yet realistic goals connected to the business value of the company. For example, one of fintech N26's objectives is to transform retail banking on a global scale, while the aim of retail company Zalando is to become the "starting point for fashion".

The key results are the "hows" – measurable milestones, which once achieved in full, the objective is reached in full as well. You either deliver on a key result, or you don't. For example, a key result at the company level for N26 is to bring banking services to over 50m customers world-wide; Zalando measures its success by growing its gross merchandise volume on their platform to more than €30bn by 2025. Other typical key results could be to "increase the net promoter score by 10 points" or "increase employee engagement scores from 3.0 to 4.0".

A scale-up's executive team ideally defines 3–5 top company objectives in each quarter, with 3–5 key results, each at the maximum. The annual OKRs of an example neobank could be as follows:

- **Objective 1: Become the largest neobank for SMEs in Europe**
  Key results: reach 200,000 customers in Germany, launch beta product in Italy and reduce average monthly customer churn from 3.5% to 2.5%.
- **Objective 2: Become the most popular bank for SMEs in Europe**
  Key results: increase Net Promoter Score by 10 points, increase conversion sign-up to completion by 5% and increase net revenue retention from 110% to 120%.

- **Objective 3: Build a secure and compliant bank**
  Key results: reduce institutional fraud requests by 50% and solve all regulatory remarks from the last audit.
- **Objective 4: Hire and retain the best team**
  Key results: hire five C-levels and senior executives and increase employee engagement score from 3.0 to 4.0.

Typical top company OKRs usually fall into the following categories: growth and financial performance (e.g., monthly recurring revenues), sales & marketing (e.g., customer acquisition costs), customer experience (e.g., NPS), process efficiency & cost savings (e.g., throughput time), team (e.g., eNPS), products & services (e.g., average rating on Amazon), compliance (e.g., outstanding post-audit issues), security (e.g., mean time to detect), technology platform performance (e.g., uptime) and sustainability (e.g., waste recycling rate).

The executive team has to understand that stellar execution starts with having a clear company 'North Star'. After all, OKRs operationalize direction. One European travel company we know runs a very condensed OKR approach. In the first week of each quarter the executive team develops the top company OKRs by Tuesday. Then, each division—such as product, technology, marketing and operations—defines their OKRs based on the company's direction, usually by Thursday. Full company alignment of all OKRs is then done on Friday in an all-hands meeting, with the process, therefore, taking one week in total.

When setting up an OKR system, these are the key pitfalls:
- **OKRs are not ambitious enough**
  Ambitious but yet specific goals can lead to unparalleled performance – this is one of the most validated hypotheses in management literature with more than 1,000 <u>studies</u> on it. Ideally, teams only meet ~70% of the OKRs. If they constantly achieve 100%, the goals were likely not ambitious enough.
- **Key results are phrased as activities, rather than measurable outputs**
  Key results that "analyze," "assess," or "explore" are weak. Activity-based key results such as "Analyzing ways to boost conversion rate" are inferior to output-focused key results. These are either based

on a quantitative metric (e.g., "Improve the Net Promoter Score by 10 points") or a qualitative assessment (e.g., "Launch a closed beta product version in the US").

- **OKRs are set top-down**
  Having a founder write OKRs for the marketing team or a CMO write OKRs for the performance marketeers takes the sense of ownership of the teams away. The person who delivers on the OKRs should be the one to write the first version of it. The OKRs are then usually refined together with the respective manager.
- **There are too many key results**
  Defining more than five key results per objective can create a risk that the teams will become unfocused. The fewer key results needed to fully capture the objective, the better.
- **There is no OKR tracking in place**
  At the end of the performance period (e.g., each quarter), each team ideally scores the progress of each key result with their respective manager. Typical tools that can be used for this include plai.team, Perdoo and Workpath.
- **OKRs are connected to bonuses**
  Making bonus pay-outs dependent on achieving OKRs disincentivizes teams to agree on stretch goals. For *Star Wars* fans, <u>here is</u> a great description of how to do it using OKRs (objectives and key results).

Bonus: For Star Wars fans, here's a great description of how to explain this in an easy way to your teams. And if you'd like to find out more about how to take your startup's execution abilities to the next level, be sure to check out "Measure What Matters" by John Doerr.

Recommended publications:
- John Doerr (2018). *Measure What Matters: How Google, Bono, and the Gates Foundation Rock the World with OKRs*.
- Reid Hoffman (2018). Blitzscaling: *The Lightning-Fast Path to Building Massively Valuable Companies*.

Watch our video on the Six Dimension of Direction by scanning the QR code or following this link: https://youtube/-EXteEwjuH4.

How to get your company value proposition right? Watch our video by scanning the QR code or following this link: https://youtube/ mx9D7AbNjP4.

Definitions

- **B2B**: a business-to-business company is one that provides products and/or services to other businesses.
- **B2C**: a business-to-consumer company is a company that provides products and/or services to individual consumers.
- **Company purpose**: a statement that describes why a company makes the planet a better place.

- **North Star metric**: the primary metric that sets the direction of your company's focus and encapsulates the key values you offer to customers/end-users; for example, number of nights booked (Airbnb) or daily active users (Facebook).
- **Unicorn**: a term derived from the venture capital industry to describe a privately held startup company with a valuation of USD 1 billion or greater.
- **Value proposition**: a statement that describes features and services that solve few key unmet needs for specific target customers uniquely well.

2 Environmental, Social and Governance Criteria as Drivers of Business Success

With Johannes Lenhard and Hannah Leach

Key pitfalls for scale-up builders: !

- **Seeing ESG as a side topic or ignoring it altogether**
  If a startup fails to incorporate environmental, social and governance factors into their strategic decision-making process early on, it can be difficult for the company to realign its values, practices and operations to reflect ESG when scaling. While it may take time for the consequences to materialize (e.g., during an IPO or the sale of the company), the rot will set in immediately in the company's culture, team structure and internal processes – which can be difficult to reverse. Numerous studies have shown that having a strong stance on ESG correlates with higher-equity returns.
- **Greenwashing through superficial actions or narratives**
  As it has been shown many times, treating ESG as a checklist, matter of compliance or surface-level reporting issue is rife with public pitfalls for scale-ups. It is essential to avoid falling into the trap of embracing ESG-marketing narratives without actually taking action.
- **Neglecting a comprehensive, always-learning view**
  ESG can be a moving target for startups and scale-ups. While this chapter presents the best practices at the time of publication, this is a rapidly developing field, making it all the more important to keep up to date with ESG practices.

Deliveroo's IPO in March 2021 was one of the most hotly anticipated (and biggest) tech IPOs in a decade on the London Stock Exchange. The delivery company, which had been at the forefront of bringing the gig economy to Europe, was (temporarily) valued at just under GBP 10 billion. The IPO ended up being a disaster: Deliveroo's stock dropped 30% on the first day, wiping out nearly GBP 2 billion of the company's value. The reason? Institutional investors, including Aberdeen Standard and Aviva, were concerned about the long-term risks associated with the company and outright refused to buy the stock. They believed Deliveroo had not built a sustainable business either in terms of its revenue model or – more importantly – its "self-employed" workers (i.e., individuals earning the minimum wage with no social benefits). According to Andrew Millington, Head of UK Equities at Aberdeen Standard: "We wouldn't be comfortable that the way in which [Deliveroo's] workforce is employed is sustainable."[15] The message is clear: investors are now taking environmental, social and governance considerations much more seriously – as Deliveroo found out when it failed to factor the "social" aspect into its public offering.

What is ESG?

ESG principles focus on three types of consideration when building a company. In turn, these can be further broken down into different subsectors:

- **E – Environmental:** Up until now, this has primarily been broken down into carbon emissions (driven by energy consumption and travel policies, for instance), as well as waste management processes and the supplier's footprint. The focus is usually on three "scopes" (see the graph below).
- **S – Social:** The core focus here is on practices revolving around diversity, equity and inclusion (DEI), part of which involves assembling a team that is diverse in terms of how it thinks and is truly inclusive of all cultures, genders, ages and sexual orientations. "S" also includes considerations regarding the unintended (societal) consequences of a product or service. One concrete example here is Airbnb's efforts to counteract biases that make it harder for African-American guests to rent rooms through their platform.[16] This also includes more general considerations at the level of the team and work environment (pay gaps, impact on the local community, etc.).
- **G – Governance:** This refers to the internal "governance" of a company that impacts decision-making and includes the distribution of shareholder rights, the role and composition of the board of directors, the stated purpose of the business and conflicts of interest.[17] It also includes transparency and accountability and involves measures such as keeping accounts in good order and regularly making them available to investors, as well as pursuing transparent and ethical business practices. The Volkswagen emissions scandal and Facebook's misuse of user data and possible election manipulation are two examples of a lack of proper internal governance.[18]

When it comes to startups and scale-ups specifically, nine areas constitute the "universe of ESG" (see Figure 10).

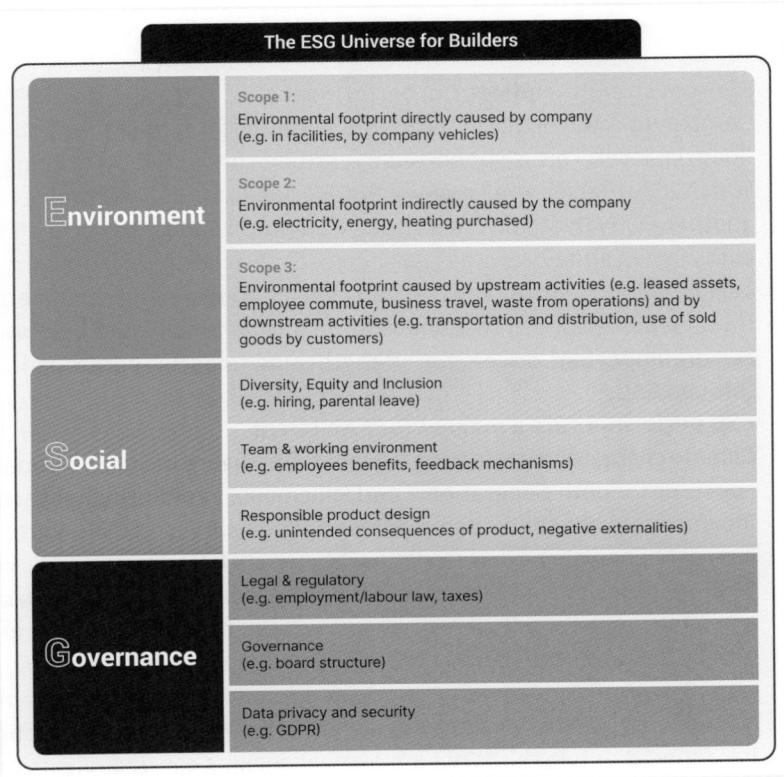

Figure 10: The ESG Universe for Builders

Why is ESG important for growth company builders?

ESG principles have become more important over the past few years when building and/or investing in a technology company. According to a recent poll, over 70% of major VCs and 60% of angel investors have stated that they expressly factor ESG criteria into their decision-making process.[19] For example, in Berlin, a group of 30 VC funds, including Cherry Ventures, Earlybird and Holtzbrinck Ventures, have updated their term sheets to include a "sustainability clause," which requires their portfolio companies to measure and improve their environmental footprint. Similarly, major scale-ups, such as DeliveryHero and BlaBlaCar, have signed a "green pledge."[20]

There are several reasons that startup builders should take ESG seriously:

- **ESG can strengthen financial performance**
  Companies rated highly in terms of ESG outperform their peers on a financial level. This is supported by a study conducted by Morningstar in 2020 that featured nearly 4,900 European funds.[21] According to another study by McKinsey, a strong ESG proposition also correlates with higher equity returns. Saving costs through reduced energy consumption, boosting the company's reputation among customers through the release of sustainable products and motivated employees are important drivers for strengthening financial performance through ESG.[22]

- **ESG performers are a magnet for AAA talent**
  Climate change and protecting the environment are the top personal concerns for both Generation Z and Millennials, ranking higher than income inequality and unemployment. When surveyed by Deloitte, 42% of Millennials have stated that they would be willing to deepen their relationship with a business whose products or services had a positive impact on the environment or society.[23] Out of this focus group, 10% even stated that they would take a pay cut of USD 5,000–10,000 to work for an environmentally-friendly company. Inclusion and diversity are other aspects that are highly valued. Glassdoor has found that two thirds of employment seekers consider diversity to be an important criterion when evaluating job opportunities.[24]

- **ESG is a driver for customer growth**
  Placing a specific focus on environmental business practices can help attract customers.[25] For instance, according to BCG, 95% of consumers believe their actions can have an effect on mitigating climate change and addressing sustainability concerns on a broader level. Many consumer companies have taken action in response to these beliefs. Fashion retailer Patagonia – a long-standing and outspoken proponent of strong environmental policies and a certified B Corporation – has experienced phenomenal growth in continuing to expand its social mission.[26] Similarly, McKinsey has found that customers are increasingly willing to "go green" when it comes to consumer choices. More than 70% of the customers that they surveyed were willing to add up to 5% to the price for a more sustainable product (including for cars, buildings or electronics).[27]

- **Being strong on ESG increases the likelihood of VC (and buyout) investments**
  As of 2020, approximately 7 out of 10 major VCs in Europe incorporate ESG into their investment decision process, while over 60% measure their firms' performance using ESG metrics.[28] The Deliveroo case mentioned above, Uber's post-IPO share price drop due to allegations of a culture of sexism and racism and WeWork's IPO failure are three prime examples where ESG-related concerns led to funds or shareholders *not* investing. At the same time, demand is increasing rapidly for "sustainable investing." In 2020, over 250 European VC/PE funds have recently changed their strategy to focus on this by pushing asset allocation in "sustainables" to a record high of EUR 1.1 trillion. Larry Fink, the CEO of BlackRock, goes as far as to claim that "over time, companies and countries that do not respond to stakeholders and address sustainability risks will encounter growing skepticism from the markets and in turn a higher cost of capital."[29]

- **Building with ESG in mind reduces regulatory risk**
  More comprehensive ESG regulation is increasingly forcing investors and companies to consider, implement and report on ESG factors.[30] Several regulators in the European Union have already made steps in this direction. One of these regulates public suppliers in the UK needing to adhere to the social value framework, which is closely aligned with ESG principles. In the EU, investors have to report on a comprehensive SFDR framework, which was introduced in March 2021 (requiring participating VCs to report on indicators, such as greenhouse gas emissions, the gender pay gap, board diversity, whistleblower protection and human rights performance). Meanwhile, in the United States, the SEC has also already announced comprehensive ESG regulation.[31]

Ultimately, ESG is not only the right thing to do, but it makes for a strong business case. Now, let's dive into several concrete practices that can be implemented straight away.

Environmental

Practice 7: Measuring, reducing and offsetting your environmental footprint with clear responsibilities and targets

In 2019, several founders and executives of big tech companies and scale-ups – including the founders of Zalando, TIER Mobility, Flixbus and Delivery Hero – came together in Germany to discuss the impact they were having on the environment. They wanted to contribute toward reaching the world's climate targets and a regenerative economy. This is how the community called Leaders for Climate Action was born. The community consists of around 1,000 tech scale-ups and venture capital investors who are dedicated to *acting* on measuring, reducing and offsetting their carbon footprint. They have established a green pledge for scale-ups, including a set of three binding steps (reported on and reviewed annually) that form the core of any good environmental effort, including data collection, carbon footprint measurement and carbon offsetting. The pledge also encompasses a clear move toward reduction in the medium term. Ecosia, one of the largest alternative search engines in the world, is certainly benefiting from this. The company managed to leverage its position in being a sustainable alternative to Google and Bing. With the ad revenue that Ecosia generates, it plants trees around the world – at least two in the time it takes to read this page.

With the Climate Action Guide, Ferry Heilemann published an excellent book on suggestions for companies to deliver on climate targets. We encourage every startup builder to read it. The following building blocks can boost a scale-up's "E" performance:

- **Making climate carbon reduction goals part of your annual OKRs**
  From Apple to Amazon and Google to Microsoft, a number of big tech companies have announced ambitious carbon-neutral and net-zero targets for their businesses and supply chains. Apple, for example, is committed to making its supply chain carbon neutral by 2030.[32] Microsoft is aiming to become carbon *negative* by 2030.[33] Many scale-ups have moved in this direction, too. In the United States, scooter giant Lime has set a 2030 net-zero target for all 30 countries in which it operates, with plans to transition its entire charging network to renewable energy sources and exclusively use electrical cars for its ops

team fleet.[34] In early 2021, the Amsterdam-based platform WeTransfer announced that it wants to cut its emissions by 30% over the next five years.[35] VMWare, a virtualization technology company, built a meter that clients can use to monitor their energy usage and carbon footprint at their data centers and has partnered with an environmental organization that helps the company plant trees.[36]

- **Appointing a climate officer, head of sustainability or a "carbon footprint hacking" team to make responsibilities clear**
  In the past year alone, the German scooter company Tier, fashion resale app Depop, meal replacement startup Huel and fitness apparel brand Gymshark have all appointed sustainability leaders and teams.[37] A sustainability hacking team (or a "carbon-footprint hacking team") is a cross-functional squad with an involvement in Product, HR and Supply Chain. This team works together with the climate officer or sustainability lead, who drives the topic forward and reports directly to top management. Establishing both a clear top management lead and a functional team can be a key to driving change with strong responsibilities and OKRs that have been broken down.

- **Identifying, measuring and benchmarking key (carbon) footprint drivers**
  Understanding a company's carbon footprint is known as "carbon accounting." Until recently, most companies were using Excel sheets to make very rudimentary estimates (if at all). Today, tools provided by companies like Planetly and PlanA can do this and will establish a system of continuous measurement, reporting and assessment. Ideally, CO_2 footprints should be calculated for every product the company produces, leading to the establishment of clear reduction responsibilities for each of them. Top management attention should focus on these numbers and agree on targets at least once per quarter. They should also be part of any external reporting to establish a culture of transparency and accountability.

- **Reducing the carbon footprint**
  Reducing a carbon footprint is a long-term journey and one that can be approached in various ways. One "quick win" that can, in some cases, create a 15–30% reduction in the carbon footprint is to focus on energy efficiency and reduction by switching to a renewable energy provider, encouraging the workforce to switch all devices off overnight (including heating and lighting) and potentially switching to smart heating. Other worthwhile options to explore here include

only buying energy-efficient office equipment (e.g., AAA label in Europe, Energy Star–certified in the United States), sourcing green cloud services (e.g., pausable data centers) and purchasing renewable energy credits. It is also worthwhile to consider implementing a no-printing policy. The average employee in Western high-income countries, such as the United States, Germany or the UK, prints between 0.5 and one tree per year.[38] This can be radically reduced by switching to a paperless office. Finally, it is important to reexamine the company-wide travel policy to see if it can be revised. Every meeting should be remote by default. If travel is necessary, establish clear rules, like travel by train instead of plane and bundle group meetings abroad together. Another measure is to incentivize people to switch to traveling by bike rather than car (e.g., thanks to a cycle-to-work program or bike leasing).

- **Reducing the footprint of your supply chain**
  The carbon footprint is driven by the supply chain, as the purchase of goods and services has an environmental impact. A good starting point is to review suppliers in terms of their own climate action. The US Environmental Protection Agency has developed a good questionnaire for this.[39] Two concrete aspects to consider across a supply chain are to *source locally* wherever possible (with ships>trains>planes when inbound logistics are necessary) and to *decrease the footprint of packaging*. The latter applies across a supply chain and is especially important when it comes to the volume of packaging and plastic usage. Walmart has rolled out a comprehensive playbook for "sustainable packaging"[40] and more and more startups are providing solutions in this field.[41]

- **Creating internal carbon pricing**
  A good tool to facilitate change (and distribute responsibilities) across your scale-up is "internal carbon pricing." So far, 28% of companies across Europe are using a tool to devise internal budgets for carbon emissions (and reductions) across various functions. These budgets should be treated like financial budgets and should lead to undisputable responsibilities within the organization, thus enabling the work to be distributed beyond a sole climate officer.[42] At the core of this is an internal carbon fee – a voluntarily monetary cost per ton of carbon emissions – which allows companies to generate revenue internally through carbon-emitting activities.[43] These financial resources can then be reinvested into carbon offsetting programs.

Internal carbon pricing has been shown to lead to a reduction in carbon-emitting activities by acting as a disincentive to conduct such activities in the first place.[44] When Microsoft introduced an internal carbon fee – requiring its business functions to include the cost of carbon in its annual budgets – it led to widespread behavioral change as business functions sought to reduce emissions.[45]

- **Offsetting your footprint**
  The general rule concerning a company's footprint needs to be very clear. Reduction always needs to come first – off-setting is a temporary matter of last resort. The most widespread means of off-setting target forest recovery and protection of forests, as well as many (software) solutions to help to "automate" the process of off-setting a carbon footprint (e.g., Planetly.org, my.climate, firstclimate.com, planaearth.com). Ideally, this is done as locally as possible to maximize the impact on the local community. Several scale-ups and start-ups have implemented off-setting as part of their offering to their customers, which is something that takes this to the next step. For instance, Shopify launched an app that allows merchants to choose to offset the carbon emissions on their deliveries.[46] Similarly, Stripe Climate allows its customers to contribute a portion of the revenues they generate through Stripe directly to carbon removal programs.[47]

Social

Practice 8: Building a culture that embraces diversity and inclusion

To drive diversity, equity and inclusion, a growth company leader does not have to believe in a good cause – just in the profit and loss statement. The more women and people from a diverse set of ethnic backgrounds that work as leaders in a company, the higher its EBIT margin. This has been confirmed by several studies conducted by McKinsey & Company.[48] According to these analyses, companies in the top quartile for gender diversity on executive teams were 25% more likely to have an above-average profitability than companies in the bottom quartile. For ethnic diversity, the impact is even higher. Companies in the top quartile for ethnically diverse executive teams have a 36% higher likelihood for above-average profitability.

Deloitte Insights created a four-phase model that shows a possible path for a maturing diversity and inclusion driven company (see Figure 11).[49] Leaders in the field see the path to increase DEI (diversity, equity, and inclusion) as a movement toward leveraging differences in thinking within the team to create business value.

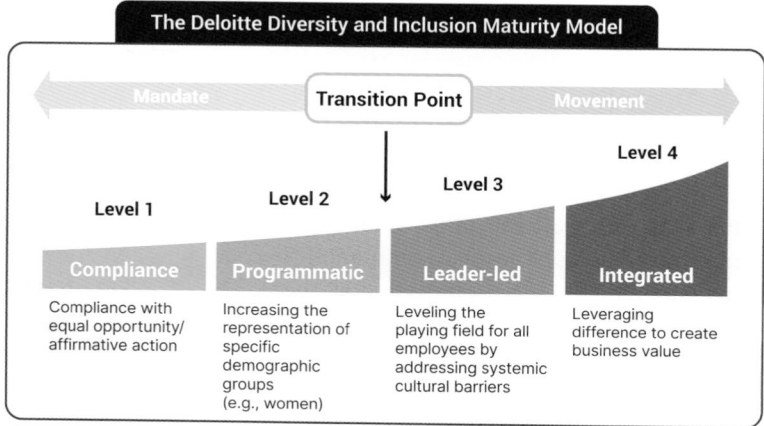

Figure 11: The Deloitte Diversity and Inclusion Maturity Model
Source: Deloitte Insights

There are several potential building blocks that can help to become a DEI-driven company.

- **Getting a dedicated DEI person on board early**
  This DEI expert, for example, as part of the people team, can co-design the DEI strategy, setup training for hiring managers to avoid unconscious biases, write inclusive job descriptions and lead initiatives and mentoring programs. A service provider performing an external audit could be a first step (e.g., the non-profit organization Inklusiiv or consultancies like FairHQ offer this).
- **Setting measurable DEI goals**
  For instance, the HR-toolbox multi-billion-dollar scale-up Gusto made DEI a top executive priority early on. They regularly publish dedicated diversity reports and set out concrete and measurable DEI goals across the team. Their 2016 goal was to "increase the percentage of Black and Hispanic Gusties to 10%," and they also

worked actively against pay gaps.[50] In particular, the priority-setting of the founding team shot Gusto into what Deloitte calls the "integrated phase," where the whole organization is united behind the DEI agenda.

- **Reporting on progress transparently**
Important DEI metrics include staff ratios of gender, ethnic diversity and socioeconomic background, among others, for executives, as well as non-executive leaders, within each function. An assessment of DEI roadblocks, such as insufficient applications from women in specific positions, also counts. CultureAmp, a platform that works with companies to collect, understand and act on employee feedback, suggests integrating DEI questions into the regular people engagement survey (e.g., "I can voice a contrary opinion without fear of negative consequences" and "Perspectives like mine are included in decision making").[51] They also set a target benchmark score for responses and suggest paying close attention to the discrepancy between demographic groups. All of the data should be shared transparently and openly to facilitate dialogue.

- **Focusing your talent acquisition on DEI early**
When the marketplace Etsy was scaling up, they faced tremendous challenges to recruit a (gender) diverse engineering team. To solve this, they did not only restructure their interview process and retrain the recruiters, but they also partnered with *HackerSchool,* an engineer camp, to provide free training for female engineers.[52] The key levers here include: inclusive public communication in marketing, public messaging and recruiting, as well as job descriptions that target all gender and ethnic backgrounds. A powerful starting point to counter unconscious biases (beyond making training mandatory) is to staff all hiring committees with at least 30% women and one person from a non-white background.

- **Becoming a truly parent-friendly company**
Becoming accessible to parents is a particularly important factor for creating gender balance. Allowing both moms and dads to perform at work and spend time with their family helps to become a magnet for AAA talent. There are several options to pursue. Enabling all leaders to work part-time and granting up to two months of unpaid vacation per year is a first step. And, particularly after Covid-19, the time has never been better to become a "remote first" company. For example,

the German SaaS startup Solvemate kept its HQ in Berlin but has allowed all of its employees to now work wherever they want. Every eight weeks, they organize a three-day "homecoming" for planning and team alignment. They pay gross salaries based on German standards within Europe and the employer contribution to social security in the respective countries. The big advantage is that talent acquisition pools suddenly multiply in size if you are not dependent on specific cities. If you are, you need to open a local business unit and pay taxes in the respective country. Digital team alignment then plays a much bigger role: a virtual coffee kitchen where you can meet spontaneously, an updated slack status to show that you are available or a "camera on" policy in meetings. The Swedish music-streaming service Spotify has also recently announced its "Work from Anywhere" initiative by letting employees elect their work mode (remote or in the office) and location of work.[53] Many major US companies, such as Airbnb, Google and Shopify, have also transitioned to either remote-first or fully distributed over the last year. A financed daycare spot, a nursing room in the office and emergency babysitting (e.g., during Covid-19, HR scale-up Personio provided financial support for external childcare) are additional options that can help parents succeed.[54]

Governance

Practice 9: Establishing internal governance that facilitates growth, compliance, and employee representation

The planned WeWork IPO made the setup and structure of the company's governance publicly transparent. The verdict of some observers: "WeWork is a Corporate Governance nightmare."[55] The result: a cancellation of the IPO. Self-serving behavior amongst the founding team (e.g., the founder was leasing the trademark for "We" to his own company) and a lack of board diversity and independence were some of the reasons behind this.[56] WeWork provides a strong case for why it is essential for scale-ups to be proactive with implementing strong corporate governance practices. The goal of good governance is not only to minimize internal and external risks but also to maintain the long-term value and growth trajectory of the company, particularly as one looks toward an exit.

Here are some possible options to set a scale-up on a good-governance basis:

- **Building an independent and diverse board**
  In a 2015 study of over 6,000 US-based startups, the value of some degree of independent control over the companies became clear.[57] Startups in which the founders were still in control of the board of directors and/or on the CEO seat were significantly less valuable than those in which the founders had given up some degree of control. Each additional level of founder control, such as controlling the board and being the CEO, reduced the pre-money valuation by roughly 20%. This applies in particular for startups that are three years or older. Some degree of external control and "friendly challenging" usually contributes to the process of raising the hiring bar and thinking through trade-offs around strategic choices more explicitly, such as with market and product expansions. A capable board with some control rights can help to more quickly bring in the appropriate skills for the various phases of growth on regulation, fundraising, organizational scaling, etc. A diverse board is of relevance as well. Having at least one woman and one person from a minority ethnic background in a board of six might be a possible goal. Diversity on the board level is not only important to ensure the consistency of a DEI strategy, but it can also help with diverse representation more generally and, by extension, better decision-making.[58]
- **Protecting and empowering employees within the workplace**
  Amazon and Google have both been massively under attack for a lack of consideration toward their employees. Google has been criticized for their "two tier employee system," where the ~50% of its workforce that are contractors and temporary workers are paid less, treated differently and receive none of the benefits Google offers to its direct employees.[59] At Amazon, its warehouse employees are protesting about unsafe working conditions and lack of protection.[60] The key issue to solve here is to give employees a voice to keep employee retention up and ensure that decision-making remains fast. A formal workers' council with "decision cycles" of weeks,

which is standard in a corporation, is often not the right answer for a fast-moving startup. However, ignoring employee representation can also backfire substantially.

This is often particularly relevant in front-office or back-office teams, such as customer service. Some startups solve this by letting each customer service team elect one "employee representative." These colleagues collect improvement suggestions for the work environment and meet with the customer service leadership once a month to discuss specific suggestions on how to improve working conditions. This could include anything from taking personal preferences into account when scheduling shifts, organizing child care or ensuring that free lunches are delivered. These may seem like minor things, but they are nevertheless important. Alongside its legally regulated workers councils, Zalando, a German eCommerce company, set up the Zalando Employee Participation (ZEP) program in 2015.[61] This is a voluntary employee participation committee that enables employees to participate in business decisions related to their work and company culture. It is designed as an unbiased platform where employees and the business can discuss and resolve issues. The ZEP is an advisor, not a co-decider to the Zalando Management Board. These voluntary structures can help to identify employee needs and concerns early on and take a proactive response.

Recommended publications:
- Erika Brodnock and Johannes Lenhard (2021). *Better Venture: Improving Diversity, Innovation and Profitability in Venture Capital and Startups*.
- Emily Chang (2019). *Brotopia: Breaking up the Boy's Club of Silicon Valley*.
- Ferry Heilemann (2021). *Climate Action Guide*.

PEOPLE & MINDSET

3   People (HR) Excellence

Attracting, Developing and Retaining an A+++ Crew

With Constanze Buchheim, Manjuri Sinha and Chris Bell

Key pitfalls for scale-up builders   !

- **Failing to understand that an AAA team is one of the best predictors of business success**
  Some tech company teams believe success comes primarily from getting the product and technology right. While this matters, hiring and retaining an outstanding crew is mission-critical, too. Evolving from a startup to a scale-up calls for the crew to create an impact quickly in an environment with limited resources. Without the AAA team, this growth journey can end fast.
- **Lowering the recruiting bar due to time pressure**
  The pressure to quickly fill open positions can lead some scale-ups to choose internal or external candidates that are available but do not have enough potential to scale. Senior leaders in particular should have ideally scaled tech companies before they are hired. Some companies put people with no leadership experience in senior management positions. This usually only works if they are exceptionally talented and coached intensively (see Practice 12).
- **Copying people and culture "best practices" from shiny brands**
  Copying measures that Netflix or Amazon have taken is often not the path to creating the next unicorn. It is key to understand specific business goals and then design a "people perspective" that contributes to achieving them.
- **Failing to mobilize the organization in terms of recruitment and organizational development**
  Some people teams try to solve the various "people" challenges of a scale-up by drawing on the people team's limited resources. They fail to appreciate the importance of building partnerships throughout the company by enabling and supporting business functions. In particular, topics such as hiring more female leaders and instilling a culture of diversity and inclusion should be the responsibility of every leader, not the people team alone.

- **Failing to develop candidate "sourcing" capabilities that amaze**
  Some scale-ups rely too heavily on inbound applications. The single most important strength of a people team in a growth company is to be able to source great candidates (see Practice 13).
- **Dismissing investment in values, processes or structures as "too corporate"**
  Some startups fear that values, processes and structures are not compatible with an agile startup that prioritizes a bias to action. However, all of these elements matter. Clear company values and some structures and processes are inevitable to avoid organizational chaos and inefficiency. This comes into play especially in the run-up to an IPO.

If growing a startup is akin to jumping off a cliff and assembling a plane on the way down, having an AAA team is the difference between flying and hitting the ground. They add the wings, and they fire up the engine. One of the biggest misconceptions when building a scale-up is that it is all about delivering a great product driven by a thriving business model. In particular, future unicorn companies invest heavily in people in building up their leaders. A study from Notion Capital shows that in the first two years after a USD 3–15 million funding round, future B2B unicorn companies hired six times more leaders than less successful companies and increased the (wider) leadership team from 5 to 11 members on average.[62]

Assembling and retaining an AAA crew tends to rest on fulfilling four objectives. The first is to hire and onboard talent quickly – with a special focus on great leaders. The second is to make every effort to ensure these individuals can be productive within weeks (rather than months). Once they are firing on all cylinders, the third objective is to avoid a leaky bucket scenario where your high-flyers leave the company for greener pastures. Finally, it is important to keep working to build a strong employer brand. This is captured in our formula for people-led growth (Figure 12):

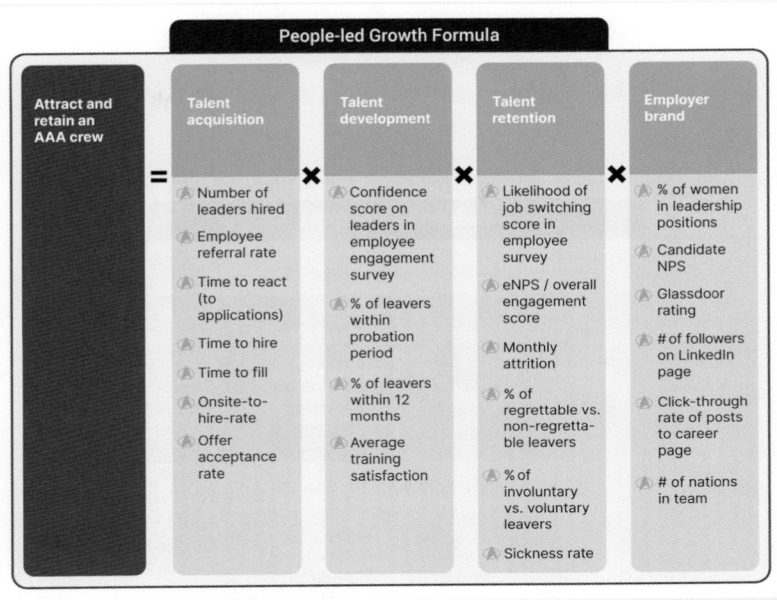

Figure 12: People-led Growth Formula

We next used this formula to create an example table of the typical objectives and key results (OKRs) (Figure 13).

OKRs

Practice 10: Establishing the right people OKRs

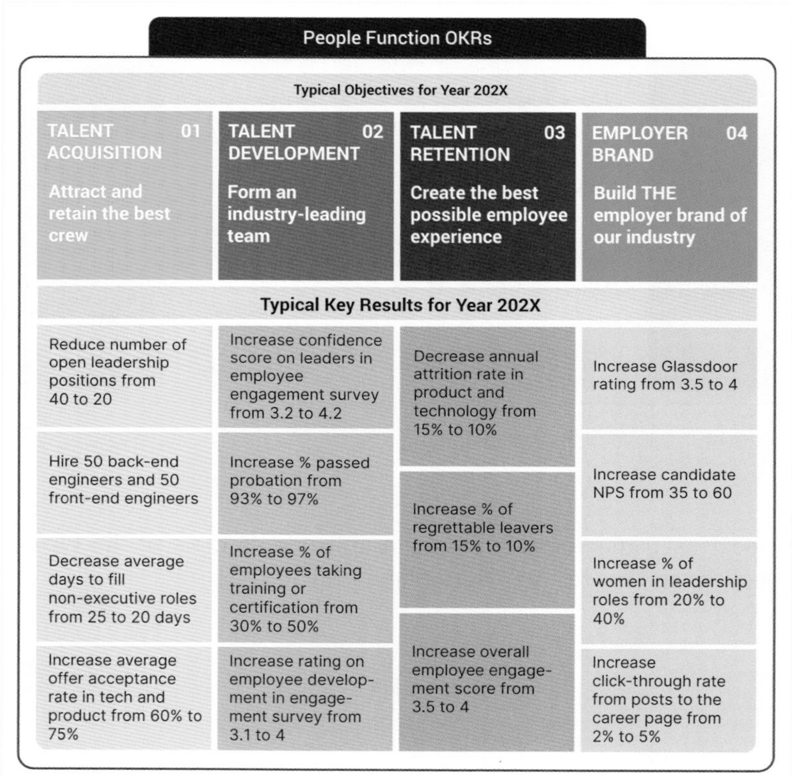

Figure 13: Typical Annual Objectives and Key Results for a People Function OKRs Team in Scale-ups

To create your own set of people OKRs, you need to select the right objectives and key results with the appropriate ambition levels for the context. This practice offers some inspiration for exactly how to do this.

01. Talent acquisition: Are you hiring quality leaders and specialists quickly enough?

For the German eCommerce company Zalando, the time between 2016 and 2017 was its high-water mark in terms of growth.[63] A massive increase in customers led the company to expand its workforce by ~4,000 employees to a total of 15,000 within one year. Hiring 1,000 additional engineers was one of the goals during this period. Zalando's recipe for success: they defined candidate personas more clearly, introduced a tool to analyze the candidate pipeline composition, tailored the job descriptions to these talents accordingly and implemented an interview scheduling tool for candidates. Additionally, they made the rejection messages much more actionable for candidates. As a result, new hires received an offer within 32 days rather than 52, the candidate NPS improved from −7 to 33, and their offers' acceptance rate rose by 30%.

When scaling, a company's recruiting team needs to excel in making quality hires in large numbers both on the leadership level (C-level and all people managers) and on the specialist level. For both levels, the recruiting team needs to have a clear overview of the number of candidates per role across the key funnel steps (see Figure 14).

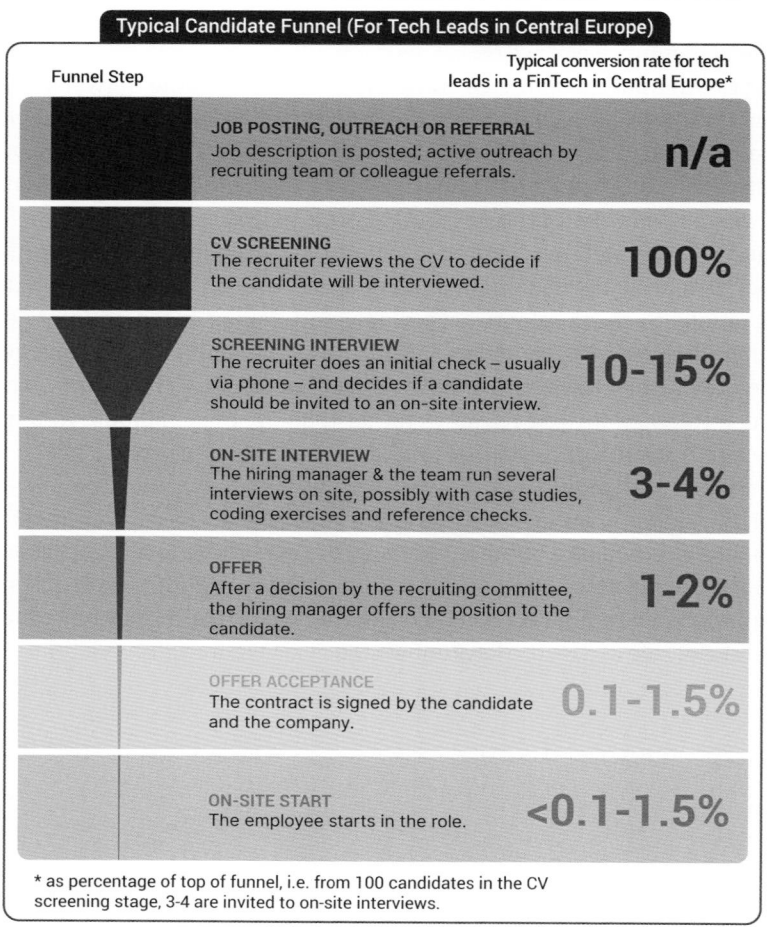

Figure 14: Typical Candidate Funnel (for Tech Leads in Central Europe)

Typical key results here include recruiting volume, speed and conversion targets. The number of open (leadership) positions and people hired is a measurement of success in volume recruitment. Speed can be tracked through the time-to-react, time-to-hire and time-to-fill rates. "Time to react" refers to the number of days until a new job applicant is sent an interview invite or rejection (3–4 days is a good rule of thumb). "Time to hire" is the number of days on average that has passed between the candidate applying for the position through to the contract being signed (a scale-up ideally aims for 20–25 days). "Time to fill" measures the number of days from when the job was posted until when the candidate starts. It is important to keep offer acceptance and onsite-to-hire (percentage of candidates invited to onsite interviews that are hired) rates on the radar, too. A very good offer acceptance rate for a tech lead in Europe is >90%.[64] A typical onsite-to-hire rate for the same type of role is 20–40%.[65]

O2. Talent development: Is your team becoming productive within weeks rather than months?

Google excels with its "just-in-time" approach for having new employees fully productive within a month.[66] On the Sunday before a new hire arrives at the office, the hiring manager receives an email alert asking them to complete five small tasks that are proven to be essential for the new hire's productivity. These actions include performing a role & responsibilities discussion, allocating a buddy to the new hire, helping them to build a social network within the company, scheduling onboarding check-ins once a month for the first six months and creating an atmosphere of open dialogue.[67] Onboarding includes two weeks of intense training on Google's way of working and expert topics, such as "The life of an ad," along with after-work drinks for bonding purposes.

Google's track record is a prime example of how important it is to invest in onboarding and ensure new hires become productive within a short time frame. It is critical to see the onboarding as a celebration or an extended welcome rather than an administrative process.[68] Two especially effective levers for onboarding new hires include a mentor/buddy system and "Gemba Walks" in which new hires work in the contact center or warehouse to gain a comprehensive understanding of the product. Other useful options include "Ask me anything" sessions with senior leaders (focusing particularly on company values), a well-structured internal how-to guide and individual one-page goal and priority plans to establish mutual expectations. Furthermore, the new hire should ideally meet the hiring manager on Day 1, then meet with them again in weekly 1:1s and as part of 2–3 feedback sessions for the first six months.

Typical key results here include the employee survey score that measures employee confidence in leaders (e.g., "I have confidence in the leaders at {Name of Company}"). The percentage of leavers within 6 and

12 months counts, too. Retaining more than 95% of your hires after the probation period is considered good for scale-ups in Central Europe. Employee satisfaction scores for learning and development matter as well. A good question for the employee survey is: "Is {Company X} an ideal place for me to foster my professional development?"

O3. Talent retention: Are you avoiding the leaky talent bucket scenario?

In 2013, a rumor shook the SaaS landscape: Salesforce supposedly lost 750 of its 3,000 salespeople.[69] With the average cost of replacing sales staff just shy of USD 100,000, that year's employee turnover alone is estimated to have cost the company close to USD 75 million. Seven years later, in 2020, Salesforce was ranked Number 6 on Fortune's list of "100 Best Companies to Work For." What led to this dramatic turnaround? Clear career paths, a strong connection to leadership, a stringent hiring process and, most importantly, a resilient monetary incentive scheme with a focus on retention.

Considering that getting a team up to speed can take up to a year, retaining employees is essential. This is applicable in particular for team members that are working with complex products and long-term B2B customer relationships. The top three reasons that a member of staff will leave a tech company are culture and management style (e.g., issues with the direct manager, a lack of autonomy and trust), insufficient career development (e.g., a lack of personal career and development plans, actional feedback and training) and inadequate rewards and compensation.[70]

Typical key results here include the score in the quarterly or biannual employee survey that measures the likelihood that the employee will switch jobs (e.g., "I rarely think about looking for a job at another company") and the overall engagement score. These are both leading indicators of employee attrition. The aim is to minimize annual attrition and a rate of 15% to 20% is considered good by many tech companies.[71] The percentage of regretted leavers is another important metric – these are employees who leave on their own accord (i.e., they are not let go by the company or rated as low performers).[72]

04. Employer brand: Is your company a shining star in the tech galaxy? The German B2B software company SAP has won more than 200 employer awards, was named the best place to work by Glassdoor in 2018 and 96% of employees would recommend the company to a friend.[73] Here's how SAP managed this: for a start, it has an inclusive employee value proposition, namely "Bring everything you are. Become everything you want." Starting in 2018, it has allowed two part-time employees to share the responsibilities involved in a single management role. In addition, all leadership positions are advertised as part-time, while a Women Leadership Excellence Acceleration Program (LEAP) has been set up to empower women at SAP and equip them with the right skills and knowledge for leadership roles.

In a scale-up, investing in an employer brand supercharges much of the work that can be done by your people function. According to LinkedIn, companies with a strong talent brand get ~30% more responses when recruiters reach out with direct messages to potential candidates in comparison to companies with weak talent brands.[74] That means that items like publishing a culture deck (think Hubspot or Netflix) to make a company's values and culture transparent,[75] caring about and ensuring a gender balance in leadership roles, employing a workforce representing multiple nations, pursuing parent-friendly arrangements, such as offering part-time leadership positions and/or remote work, etc. are essential. This type of company receives 2.5x more job applicants per job post and is able to grow its talent base by 20% more than those with a weak talent brand.

Typical key results to measure the employer brand include Glassdoor or Kununu rankings on candidate and employee experience, the percentage of women in leadership positions (gender balance), the number of different nations represented within the company and the number of followers of the company's LinkedIn page.

Organizational chart and roles

Practice 11: Defining the roles & responsibilities for a people function

For a scale-up with product-market-fit, one way to set up a people function is to establish "people partners" (or business partners) who work with the key functions and coordinate the resources of the people team for the respective functions. They draw on the capabilities of various centers of excellence, including talent acquisition, total reward, people operations and people analytics. People teams assembled to ramp up major new markets complement this function (Figure 15).

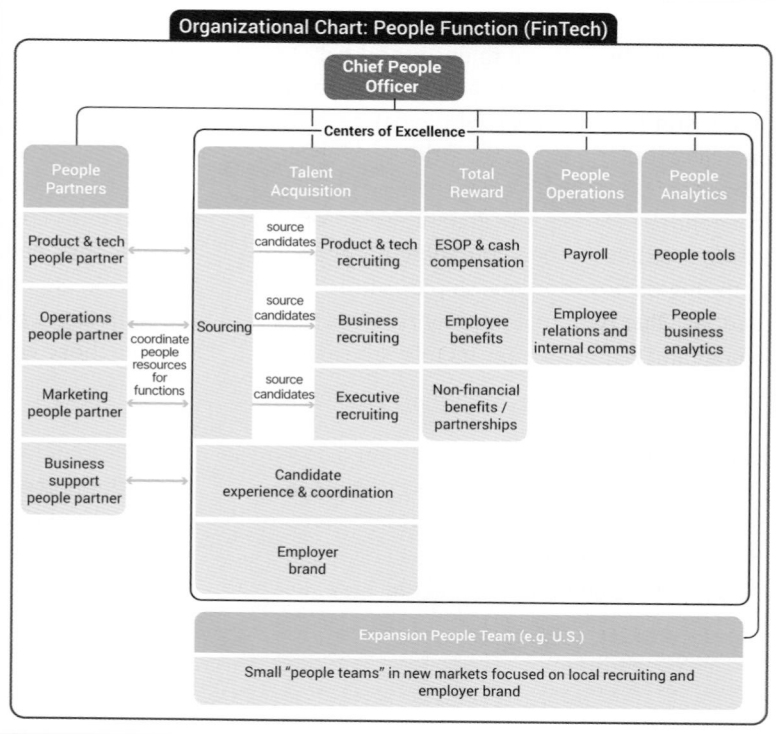

Figure 15: Possible Organizational Chart – People Function (FinTech)

Typical teams to build include:

- **"People partners"**
  While they are known as "business partners" in the corporate world, these teams work in close cooperation with leaders in each function to facilitate job leveling, promotions and appraisals, the ongoing refinement of the organizational structure and operating model and any ad-hoc people issues, such as performance management or harassment cases.

- **Talent acquisition: Sourcing**
  Many tech companies will create separate "Sourcing" teams that approach candidates with personalized outbound messages (e.g., on LinkedIn). The sourcing roles may sometimes be viewed as less valuable entry points with a lower salary within a people team. This is why some companies seek to turn this preconception on its head by paying talent sourcers a higher base salary than the rest of the people team. Sourcing is ideally one of the strongest muscles of a people team. One possible operating model is to have a central sourcing team that focuses on finding candidates for C-level and senior leadership positions, as well as critical roles with limited talent pools across all functions. Sourcers work with the employer brand to create strong candidate pitches, map the talent market and identify talent on both standard job platforms (such as LinkedIn, Indeed or Honeypot), as well as specialized content platforms (such as StackOverflow, GitHub, blogs and conferences). After a successful screening interview, the sourcers pass the candidates on to the recruiting teams.

- **Talent acquisition: Recruiting**
  One way to organize a good recruiting unit is to form separate teams for product and technology, the various business functions (e.g., marketing and operations) and executive recruiting. The recruiting teams are responsible for creating the best possible candidate experience along the individual funnel steps. This includes sending respectful rejections to unsuccessful candidates (see Practice 14).

- **Talent acquisition: Candidate experience and coordination**
  If a tech company organizes several hundred on-site interviews per month, the recruiting process may appear disorganized from a candidate's perspective if everything is not up to standard. This team ensures the time to hire remains on track at all times (e.g., less than 25 days) by guaranteeing candidates can book suitable travel

options. Tools are available for automated scheduling and on-site interview schedules are adhered to.

- **Talent acquisition: Employer brand**
  This team makes sure the company's external reputation is excellent among the candidate pool in order to prompt as many inbound applications as possible. They show the external talent market that the company is the best place to develop their career, whether by organizing employer events (e.g., regular meetups, a Christopher Street Day float), replying to comments on Glassdoor and Kununu, or publicly celebrating a strong gender balance and sending candidate feedback to sourcers, recruiters and candidate experience teams in order to improve the candidate experience.

- **Total reward**
  In a multi-country setting, the situation can quickly become complex when dealing with reward, compensation, contract and visa issues, which is why the total reward team is there to set rules and ensure they are followed. While the sourcing and recruiting teams will lead the hunt for talent, the total reward team usually ensures compensation for new employees stays within the agreed limit levels and that exceptions do not become the rule. In addition to allocating employee stock options to new hires, the team will also administer financial and non-financial employee benefits (e.g., social security contributions, student loans, partnerships with gyms, paternity leave).

- **People operations**
  The payroll team, which is responsible for ensuring employees are paid consistently and reliably, is often organized under the people operations banner. Likewise, internal communications are responsible for sending regular updates to the team or scheduling and organizing "Ask me Anything" sessions.

- **People analytics**
  When a company starts receiving thousands or even tens of thousands of applications per month, the automated people operations becomes an essential team. They are responsible for implementing and maintaining sourcing and application tracking tools (e.g., Bamboo HR, Greenhouse, TopFunnel), HR information systems (e.g., Bamboo HR, HR Cloud, Workday), candidate talent assessment (e.g., Checkr, codility, HackerRank) or machine-learning-driven interview scheduling tools (e.g., GoodTime, recooty). Tools to measure employee engagement (e.g., Culture Amp, Lattice, TINYpulse) or online

payroll tools are also important for scale-ups (e.g., Rippling, ADP). The analytics team will further support creating dashboards – possibly in co-operation with a central data team.

- **International people teams**
One way to expand into major new markets (e.g., from Europe to the United States or from the United States to South America) is to set up an international people expansion team. Members of this team will stay on location in the new market for 3–6 months and are responsible for filling the first 15–20 roles in addition to building up the local recruiting team. They are the ones to ensure the culture is exported to the new markets. Local activities often focus on recruiting and nurturing the employer brand as part of local events and local digital platforms. All other functions, such as rewards and people operations, can often be organized as a single global team.

Practice 12: Scaling the right people roles at the right time

Like other business functions, scaling up the people team is a journey of specialization:

- **Startup phase**
Here, recruitment is often driven by an executive assistant, with hands-on support from the founders and key leaders. It is critical to quickly lay down the foundations of the people function during this phase by sharpening the skills of the recruiting team and hiring recruiters with strong networks and the experience to actively reach out to potential candidates. Working with recruiting process outsourcers to get additional recruiters on board is an option, along with working with executive recruitment agencies to fill leadership positions. Another key element is to establish the people operations team (especially payroll) on firm foundations.

- **Early growth phase**
Building up a full-scale talent acquisition team – and recruiting from candidate sourcing – is essential in this phase. Strengthening the employer brand team to facilitate the build-up of a strong external reputation in the market and investing in a well-organized overall recruiting process reduces the time to hire while enabling the startup to secure the best possible talent on the market. Building up at least 1–2 talent analytics colleagues also helps at this time.

- **Late growth phase**
  This is the latest possible phase in which the "people partners" need
  to be established so that they coordinate well with the functions. This
  is also the latest point to invest in transparent job leveling, systematic appraisal and promotion processes. Here, a systematic approach
  to building up teams in new markets via a people expansion team is
  also important. In this phase, the people function usually needs to
  be strong enough so that there is no need to make use of outsourcers
  for the recruiting process – and partnerships with executive recruiting agencies need to only focus on roles with limited talent pools and
  insufficient networks. Ideally, the in-house executive recruiting team
  is so strong at this point that agencies are not needed at all.

Now that the organizational structure is in place, we can turn to the "people practices" that facilitate the smooth transition to a well-functioning
scale-up. The key practices revolve around **recruiting and candidate experience**, with a focus on sourcing, evaluating and "closing" candidates,
organizational development, **employee experience** and designing **employee stock option programs**.

Recruiting & candidate experience

Practice 13: Building the candidate sourcing muscle

Sourcing quality candidates is the core added value of a recruiting team.
People teams need to become candidate hunters, not just administrators
of the recruiting process. Getting a high number of quality candidates at
the top of the recruiting funnel counts here. Not enough incoming quality applications? One answer is to turn to proactive candidate outreach.
According to LinkedIn, 85% of the users on their platform are willing to
talk about potential new opportunities.[76] In other words, if the candidate
response rate to proactive requests from the company's side is just 30%
or if the number of incoming applications for a job posting is very low, this
is an indication that something may be wrong with the sourcing.

Here are typical pitfalls to avoid:
- **The "candidate intake process" is rushed and superficial.**
  If the recruiting team is not precisely briefed on the exact role and
  desired type of candidate, a company will end up with either too few

candidates or a pool of candidates with insufficient skills. Here are the key questions the hiring manager usually needs to discuss in a meeting with the recruiter before starting the recruiting process:

- Basics:
  What is the title of the role? Who is the hiring manager? Where is the job located? What salary range are we willing to pay? To whom does the role report? How large is the team that the candidate will lead (currently and in the future)?
- Goals:
  What are the objectives/OKRs for the role? How will success be measured over the first six months and the first year of employment?
- Responsibilities and tasks:
  What are key responsibilities and tasks?
- Ideal candidate:
  Can you describe the ideal candidate? What top experience and hard skills do they need? What is required and what is nice to have?
- Candidate pool:
  Which industries and companies should we reach out to in order to find candidates? What companies should we not reach out to? Are there any internal candidates?
  For a template of a good intake sheet, see *The Builder's Guide* public resources here.

- **The outreach messages are not personalized enough, too transactional or not delivered on the right platforms.**
  The company always applies to the candidates as well. The best people are virtually always already employed and rarely, if ever, scan traditional job boards, which is why it is necessary to reach out to them on the platforms where they are active. While LinkedIn is one of the most important outreach platforms, tech and product talent tend to frequent specialized recruiting sites like Honeypot, as well as the comment sections of GitHub, StackOverflow and OpenSource. It is important to consult conference speaker lists as well. Messaging them should never be a copy & paste exercise. Messages should include references targeting their personal situation, demonstrate genuine interest and recognize their work. Best-in-class outreach could even be in the form of a short, personalized video ("Hey Carmen, I saw your recent blog on LinkedIn and I'm interested in speaking to you about it. . .").

- **"Multipliers" or "network nodes" are not used enough for direct outreach.**

  Everyone on the planet is connected to everybody, at most through six rounds of introductions.[77] Some of these people are "network nodes," with many connections to relevant candidates (known as the "small world phenomenon"). It can be helpful to find potential candidates by asking these network nodes if they know anyone with relevant experience in, for example, scaling up a design team in a tech company. While they may not know somebody personally – or may not be interested in the position being pitched – they can be references for others. This in turn increases the likelihood of finding a match.

- **Job descriptions are boring and unspecific and fail to entice candidates.**

  A good job description needs to be seductive and sweep candidates off their feet. The aim is to excite quality candidates from diverse backgrounds while weeding out unsuitable candidates from the start. This is why the job description should be crystal clear: while 72% of hiring managers contend this is the case, only 36% of candidates agree.[78] Here's how to do it: the job description should be able to fit onto an A4 sheet of paper. It should deliver the necessary information without boring the reader with lengthy explanations in corporate speak. Best-in-class job descriptions usually follow the pattern outlined in Figure 16.

	Typical Dimensions of a Job Description	
DIMENSION	**WHAT IS IT?**	**EXAMPLE**
INSPIRING JOB TITLE	Innovative, modern titles can attract candidates who are motivated to work in vibrant environments. For engineering titles the rule of thumb is to keep them clean and simple in order to increase the chances of being found online.	Customer service agents = "customer experience associates" Associate cloud technicians = "cloud infrastructure architects" Business development interns = "entrepreneurs in residence"
COMPANY JOURNEY AND PURPOSE	The first section often refers to the company's compelling purpose. Why does the company make the planet a better place?	"HelloFresh is on a mission to transform the way the world thinks about home cooking. Forget the hassle of supermarkets or the tiresome process of planning your weekly meals. We deliver to your door all the ingredients, instructions and inspiration needed to make delicious meals at home, from scratch." (HelloFresh)
CURRENT TURNING POINT	The second section describes the current challenge the company is facing, and explains their growth history and current needs.	"Now we're on fire. Exponential growth, global distribution, an ever-expanding product portfolio that goes well beyond ovens, and a growing community of Ooni-lovers around the world who sing our praises and treat their friends and family to epic pizza. We're at that perfect stage of growth where we're still small enough for you to make a major difference while big enough to have the resources to do amazing things." (Ooni Pizza Ovens)
CALL TO ACTION	In this section candidates from diverse backgrounds are urged to apply.	"Ensuring a diverse and inclusive workplace where we learn from each other is core to Slack's values. We welcome people of different backgrounds, experiences, abilities and perspectives. We are an equal opportunity employer and a pleasant and supportive place to work. Come do the best work of your life here at Slack." (Slack)
SUMMARY OF ROLE	Relevant, interesting responsibilities and tasks are described here. They should be specific enough that the candidate knows what to expect, but broad enough to be able to adjust them to a dynamically growing company.	"Design, develop, roll out and maintain robust data pipelines which back our auction and personalization systems Work with data scientists and economists to develop and productionize estimation and prediction models Create tooling to automate data workflows Implement high-performance and scalable data processing systems" (Zalando, data engineering role)

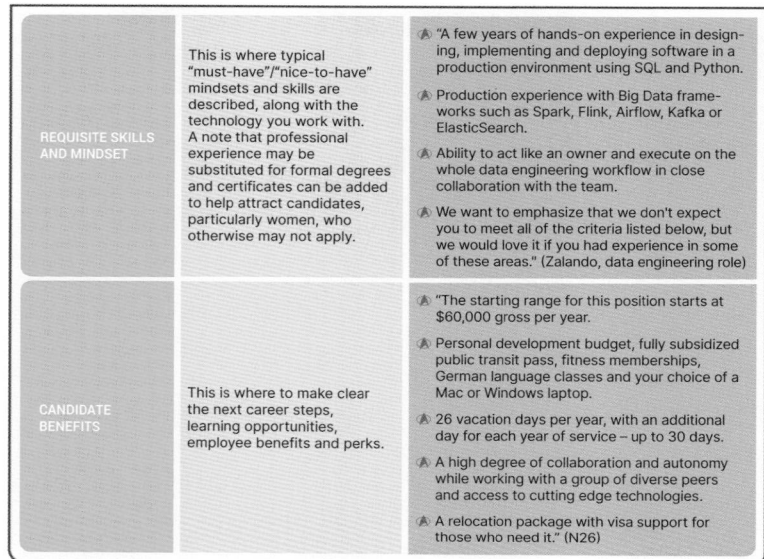

REQUISITE SKILLS AND MINDSET	This is where typical "must-have"/"nice-to-have" mindsets and skills are described, along with the technology you work with. A note that professional experience may be substituted for formal degrees and certificates can be added to help attract candidates, particularly women, who otherwise may not apply.	▲ "A few years of hands-on experience in designing, implementing and deploying software in a production environment using SQL and Python. ▲ Production experience with Big Data frameworks such as Spark, Flink, Airflow, Kafka or ElasticSearch. ▲ Ability to act like an owner and execute on the whole data engineering workflow in close collaboration with the team. ▲ We want to emphasize that we don't expect you to meet all of the criteria listed below, but we would love it if you had experience in some of these areas." (Zalando, data engineering role)
CANDIDATE BENEFITS	This is where to make clear the next career steps, learning opportunities, employee benefits and perks.	▲ "The starting range for this position starts at $60,000 gross per year. ▲ Personal development budget, fully subsidized public transit pass, fitness memberships, German language classes and your choice of a Mac or Windows laptop. ▲ 26 vacation days per year, with an additional day for each year of service – up to 30 days. ▲ A high degree of collaboration and autonomy while working with a group of diverse peers and access to cutting edge technologies. ▲ A relocation package with visa support for those who need it." (N26)

Figure 16: Typical Dimensions of a Job Description
Sources: Ongig, Careers pages on HelloFresh, Ooni Pizza Ovens, Slack, Zalando and N26

N26, Slack, HelloFresh and Facebook are all known for their inspiring job descriptions. See *The Builder's Guide* public resource page <u>here</u> for examples.

- **You do not sufficiently leverage referral programs to boost your candidate pool.**

  Good people know and attract good people. According to LinkedIn, referrals are the top source for quality hires.[79] What's more, the time to hire for referred candidates is 25% lower on average. Once employed, they tend to stay longer, have more job satisfaction and generally tend to produce higher-quality candidates and culture fits.[80] Lever, a US-based recruiting platform, found in one study that referrals are almost 10 times more likely to be hired than direct applicants.[81] A formal "employee referral program" can often pave the way for this. Typically, scale-ups pay USD 1,000-3,000 per hired referral who passes the probation period.

Practice 14: Evaluating candidates in record time while creating an outstanding candidate experience

While a company may receive many quality applications, it can still lose candidates during the evaluation stage. Over 80% of job applicants say that a negative or positive interview experience can change their mind about a company they previously liked or doubted.[82] The idea here is to create a candidate experience so good that all candidates, even the ones who are ultimately rejected, become promoters of the company.

Typical pitfalls here include:

- **The recruiting team does not apply to the candidate**
  If the candidate does not feel that the evaluation is a two-way decision-making process, the company will be perceived as arrogant. Some companies fail to understand that the best talents are sought after by many competitors. Just as growth companies are evaluating if the candidate is the right fit for the company, the candidates are deciding if the company is the right fit for them. Everyone – through to C-level and the CEO – should be a part-time recruiter at the company and play a part in ensuring the candidate's experience is optimal.[83]

- **The interviews are repetitive and do not assess multiple facets of the applicant**
  The candidate's experience will suffer if the candidate is asked similar questions during each interview at the company and their skills and traits are not assessed properly. Instead, every interview should test a different set of skills, and the interviewing process should be coordinated and built upon during each subsequent step. Typical interview topics include a cultural and value fit, a skills-based interview with case studies and a test for coding exercises. Amazon's last interview is a "bar raiser." In this interview, a trained Amazon interviewer from another business unit that is not associated with the team is brought in to offer an objective view during the interview. These bar raisers are more impartial and can better assess if the candidate genuinely lives up to the company's leadership principles.[84]

- **The logistics of the recruiting process are broken**
  For many candidates, the number-one point of frustration is the lack of response from employers.[85] Other typical problems include interviews being frequently rescheduled, the response rate between the screening interview and on-site interview being measured in weeks

rather than days, the candidate not being informed whether travel expenses are reimbursed, as well as the name of the interviewer and the case studies not being communicated soon enough. This is why it is essential to have a recruiting coordination team with a designated recruiter to oversee this process.

- **Assessments and offer decisions are shared in writing**
  If the results of an interview are shared among the interviewers only in writing, it may affect the quality of the hiring decision. A live discussion involving all the interviewers allows them to exchange and reflect on their assessments, compare candidates, refine their judgment and arrive at a joint decision. This taps into the "wisdom of the crowd" and makes it more likely that the right candidate will be employed. Having at least one woman on the panel is important to counter any unconscious bias against female candidates.

- **A junior team vetoes candidates, as they want to keep working directly with the hiring manager**
  This can happen when the hiring manager is a CXO, director or head and a top people manager. The "pirate ship" team from the early days may want to continue working with this person directly and sabotage the recruitment funnel in the process. It is essential to mitigate this by making it clear that the team may offer their recommendations, but the hiring manager is ultimately responsible for the decision.

- **Rejection messages are not personalized**
  Sending a rejection message that feels to the candidate like they have received an impersonal template can end up adversely affecting the employer brand. A personalized rejection communicates to the candidate that the company intends to stay in touch with them for other roles, appreciates the time and effort they have spent on the process and provides links to resources that will help the candidate with their job hunt. For some examples of inspiring rejection messages, see *The Builder's Guide* public resources here.

- **Insufficient tool support**
  Without a proper applicant tracking system (ATS) and scheduling tools, hiring staff efficiently at high volumes is simply not possible. The recruiting teams need to be equipped with a well-functioning ATS that has CRM-like features to track and manage the inflow of candidates throughout the process. They also require access to sourcing and job posting tools, such as LinkedIn Recruiter, Honeypot, The Muse, Hired, Workable People Search and more.

Practice 15: Boosting the offer acceptance rates

A contested talent pool can often lead to offers being declined. This is where making the effort to "close" candidates comes into play. This phase is often severely underestimated, despite an employer being at their most vulnerable here. During this phase, a candidate will have informed their current employer of the situation, and this employer may seek to change the candidate's mind with a strong offer.

Typical pitfalls in this phase include the following:

- **You take a "no" for a "no"**
  Persistent follow-ups showing appreciation for the candidate can often turn an early "no" into a successful new hire. This appreciation should be shown over months. It is also important for the hiring manager to make regular follow-up calls and emails (with an appreciative tone), and even share relevant blog posts, podcasts or books with the candidate. A proactive call by the CEO or founder is another avenue to explore.
- **The candidate's living situation is not properly taken into account**
  If a candidate needs to relocate, find a place to live or support their partner's search for a job, it is important to extend assistance in this area.
- **You do leverage neutral parties enough when looking for candidates**
  Neutral refers to everybody from venture capitalists to mutual acquaintances. If a VC shares the story of why they decided to invest in the company and why they believe in it, this can be a powerful boost during the pre-closing phase.
- **Your recruiting team is not being incentivized in the right way**
  If monetary incentives are the method used to boost, performance is contested. What usually pays off is to agree on clear goals (e.g., recruiting targets) and measure them in regular performance and learning dialog sessions that form a basis for appraisal and promotion. However, if a people team chooses to work with bonuses, one option is to put an amount of money in a virtual pot each time a new hire passes their probation period. The pot is then spent on an event that recognizes the efforts of the team every six months, and the remainder is shared amongst the recruiting team. People team leaders can be rewarded separately (e.g., by issuing a bonus for meeting their hiring targets). For example, a team manager could receive a

100% bonus if a team leader meets their hiring goals for the quarter (and the number of contracts signed with >95% passing during their probation period). If they do not meet their goals, the bonus is paid pro rata only.

Organizational development

Practice 16: Establishing a strong job architecture with clear levels, career paths and tracks

In most surveys on why millennials leave their companies, one of the top three reasons is "a lack of career development opportunities."[86] Once a company enters the later growth stages – usually beyond 300 FTEs – taming the "zoo" of different job titles and salary levels starts to matter more. While in a startup a certain degree of chaos regarding the job architecture is common and accepted, a growing scale-up should aspire to live up to higher standards. Series C is usually a good time to start, because this phase is often when the people function becomes more formalized.[87] Using a job leveling exercise to refine and streamline the job architecture is considered good practice, as this will provide transparency on possible career paths and perceived fairness when it comes to salaries and promotions. Job leveling refers to classifying all jobs within the company according to a specific level, which is usually tied to a salary band and a title (manager, senior manager, director). The job levels can be used to set a baseline salary and determine a position's eligibility for different kinds of short and long-term reward programs, bonus targets and equity grant guidelines.[88]

There are four essentials to a healthy job architecture:
- **Creating clarity on the key dimensions of a job architecture**
  - *Job families*
    These are jobs that belong to a similar domain involving similar work, skills and knowledge. Engineering and finance are two typical families, while a sub-family would be front-end development or accounting.[89] The job evaluation service company Gradar provides a good overview of typical job families.[90]

- *Job titles*
  These refer to the individual roles and titles within job sub-families (e.g., Head of Customer Service or Senior Manager Performance Marketing).
- *Levels and related pay grades*
  Each job position needs to be allocated to a particular level (e.g., from L1 to L10). For example, the Head of Customer Service could be on Level 6, while the Director of Performance Marketing is on Level 7 and a CXO is on Level 10. The level is usually linked to an overlapping salary range (i.e., a high-performing L6 may earn more than an L7 who has recently joined the company). The range midpoints for each pay grade are often at least 10–15% apart from each other.[91]
- *Career tracks*
  Some employees are outstanding experts in their field, but they are either unable or do not want to manage people. For these colleagues, some companies create "expert tracks" that facilitate career advancements and salary rises without them having to manage more people each time (see below for details).
- **Building a unified leveling system that maps jobs to levels for all functions**
  This should include mapping positions to the relevant job levels. In functions such as Operations – which have employees with lower entry qualification hurdles on the payroll – entry-level jobs usually start at Level 1. By contrast, in functions such as marketing – where employees usually start with the equivalent of a Bachelor's or Master's – the entry positions are grouped in higher tiers (see Figure 17).

		Engineering	Marketing	Operations
Business Leadership	10	Chief Technology Officer (CTO)	Chief Marketing Officer (CMO)	Chief Operating Officer (COO)
	9	VP of Engineering	VP of Marketing	VP of Operations
Management and Professional	8	Director of Software Development	Director of Marketing	Director of Operations
	7	Head of Software Development	Head of Marketing	Head of Operations
	6	Senior Engineering Manager	Senior Marketing Manager	Senior Operations Manager
	5	Engineering Manager	Marketing Manager	Operations Manager
Entry Level and Support	4	Senior Software Engineer	Marketing Specialist	Operations Supervisor
	3	Software Engineer	Marketing Analyst	Customer Experience Specialist / Team Leader
	2	-	-	Customer Experience Senior Associate
	1	-	-	Customer Experience Associate

Figure 17: Building a Unified Leveling System
Source: Radford, 2018; ONGIG

- **Establishing leadership and an expert track as two equally valued career paths**
  For experts who cannot or do not want to lead people, an expert track is a good option, as it enables the company to retain top experts without forcing them into leadership roles. A major pitfall here is seeing the expert track as "second class." Employees embarking on an expert track need to have the opportunity to reach the highest possible level, similar to CXO positions on the leadership track and with comparable compensation (see an example of an expert track in Figure 18).

Example of a Dual Track for the Engineering Job Family

LEVEL	EXPERT TRACK	LEADERSHIP TRACK
10	Fellow Engineer	CTO
9	Distinguished Engineer	VP of Engineering
8	Senior Principal Software Engineer	Director of Software Development
7	Principal Software Engineer	Head of Software Development
6	Senior Staff Software Engineer	Senior Engineering Manager
5	Staff Software Engineer	Engineering Manager
4	Senior Software Engineer	Engineering Team Lead
3	Software Engineer	

Figure 18: Example of a Dual Track for the Engineering Job Family
Source: Brandwatch, 2020; Buffer, 2019; Levels.fyi, 2021; Radford, 2018; Proton, 2021[92]

- **Getting the leveling process right**
  Job leveling often provides mid-term benefits but short-term pains, as it can trigger discussions regarding fairness and perceived appreciation for achievements. When doing so for the first time, it is essential not to conflate the leveling exercise with a salary adjustment. The latter can be done once the levels are established. Here is one possible blueprint:
  - Announce the leveling exercise transparently to all employees (along with the goals and the process).
  - Build a level rubric – the graphs above can serve as inspiration.
  - Add all current job positions for all functions to one spreadsheet (positions only, no employee names).

- Hold multiple leveling workshops with functional leaders and CXOs to assign their jobs to the new levels.
- Coordinate with the CXOs on the levels for each function.
- Communicate the new levels to the employees with an implicit (not explicit) option to give feedback in case of major errors.
- Log the levels in the employee database.

When assigning a job to a specific level, the following criteria typically apply:[93]
- **Mastery**: the degree of functional knowledge or technical skills required for the job (e.g., coding, programming languages, etc.).
- **Scope and impact**: the degree to which duties and responsibilities influence the company's overall success (e.g., core changes to product features, decisions regarding company direction, etc.).
- **Leadership, influence and collaboration**: the degree of stakeholder management, collaboration and influence over other teams and the function.

Practice 17: Putting fair appraisal and promotion processes in place

Employees who believe promotions to be fair and transparent are more than twice as likely to consider remaining at the company in the long term.[94] The opposite is also true: poor promotion and appraisal management can quickly lead to high employee turnover. Here are the three major pitfalls to avoid when designing an appraisal and promotion process:
- **Inconsistent appraisal frameworks that change too much over time**
  The type of assessment framework employed is less important than ensuring consistency and stability over time. Here's an example: Amazon has 14 leadership principles. While this may not be the most condensed framework ever developed, they are applied consistently in hiring and in promotion decisions. With this, every applicant and every promotion candidate is assessed based on these values. One widely used appraisal framework assesses employee performance in a role compared to growth trajectory (see Figure 19). Performance can refer to the degree to which the employee delivers on

their agreed OKRs, shows measurable business results and/or puts together a committed team. The growth dimension may refer to the degree to which the employee has shown the ability to assume increasingly complex and ever-broader accountability, as required by the next job level (e.g., by building up a team of interns and leading them while still fulfilling an individual contributor role). While excellent performance should be rewarded with higher salaries and bonuses, it **should not** directly lead to a promotion – stellar individual contributions are not enough in themselves to pave the way for progress along the leadership path.

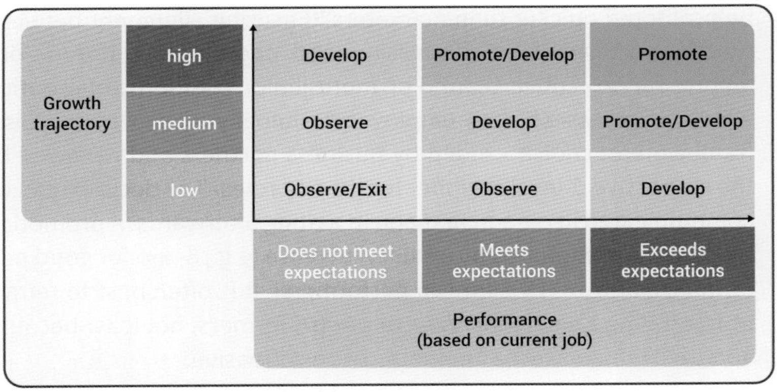

Growth trajectory	high	Develop	Promote/Develop	Promote
	medium	Observe	Develop	Promote/Develop
	low	Observe/Exit	Observe	Develop
		Does not meet expectations	Meets expectations	Exceeds expectations
		Performance (based on current job)		

Figure 19: Employee Performance and Growth Trajectory
Source: Adaption of Cornerstone, 2020[95]

- **Insufficient use of multiple sources to inform decisions regarding promotion**
  An appraisal and the decision as to whether an employee should be promoted should never be the responsibility of a single direct manager. Instead, the appraisal process should be built around multiple sources: the direct line manager, who interviews several coworkers individually, the dotted line manager (if available) and a self-assessment by the employee. The employment platform Indeed has a good self-assessment framework in the form of the following questions:[96] "Are there parts of your job you wish you could do less or more of? What contributions or achievements have you made

during the review period? Do you have skills that are not being fully utilized in your current role? How would you improve your department? How could you improve your performance? What is the one thing you need from your manager more than anything else to help you grow? What skills could you develop through education, training or mentorship?" It is often worth encouraging employees to seek out the opinion of 4–5 peers and other stakeholders when completing the self-assessment.

- **Insufficient refinement process with a group of decision-makers**
Ideally, there should be a similar standard in place across all levels when making decisions regarding a promotion. Otherwise, employee engagement may be adversely affected (if, say, engineers tend to be promoted quicker than marketers). Ensuring alignment between functions comes from discussing and coordinating promotions among the executive team. For more junior positions, one option would be to assess each employee biannually using the appraisal framework of choice – aided by business partners and reviewed by the respective C-level member for the key roles. The decision can be communicated in person first and in writing afterwards. A promotion is usually accompanied by a salary increase (e.g., 5–8% for good performance and 10–15% for top performers). It is often best to refrain from offering a salary increase to low performers, not least because a 1% to 2% increase may come across as offensive.

Employee experience

Practice 18: Driving employee happiness by enabling meaning, mastery, psychological safety, autonomy and community

Work in a thriving growth-stage startup can be both fun and demanding. After all, autonomy is high, while the learning curves are refreshingly steep. The trade-off here is that communication never seems to stop across any of the channels, many leaders seem to be online and working 24/7, and the pressure to deliver is often extremely high. In this kind of environment, shaping the employee experience is the key to retaining your teams and instilling lasting beneficial values. While the process here is different for every company, there are usually several elements a company can provide or facilitate to boost the employee experience:

- **Purpose and meaningful work**

  SpaceX's "Turn humanity into a multiplanetary species," Nike's "Bring inspiration and innovation to every athlete* in the world (*if you have a body, you are an athlete)" and Square's "Empower everyone to participate and thrive in the economy" are prime examples of a great purpose. According to multiple surveys, one of the top career goals for many Millennials is to have the chance to work on solving social and/or environmental challenges.[97] It is important to make the following question crystal clear: Why, exactly, does the company make the planet a better place? It is also essential that leaders connect all team members' tasks to the overall purpose. Are you building a FinTech that aims to enable millions of women to become investors? Every software developer, for example, should then understand that every line of code contributes to this purpose. The examples in the North Star chapter (see Practice 1) and the values outlined in the ESG practices (see Practices 7, 8 and 9) are strong starting points.

- **Mastery**

  Amazon has pledged USD 700 million for its "Upskilling 2025" program that aims to train its employees with future highly in-demand skills, including a "Machine Learning University," an Amazon apprenticeship and training and certification for AWS.[98] Companies including Google and IBM have invested in creating massive open online courses on sites such as Udacity or Coursera that teach current employees specific skills in fields such as machine learning, while sourcing potential talent from the vast pool of online learners. People often seek to become a better version of themselves. According to one survey, nine out of ten employees say that upskilling annually is the minimum required to be able to remain operationally effective in the digital age.[99] Team members often ask for different options – development budget, a training catalog, coaching, mentoring and/ or ongoing feedback – that will allow them to build up their skills accordingly.

- **Psychological safety**

  According to several studies conducted by Google, psychological safety is the number-one factor that underpins any high-performing team. The safer each team member feels with the rest of the crew, the more likely they are to admit mistakes, partner with others on specific key tasks and take on new roles. Google found that team members who feel psychologically safe provide benefits in four ways: they are less likely to leave the company, they are more likely to seek and incorporate diverse ideas from their teammates, they bring in more revenue overall and executives rate them as effective twice as often.[100] Netflix reached a similar conclusion, which is why it facilitates self-improvement in an environment where every team member tries to help each other grow.[101] Part of this comes from being honest. Managers are encouraged not to blame employees if they make a mistake but to turn the mirror on themselves and ask where they could have improved the starting situation (e.g., by linking the task to a company goal, assigning a level of priority, focusing on a key metric, etc.).[102] And measuring psychological safety counts, too. Some teams at Google measure this in surveys with questions such as: "How confident are you that you won't receive retaliation or criticism if you admit an error or make a mistake?"[103]

- **Autonomy & clarity of roles**
  When it comes to granting autonomy to employees, Netflix believes in the motto of "Context before control." For example, take the company's vacation policy, which encourages Netflix employees to take breaks when they need them.[104] This unlimited vacation time may sound radical, but tech companies such as Netflix, LinkedIn, Buffer and Kickstarter all have this initiative in place. For these companies, the focus is on employees getting things done rather than on how much time they work.[105] One danger to manage is that people are actually discouraged to take a vacation – stating a minimum vacation, which everyone should take, is one option here. Enabling the team to focus is part of this as well. For instance, a growth-stage startup could introduce "get things done" days (i.e., focused periods with no meetings or calls and a remote-first policy). When Instagram's Head of Engineering noticed the lack of decision-making transparency in its rapidly growing teams, he decided to use the RACI framework, which defines in advance who is **R**esponsible, **A**ccountable, **C**onsulted and **I**nformed about a project. They implemented a *responsibility assignment matrix*. As a result, engineering's scores improved by 10%, making it among the highest across Facebook, while the division scaled from 100 to 600 people.[106]

- **Community**
  Creating a community that employees strongly identify with is important. Many growth-stage scale-ups will tend to do some of the following to reinforce this community identity: create a culture of recognition (in which successes are celebrated), hold regular team events – in an off-site location – establish and use online communication channels (e.g., Slack) for ongoing communication among leaders, create shared environments with a casual atmosphere, build a Wow! wall encouraging peer-to-peer recognition,[107] put on free breakfasts or after-work drinks and provide access to a gym and other health facilities to bring the people together.[108]

Employee stock option programs

Practice 19: Building the right employee stock option program

(Note: The content here is intended for general information purposes only. It is not legal advice. For more details on growth term sheets, see Chapter 12.)

The startup life promises much: personal development, autonomy, the chance to build a company that changes the world for the better. What it often cannot promise is the highest salary. This is why many startups offer employees a slice of the pie in the form of an Employee Stock Option Program (ESOP). Employees accept a lower base salary in exchange for ownership of the company—and a rich reward if the startup goes public or is acquired. Giving as many employees access to a stock ownership program matters on several levels. For one thing, it makes hiring easier: new hires with at least a few years of professional experience will expect to receive this option. It also boosts retention rates, as the program's value vests over several years. Finally, it puts all employees on the same path toward the same goal: building a lasting, valuable company that delights customers. Index Venture has published an excellent guide on designing ESOP programs for European entrepreneurs.[109] Local tax laws have a strong say as to the type of stock option program you may design. The following programs are common: stock grants (employees receive shares directly), stock options (employees receive the right to buy shares at a certain price and date), and virtual stock options. Virtual shares are an especially popular choice. They essentially constitute a bonus payment in the event of a successful exit or an event that triggers the payments to all employees and investors (usually an IPO or a trade sale to an acquiring entity).

ESOP schemes tend to incorporate the following dimensions:
- **Number of shares**
  This is the number of shares from the ESOP pool, which are fully allocated to the employee after the vesting time frame. It is expressed as a percentage of the company or in absolute valuation terms. **What is common?** The percentages offered vary widely based on experience and investment round. The more experienced and the earlier the hire, the higher the number of shares. Index venture published some guidelines on the number of shares to allocate.[110]
- **Vesting schedule**
  To prevent an individual from exiting a startup too soon, companies allocate more and more shares to employees over time. This schedule is sometimes "back-loaded." As an example, Amazon gives its employees 10% of their shares in the first year, 20% in the second, 30% in the third and 40% in the fourth.[111] **What is common?** A typical vesting time frame is three to four years, with monthly or quarterly vesting and a certain degree of back-loading being common.
- **Strike price**
  If an employee joins a startup early on, they should receive a greater reward than a person who joins much later. This is why a so-called strike price (or exercise price) exists: it prevents latecomers from cashing in on the value others have created. If, for example, a share is priced at USD 1,000 when a new hire signs a contract and the price has risen to USD 20,000 when the company is bought four years later, the value that specific employee has co-created is USD 19,000 (i.e., the current share price, which is USD 20,000, minus the strike price, which is USD 1,000). In the case of an exit event, the employee, therefore, receives USD 19,000 for each share. This is a standard logic employed by startups. **What is common?** It is recommended to use the strike price of the previous funding round. While there are cases where the company will offer a higher strike price, this should only be considered if there is clear evidence of a higher current share value (e.g., a signed term sheet from a new investor with a higher valuation).

- **Cliff period**
  A cliff is the period an employee has to wait until they receive their stock options. For a one-year cliff, all their options from the first 12 months vest collectively at the start of month 13. From that point on, they will receive their shares on a monthly or quarterly basis depending on the agreement. **What is common?** A 12-month cliff is the industry standard. An employee may be able to negotiate this down but only in exceptional circumstances.

- **Accelerated vesting**
  In the event of an exit or a change in ownership, an employee stock ownership package should contain a clause covering what should happen. All unvested shares may be allocated to the employee at once. Alternatively, only those shares that apply to the exit will be vested. Employee acceleration across the board is considered poor practice, as it sends out the message that an acquisition is the end of the road.[112] **What is common?** For leadership roles in particular, accelerated vesting is common.

- **Bad leaver/good leaver clauses**
  If an employee breaks the law and is fired (e.g., due to fraud or embezzlement), they will usually need to transfer back all their shares. If, however, they decide to leave the company on their own terms within a given time frame (e.g., within four years), they will either have to transfer back all unvested shares or all shares. If an employee is let go due to non-legal reasons, the employee can usually keep the vested shares. **What is common?** There is no common scenario here. However, most consider it fair that employees who leave may keep some of the shares after a certain time period (e.g., two or three years).

Recommended publications:
- Laszlo Bock, (2016). *Work Rules!: Insights from Inside Google That Will Transform How You Live and Lead.*
- Andrew Grove (1995). *High Output Management.*
- Ben Horowitz (2019). *What You Do Is Who You Are.*
- Daniel Pink (2011). *Drive: The Surprising Truth About What Motivates Us.*

Definitions

- **Accelerated vesting**: the process through which a vesting schedule is sped up to entitle the recipient employee to ownership of the vested stock faster than originally planned; typically used during acquisitions or IPOs to protect employee compensation and thus encourage employee loyalty.
- **Appraisal**: an assessment of an employee's performance in their job, which is used to identify skill gaps and training opportunities, possible promotions and pay rises, and terminations of employment.
- **ATS (Applicant Tracking System)**: a tool for helping companies to organize job applications and the recruitment process to maximize efficiency in hiring new staff.
- **Career tracks**: the pathway through an occupational field within an organization – usually there is at least a managerial track with people leadership responsibilities and an expert track without.
- **Cliff period**: a defined period of time after which an employee begins to take ownership of money, stock or other assets that are given to them by their employer; the employee will have no entitlement to the money, stock or other assets until the cliff period has been completed in its entirety.
- **cNPS (Candidate Net Promoter Score)**: a measurement of the experience that candidates have during a company's recruitment process, assessed by asking candidates how likely they are to recommend the company to friends and family.
- **eNPS (Employee Net Promoter Score)**: a measure of employee satisfaction, assessed by asking employees how likely they are to recommend their place of work to friends and family.
- **ESOP (Employee Stock Ownership Plan)**: an employee benefit plan that gives employees the ability to participate financially when the company is floated on a public stock market or is acquired.
- **Job architecture**: the organizing principles and hierarchy of jobs within a company, including job titles, pay grades, career paths and career tracks.
- **Job families**: groupings of jobs that involve similar types of work, skills, knowledge and expertise. Useful for defining career tracks, setting pay grades and building training programs.

- **Job leveling**: the process to ensure comparability in terms of payments and career promotion between similar jobs.
- **Onboarding**: the process of inducting newly hired employees into a company, orienting them in their role and responsibilities and helping them adapt to the company culture.
- **Onsite-to-offer rate**: the percentage of hires from all candidates invited to onsite interviews and one metric on the efficiency of a company's recruitment process.
- **Regretted attrition**: the percentage of employees who leave on their own accord, not counting those which the company lets go and those rated as low performers.
- **Strike price**: the pre-agreed price defined in an Employee Stock Ownership Plan that an employee must pay to purchase stock in the company.
- **Time to fill**: the average number of days from when a job is posted until the new hire starts.
- **Time to hire**: the average number of days from when a candidate applies for a position until the contract is signed.
- **Time to react**: the average number of days from when a candidate applies for a job until they are sent either an interview invite or a rejection.
- **Vesting schedule**: a timetable that sets out when employees take ownership of stock or other assets given to them by their employer under their employee compensation plan; ownership is usually assumed in stages over a period of time to encourage employee loyalty.

How to avoid the seven key pitfalls in building up an AAA team? Watch our video by scanning the QR code or following this link: https://youtube/l1NqBpaiM_Y.

How to set up a people team that can scale? Scan the QR code or follow this link to find out: https://youtube/edwB9SkO_gY.

4   Scale-Up Mindset

Principles to bridge organizational silos

With Johannes Lenhard

Key pitfalls for scale-up builders   !

- **Ignoring the risk of organizational silo-building for too long**
  With rising complexity in each scale-up function, it is natural that the teams start looking inward. Ignoring this for too long can lead to a non-aligned direction and lack of execution.
- **Lack of customer experience focus**
  Customer experience will be interpreted differently by each team. Not having measurable experience goals (e.g., with company-wide NPS targets that align the teams) is one key pitfall to avoid (see Practice 20).
- **Thinking in "or" rather than "and"**
  Often goals seem to conflict (e.g., growth vs. profit, speed vs. quality) and many teams discuss these as "either. . . or." A successful scale-up will always try to reconcile seemingly contradictory goals (see Practice 21).
- **Lack of learning cycles**
  "Idea meritocracy" and psychological safety are often introduced as elements of a scale-up's culture too late (see Practice 22)
- **Insufficiently enabling teams to work autonomously**
  With rising size, the interconnectedness of teams will increase. Actively delegating decision power (e.g., with cross-functional product and tech teams, growth hacking teams or independent service teams) will often boost productivity and employee morale (see Practice 23).

In a startup, the generalists are the queens and kings. However, in scale-ups, specialists start counting more. For example, while the paid marketing generalist was sufficient in the early phase, now the company might need an expert for paid advertising on Instagram. The primary issue that often emerges in this transition is that increasingly complex scale-up functions start forming organizational "silos," which can lead to a lack of cross-functional collaboration and alignment.

To ensure continued cross-functional collaborations in the scale-up phase, the following four principles are needed to bridge organizational silos and get teams to collaborate effectively:

- **Obsession with customer experience**
  Improving key customer journey experiences as a top priority for leaders.
- **Impossible-is-nothing**
  Setting an impossible-is-nothing attitude by thinking in terms of "and," not "or."
- **Learn-it-all beats know-it-all**
  Embracing learning cycles by establishing psychological safety and an idea meritocracy.
- **Autonomy to act**
  Empowering cross-functional teams to make decisions rapidly and independently.

Obsession with customer experience

Practice 20: Improving key customer journey experiences as a top priority for leaders

Amazon is the prime example of a company with an obsession with customer experience. CEO Jeff Bezos and his teams consider themselves to be the world's most customer-centric company – a path they have followed since its early days as a book retailer. Customer obsession is enshrined as the first and most important principle of Amazon's 14 leadership principles. For example, before building any technical product, each product team writes a press statement that includes hypothetical customer quotes to work backward from the desired outcomes delivered to the customers. As rumor has it, Amazon CEO Jeff Bezos even left an empty chair in his executive team meetings to symbolize the importance of the customer when the company was still scaling up. Overall, 90% of what Amazon is building is a result of customer feedback, with the other 10% coming from industry trends and data insights.[113]

This obsession with customer experience makes sense. Companies with an industry-leading Net Promoter Score (NPS) grow by more than 2x on average in comparison to competitors with an industry-standard NPS.[114]

Growth is frequently driven by so-called "promoters" (i.e., customers that rate companies with a 9 or 10 (on a scale from 1–10) on the Net Promoter Scores survey). For example, loyal clients of retail banks are three times less likely to switch to a different provider within one year, have a 20% higher wallet share and are twice as likely to refer their bank to friends and family – in comparison to detractors (customers with a low NPS).[115]

In many tech companies, leaders will claim that everything they do is about improving the customer experience. In reality, they are measuring their success very differently: e.g., based on new customers per month (Marketing), usage rates (Product) or contacts per customer (Operations). This is why it is often important to instill a Chief Customer Officer mindset among every leader and have them work toward turning customer experience (CX) into the lifeblood that pumps through the heart of the company. Ideally, every leader should view exceptional customer experience as one of their primary goals, one that is on par with growth, profit, revenue and cost savings. This also applies to the executive team.

In particular, there are three building blocks that matter:
- **Build a shared perspective across all functions along key customer journeys**
  Sometimes product teams start drawing "user journeys" in one corner of the company while the customer operations teams develop their own version of "customer journeys" in the other corner. The result: the teams will not share the same perspective on how customers view their interactions with the company. They will have internal difficulties in aligning initiatives and might fail to work together toward customer success. Customer journeys can be a powerful tool to prevent this. They provide a common language to prioritize work for customers. These customer journeys refer to all the steps taken by the customer to meet a specific need. For example, when opening a bank account online, the journey starts with the customer doing research before choosing an account, uploading documents, completing a video verification process and performing an initial transaction (see example below). The journeys are usually bundled into journey groups (e.g., join & onboard, money in, money out). These key journeys can be the basis for prioritizing the product development roadmap, co-creating a chatbot's answer structure, formulating website

FAQs, etc. It is essential for all leaders and teams to prioritize improving the Net Promoter Score across the key customer journeys.

The leaders of any growth-stage scale-up should have a shared overview of all key customer journeys. See Figure 20 for an idea of how this would work at a FinTech.

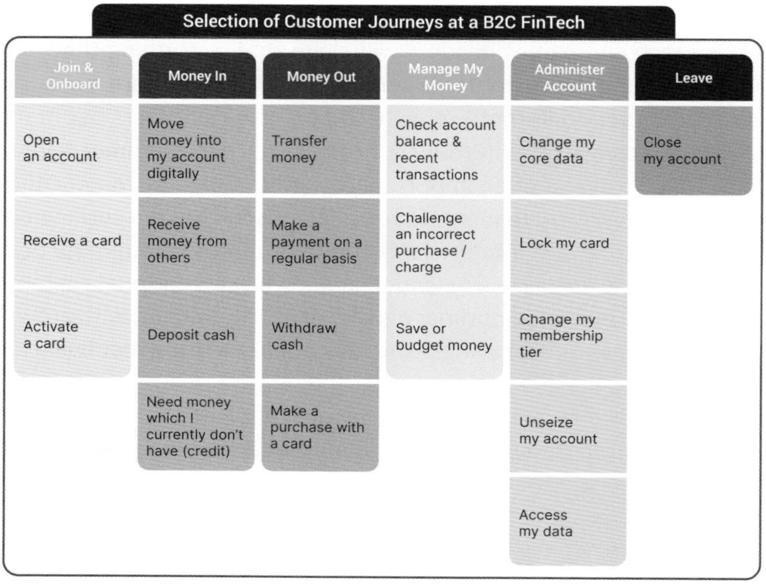

Selection of Customer Journeys at a B2C FinTech					
Join & Onboard	Money In	Money Out	Manage My Money	Administer Account	Leave
Open an account	Move money into my account digitally	Transfer money	Check account balance & recent transactions	Change my core data	Close my account
Receive a card	Receive money from others	Make a payment on a regular basis	Challenge an incorrect purchase / charge	Lock my card	
Activate a card	Deposit cash	Withdraw cash	Save or budget money	Change my membership tier	
	Need money which I currently don't have (credit)	Make a purchase with a card		Unseize my account	
				Access my data	

Figure 20: Selection of Customer Journeys at a B2C FinTech
Source: Bain & Company, internal research

- **Establish a holistic Net Promoter management approach based around customer journeys**

  Measuring a company's overall NPS is all well and good, but what truly matters is the "Journey Net Promoter Scores." Typical questions to ask here may include variations on the following: How did the onboarding NPS develop after bringing a new video identity provider into the fold?; Did the product-usage NPS improve after a new feature went live?; Did the NPS of customers using the English chatbot improve after it was relaunched? Granular measurements like this allow initiatives to be steered according to how much they contribute toward the NPS. Additionally, they help to create regular

NPS feedback loops for the executive team and use NPS development as one element of the OKR system.

- **Design (unique) customer-centricity rituals**
  Gusto, a US-based cloud-focused payroll solution provider for businesses, achieved an NPS of 75 with 40,000 customers – in the B2B space, this is an extraordinary result. Their magic formula? Besides a great product, they differentiated with a relentless focus on a great customer experience and reinforced this with rituals like sending a monthly customer voice pack featuring quantitative and qualitative metrics to the entire company, delivering CX onboarding training, issuing CX Awards that reward outstanding customer experience contributions, and putting CX on the agenda of every customer conference.[116] Another one is Clio. This legal practice management software provider holds an annual user conference that allows employees to meet customers in person. The first day is spent by developers collecting input and ideas from attendees. Then, on day two, improvements in the online software are implemented based on the feedback they got on day one. Making such rapid adjustments reflects a company's dedication to assisting its customers in their success and is often a great way of boosting employee engagement.[117]

Impossible is nothing

Practice 21: Setting impossible-is-nothing goals by thinking "and," not "or"

For a long time, tech entrepreneurs have been attracted to goals that aim to make the seemingly impossible possible. Henry Ford is a good example. In 1930, he ordered his chief engineers to build eight cylinders on an engine block. After a year of trying, they told him it was impossible. Ford's answer? "Keep going until you succeed. Time and money don't matter." The technical breakthrough came soon after, and the V8 engine was born. The "man on the moon" speech of 1961 by US President John F. Kennedy is an overstretched example, but it is one that makes the same point. In this speech, JFK announced that an American would walk on the moon by the end of the decade. At first, NASA was in a state of shock, but then its budget was boosted by 400%, the Apollo project was launched and in July 1969, Neil Armstrong took his first steps on the moon. Mathematician Katherine Johnson was also working on this project. As an African-American woman, she sought to become a pioneer in the predominantly white male domain of space travel. She succeeded, overcame racial segregation and became one of the first computer programmers at NASA. None of this would have been possible if these teams were not pushing the envelope of what is possible. Instead of aiming for gradual improvement in small steps, major progress comes when people aim for the stars. Research also proves this. These ambitious and specific goals can lead to unparalleled performance, and this is one of the most validated hypotheses in management literature.[118]

For leaders like Henry Ford, John F. Kennedy and Katherine Johnson, these goals are not a quarterly aim. Rather, they are a burning desire that consumes every waking moment. Whether setting foot on the moon or establishing a foothold in a new market, successful leaders often develop a seemingly irrational obsession with a goal and pursue it in the face of all resistance. The boxer Muhammad Ali, considered by many as the best heavyweight boxer of the 20th century, captured the idea nicely when he framed his winning mindset with an "Impossible is nothing" attitude:[119]

> "Impossible is just a big word thrown around by small men who find it easier to live in the world they've been given than to explore the power they have to change it. Impossible is not a fact. It's an opinion. Impossible is not a declaration. It's a dare. Impossible is potential. Impossible is temporary."
> Muhammad Ali

When scaling startups, these "impossible-is-nothing-goals" are often captured in a purpose that inspires and a business ambition that attracts – such as with KhanAcademy's "Provide a free, world-class education for anyone, anywhere" (see Chapter 1 for details). However, these big goals are often not enough. Scaling up tech companies requires thinking in "and," not "or." Startups need to grow rapidly *and* comply with banking compliance standards. They need to develop a two-year strategy *and* pursue short-term growth opportunities. They need to launch products in the short term *and* invest in scalable software architecture for the long run. Every function has goals that are in conflict – they help to provide a healthy tension:

- **People:** Hire 10 AAA leaders in record time *and* keep payroll costs low
  Solution: Offer attractive ESOP packages to leaders that could earn substantially higher salaries in the corporate world
- **Product:** Grow the user base fast *and* increase average revenue per user
  Solution: Launch a large feature (e.g., shared accounts for a FinTech) and make it accessible to all customers with some limitations (e.g., only two shared accounts) while offering the full feature only in the premium tier
- **Technology:** Decrease the number of high-priority bugs in production *and* increase deployment frequency per developer per day
  Solution: Invest in a continuous delivery platform that automates code quality checks and enables autonomous code deployment by the teams
- **Marketing:** Create additional customer sign-ups *and* lower blended customer acquisition costs
  Solution: Invest in non-paid, organic marketing campaigns on organic channels (e.g., Instagram campaigns)
- **Sales:** Increase recurring revenues with new business customers *and* decrease the sales costs' payback time
  Solution: Design a sales commission plan that incentivizes sales reps if customers pay upfront
- **Service operations:** Increase first contact resolution *and* reduce cost-to-serve
  Solution: Outsource transactional contacts to experienced external contact centers that are usually cheaper and more efficient when it comes to routine customer journeys
- **Supply chain:** Increase the delivery experience NPS *and* reduce cost per order
  Solution: Invest in an automated warehouse management system and in lean six sigma type process optimizations that both drive operational efficiency *and* customer experience

Putting these seemingly contradictory goals into, for example, quarterly OKRs often stimulates creative thinking that leads to solutions that can deliver on both goals in question.

While pursuing these "and" goals, it is essential to be able to state a "primary target function" at any time. For example, Amazon has put growth – rather than profit – as its primary target function for many years. The "magic free team" question helps to figure out the primary target function at the current moment of time: "After waving with a magic wand, an additional team appears out of thin air which you do not have to pay for. Which goal would you allocate your free team to work on?" Growth of a customer base or better compliance? A new feature or better scalable technology architecture? The answer points to the primary target function at this moment in time.

A note of caution on big goals: "Impossible-is-nothing goals" are all well and good. However, fraud on the scale of Enron, Worldcom, Deutsche Bank, Lehman Brothers, VW and Wirecard doesn't lead to the winners' podium but only to prison.

Learn-it-all beats know-it-all

Practice 22: Embracing learning cycles by establishing psychological safety and an idea meritocracy

When the Head of the Spanish House of Trade Nuno Garcia de Toreno painted the so-called "Salviati World Map" in 1525, he adopted a Socratic mindset. Instead of following the contemporary habit of filling in unknown territory with mythical imagery, he left large patches of it blank. Those blank patches were the unknown, and it was a call to pioneers to explore uncharted waters. Many startups and technology companies follow this "Learn it all, not know it all" path. And while "impossible-is-nothing goals" matter, Socratic modesty to embrace failure and learning cycles when building unicorns counts, too.

There are various options to instill a learn-it-all-culture:
* **Reinforcing a learning culture by celebrating errors and making blameless retrospectives part of the culture**
  Google embraces this perfectly by practicing a culture of blameless postmortems, where mistakes are systematically analyzed for their root causes and are even highlighted in monthly newsletters, postmortem reading clubs and disaster role plays.[120] For example,

after the "Shakespeare Search" on Google was down for 66 minutes in 2015, at a time of high interest in Shakespeare due to the discovery of a new sonnet, Google published an example postmortem in its SRE Handbook (to be found here). Outages or any kind of severe incidents are not simply pushed to the side, but instead are taken as inspiration for active reflection to enable improvement. The core principle is to avoid blame, understand the root cause of the problem and find a solution so that it does not happen again in the future. It is often helpful to agree that after major incidents (e.g., unavailability of services for several hours, a large-scale fraud case) the executive team discusses the learnings of the retrospectives. These can run with the following logic: writing down the timeline of events that occurred, exploring the root causes of what happened and deciding on next steps to prevent the issue from happening in the future.[121] To instill a learning culture, Google very strongly focuses on establishing psychological safety (see Practices 18 and 42 for details). The key question for them: Can team members take risks without feeling insecure or embarrassed?[122] Team and company performance can increase when everyone feels safe and that they can admit difficulties and mistakes to work on improving together. A step to instill these values across the team are mutually agreed-upon team principles (written down and transparent) and regular team exercises, such as Google's "anxiety parties" where employees write down their biggest worries and share the list with their co-workers.[123] Facebook's earlier mantra "move fast and break things" even captures this directly. If you are not breaking things, you are delivering value too slowly.

- **Spreading the "idea meritocracy"**
What counts is not years of experience or an employee's position but a curiosity for better outcomes in the customers' eyes. For example, good ideas for the product roadmap can come from anywhere – from customers, the CEO or a newly hired intern. These should be evaluated independently of the source. The intern's idea on how to improve the onboarding flow might then win against the CEO's idea for a new sign-up page. McKinsey & Company, for example, reemphasizes this with the value "obligation to dissent." It is not only the right but also the duty of everyone on the team – from intern to senior partner – to challenge suggestions that they believe are not beneficial for clients. This principle should be adhered to strictly (i.e., a young colleague is given regular time to problem-solve issues with senior leaders and encouraged to speak up).

- **Giving extra time to learn autonomously and explore ideas**
  For example, Google asks employees to set aside 20% of their time to explore side projects, while other companies will schedule several "get things done" days per month for this. During these days, no regular meetings are scheduled, and all employees have the right to decline any request from a manager in order to be fully focused on their work. As a result, the email service Gmail was launched, having originated from an employee's side project.

Autonomy to act

Practice 23: Empowering cross-functional teams to make decisions rapidly & independently

History is full of examples of technology-driven ventures that were enabled by autonomously acting teams. One of them happened on October 21, 1805. On this day, the odds did not look good for British Admiral Nelson and his crews. Napoleon's Franco-Spanish Fleet aimed to launch a land invasion, and the British fleet was the last line of defense. There were 27 ships of Admiral Nelson that stood against 33 of the Napoleon army. Britain had not been this threatened since the time they fought off the Spanish Armada in 1588. In traditional naval battles of that time, admirals arranged ships in a parallel line, fired round after round with admirals centrally monitoring the battle and issuing commands via flags – a "duel of puppet masters," reliant on centralized command and control. Admiral Nelson chose a different approach. He let his ships approach in a perpendicular way to the lines of the British fleet – with full exposure for their cannon fire at first. However, as soon as the ships hit the enemy lines, all captains were told to act on their own initiative – decentralized decision-making and critical thinking, as opposed to simple execution of central commands. His only advice: "No captain can do very wrong if he places his ship alongside that of the enemy." The results speak for themselves: zero ships were lost for the British and half of the opponent's fleet were captured. Nelson and his crew won the battle, not through superior technology or resources but through a superior mindset of decentralized autonomy.

Likewise, it is often important to consider this principle when scaling tech companies. Almost all scale-up functions lend themselves to empower teams to take decisions autonomously:

- **Product and technology**

  In a growing scale-up and cross-functional product and tech teams, one central principle is often to set up the teams to be as technologically independent as possible. Ideally, they don't have to wait for each other when touching the code base, and they should have all the capabilities in their team to launch features to customers (e.g., team members from product management, design, software development, user research and data analytics). This enables them to make decisions on prioritization and create features with a relatively high degree of autonomy.

- **Service operations**

  Some companies set up customer success teams as mini-companies, co-located in one spot, that are encouraged to collaborate and solve customer issues autonomously, as they see fit. Under this Team of Experts model (TEX), T-Mobile in the United States was able to cut service costs by 13% and boost its Net Promoter Score by 50%. These cross-functional teams can include service reps, a team lead, dedicated coaches, technology specialists for more complex inquiries and a resource manager responsible for workforce planning. Its self-organized teams of ~50 colleagues serve customers in a specific region (e.g., San Diego) with a focus on loyalty and reinforcing relationships rather than contact handling time.

- **Marketing**

  Cross-functional growth hacking teams embed autonomous decision-making perfectly. They rapidly test new ideas to drive user growth, retention and monetization through the customer acquisition funnel in an iterate-learn-scale model. A typical approach is to have a team of marketeers, product managers, interaction designers, front-end developers and data analysts to develop, test and scale different versions of landing pages, product value propositions or customer referral programs (see Practice 60).

- **People**

  When expanding to new markets, some people teams send members of the global team to the new location and let them hire the first 10–15 people together with the business team on the ground relatively autonomously, while building a localized version of a small recruiting team.

Direction and capability are two key prerequisites for granting a great degree of team autonomy.

Recommended publication:
- C. W. Goodyear (2017). *One Mission: How Leaders Build a Team of Teams*.

FUNCTIONAL EXCELLENCE
IN SCALE-UPS

5   Product Management Excellence

Launching products that create value for customers

With Johnny Quach and Sven Grajetzki

Note: The product and technology functions in startups collaborate closely and sometimes will act as a single combined function. In this chapter, we assume a product-led model in which business-focused goals (e.g., acquisition, conversion, NPS, etc.) are addressed by autonomous product and technology teams led by product managers. Technology-platform-related topics, such as security, quality assurance and reliability, are covered in the Technology chapter.

Key pitfalls for scale-up builders   **!**

- **Working with a blurred product vision or without one at all**
  Some startups do not invest sufficiently in clarifying the core issue they want to solve for their customers. A good product vision articulates the reason WHY the product exists, rather than a detailed plan on WHAT and HOW to build the product. It is important to ensure teams can always refer back to the core issue they are trying to solve and see the product as a vehicle that delivers value to customers (see Practice 27).
- **Expanding into new regions or new segments too quickly (or too late)**
  Once a company enters a new market or takes its product into a new customer segment, they are slowing down learning curves in its core business. Strong retention and operational efficiency metrics, as well as favorable unit economics in the core markets, are a good sign of a readiness to expand. However, a market that will be divided amongst few players might necessitate regional expansion sooner (see Practices 24 and 29).
- **Not focusing enough on rapidly bringing users to the "magic point"**
  The magic point is when customers realize the value of the product for the first time. This point is often hidden behind a sign-up process or lengthy tutorial. After having found product-market fit, delivering the magic point as early as possible in the customer journey is a key driver for growth (see Practice 24).

- **Failing to identify the one defining part of the product which drives user delight**
  Many scale-ups have few components of the product that truly matter to delight customers. This might be the mobile app for a FinTech or supply chain software to drive up the delivery experience for an eCommerce company (see Practice 30).
- **Focusing on shipping features over customer value creation**
  Setting up the product function purely as a feature factory involves shipping a high volume of products without actually improving the lives of your customers. A product function in a scale-up needs to combine a reliable factory that can ship the right features at the right time with missionaries who care deeply about the outcomes they achieve. Amazon's internal press statement process is a prime example of this (see Practice 28).
- **Failing to align stakeholders on a shared perspective for mid-term success**
  Some product managers do not understand the objectives and key results of the business functions they work with enough (e.g., sales or operations). Sometimes the product and the business functions will develop separate perspectives on the joint output and outcome metrics to achieve. Ideally, the product teams will work with the business functions to define OKRs and North Star metrics (e.g., reorder frequency, share of wallet), which are stable enough and do not change too much on a quarterly basis (see Practice 28).
- **Setting up product and technology teams that are too dependent on each other**
  A need to frequently shift developers between teams or a high volume of complaints about dependency conflicts are signs that the product and technology teams are not set up to be independent enough. One way to resolve this is by dividing them into tooling and product-focused platform teams, experience teams that ship features to customers and growth teams that work cross-functionally (see Practice 25).
- **Lacking strong product culture rituals**
  Failing to embed strong rituals into a product team will erode your results-focused culture. By implementing quarterly kick-offs, quarterly retrospectives and bi-weekly demo days, a company can build a strong sense of ownership within its product team. Aligning all roadmap items to company-level OKRs will reinforce the sense that product management plays a critical role in the growing organization (see Practice 27).

The best performing product management functions are central hubs for customer value, not feature factories. Of all the teams in a scale-up, the product team needs to be most closely aligned with the company's North Star metric (as discussed in Chapter 1).

Many product functions in tech startups have to deal with shifting objectives. In the early startup phase, a company will usually focus on reaching a product-market fit fast – as measured by improving retention rates on a cohort basis. Once this point is reached, many companies will "pour fuel into the fire" by investing more in customer acquisition and activation. Depending on the business model and current funding needs, monetization and internal efficiency or expansion (entering new markets and/or launching new customer segments) will become critical. This is captured in our formula for product-led growth (Figure 21):

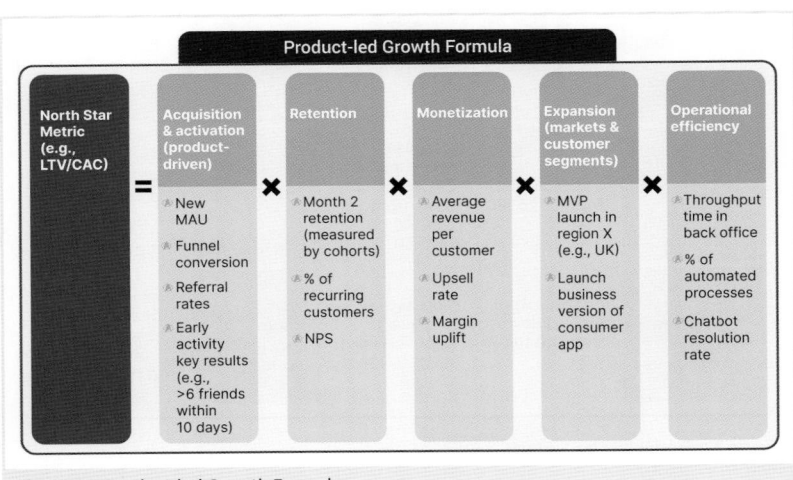

Figure 21: Product-led Growth Formula

This formula can be turned into objectives and key results (OKRs). Figure 22 is an example of a list of possible product OKRs for a FinTech.

OKRs

Practice 24: Establishing the right product OKRs

Typical Annual Product Objectives and Key results for a *FinTech* Scale-up

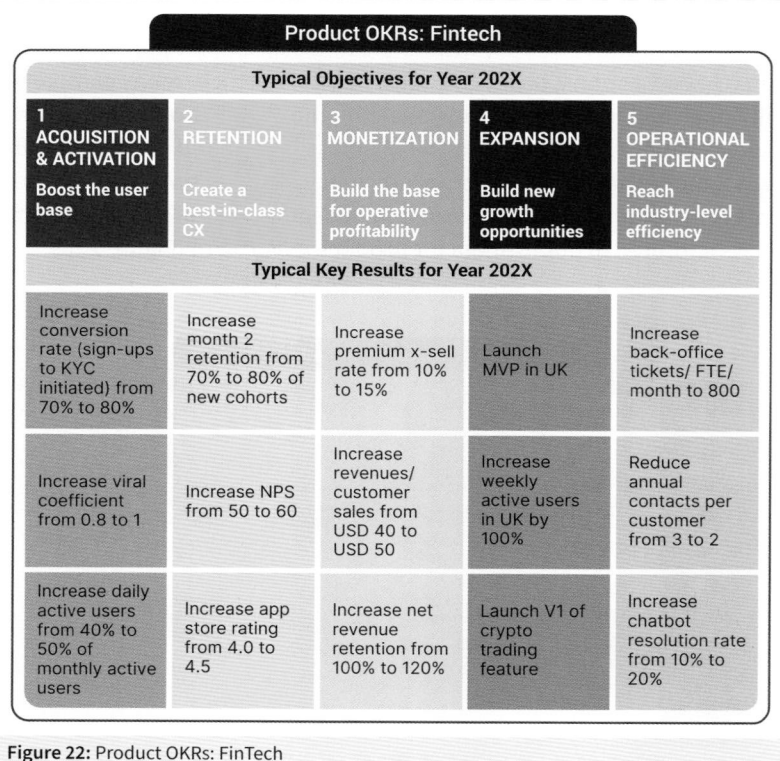

Figure 22: Product OKRs: FinTech

Now let's take a look at each objective and the key results in more detail. These objectives are illustrative of product functions. However, they will vary depending on context and can change over time.

O1. Acquisition and activation: Are your customers experiencing the "magic point" fast enough?
Bubble.io is a no-code product that allows anyone to build web applications through a visual interface. Its "magic point" is when a visitor realizes that they can build almost any web application without code by using

the service. A perfect example of reducing the space between entry and magic point is the "Edit this page to see how it works" link on the bubble. io homepage. By clicking on it, the link will send users forward to Bubble's demo editor tool that invites them to edit the Bubble homepage with the entirety of the Bubble toolkit. There is no login or sign-up necessary, which eliminates all friction for the users to a magic point.

Once the first signs of product-market fit become evident, many start-ups will pour fuel into the fire by investing in acquisition and activation. There are usually three types of fuel a product organization can choose from.

- **Move the magic point forward**
  This first experience with the product has to be valuable – otherwise, customers may never come back. Tinder understood this perfectly when it integrated with Facebook Connect early on. It made its users sign up through Facebook. The "magic point" for most dating services is when a user uploads their first profile photo and they receive attention from other users. Since connecting to Facebook gave Tinder access to a profile photo immediately, this allowed the user to reach the magic point seamlessly. Many companies try to capture the magic points using early activation metrics, with famous examples including Pinterest (at least three site visits per user in the first two weeks), Facebook (at least seven friends within 10 days) and Slack (at least 2,000 messages sent within a team).[124] For an eCommerce company, it could be one re-purchase made within 90 days, while a FinTech metric could be 10 transactions completed in the first 30 days. This is one of the most critical metrics to define as a scale-up (see Practice 60 on activation hacks).

- **Boost product-driven organic growth**
  This can include incentives for referring the service to others, with both parties benefiting or making it easy to invite non-users to try out the product. Permitting existing users to share content on social media and delivering good search engine rankings and app store ratings (often together with the marketing team) are also worth considering.

- **Improve conversion**
  Converting site visitors into active customers calls for friction to be eased in the acquisition funnel. Sean Ellis, the founder of

GrowthHackers, has a simple equation for this: "Desire – Friction = Conversion Rate."[125] Friction may be anything from a complicated sign-up procedure or payment process to a non-intuitive interface or hard-to-find links to relevant pages and/or protracted system response times. Solutions that reduce activation friction can include single or social sign-on, multiple payment options, live chat assistance, clear explanatory texts/buttons and a move toward web hosts that optimize performance. Desire can also be driven by psychological motives, such as status, achievement or a sense of belonging to a community. One example is uploading an address book to check if friends are on the platform.

Typical key results here include the share of new customers acquired through word of mouth and organic channels, funnel conversion rates (e.g., % of sign-ups becoming monthly active customers), the viral coefficient or the number of new users that an existing user generates on average.

O2. Retention: Are you constantly refining your hooks to keep your customers engaged?
The branded fitness regimen CrossFit has shown amazing retention throughout its growth journey. Originally founded in 1996, it has attracted 4 million devotees and approximately 15,000 affiliate gyms running under the CrossFit banner within less than three decades – with a member retention rate of around 85%.[126] How does the brand manage to retain such a strong core audience when it tends to take months, if not years, to reap the rewards of doing CrossFit? It does so by reinforcing users to adhere to habit-forming rituals. CrossFitters often follow a WOD ("Workout of the Day") for every session. This allows coaches to create a predictable habit-forming environment for every single session with the same members. Moreover, CrossFit, unlike going to the gym, is not a solo activity but one that is performed with other CrossFitters. The combination of a predictable habit plus a social group that reinforces that habit builds a strong retention hook.

Finding out if a habit has been established among a user base and is approaching a product-market fit is crucial. This can be done by asking customers the product-market fit question originally devised by Sean

Ellis: "How would you feel if you could no longer use [name of product]?" If more than 40% of the customers state that they would be very disappointed, it is likely that the company is approaching product-market fit (taken ideally from a sample size larger than 100).[127] If the company is not at this stage yet, this could be the result of a "leaky bucket" scenario. As Melanie Balke puts it in her blog: "it doesn't matter how much water you pour into the bucket (how many customers you acquire); the bucket won't get fuller because it is leaking water at the bottom (i.e., your customers are churning)."[128]

Typical key results here include the percentage of customers disappointed if they can no longer use the product (product/market fit survey), retention rates among new user cohorts (e.g., after 3, 10 or 30 days) and a rising Net Promoter Score paired with strong app reviews (e.g., on the Apple App Store or Google Play). Additionally, it is important to consider voluntary and involuntary user churn count. Voluntary churn is often driven by a lack of perceived product value, prices that are high in comparison to the competition and/or poor service. It can often be predicted (e.g., by looking at the % of users who stop engaging with your product). In contrast, involuntary churn is often driven by billing or payment issues, such as credit card expiration, payment information not being updated or a bank account not containing sufficient funds to make a payment.

O3. Monetization: Are you establishing a foundation for operative profitability?
Salva, a famous music producer based in L.A. whose tunes are played in clubs worldwide, quit Soundcloud in 2017. His reason: "25 million plays and zero dollars earned."[129] SoundCloud's lack of profit-making options for creators meant he was unable to sufficiently monetize on his art. It is often helpful that product teams have some accountability for monetization (such as owning a product profit-and-loss statement or the product revenue) when balancing this with long-term customer experience goals (such as retention). This can be done by creating shared OKRs between your product and marketing teams and potentially your sales team. A football team is a strong analogy here: everyone has defined roles and different skill sets, but every player – from the striker to the goalkeeper – has the potential to score a goal.

Typical key results here include the average revenue earned per user, the margin uplift of the product features, cancellation rate and the up-sell rate from free tier to premium tier.

O4. Expansion. Are you building new growth opportunities with new markets and products fast enough?
Netflix timed its international expansion to perfection. After honing its services in the US market, the streaming giant expanded across 190 countries within seven years despite national restrictions and having to source and secure content for each country (and sometimes even each region!). Now, around 130 million of Netflix's 200 million subscribers are based outside the US. eBay was less successful with its expansion. For instance, in South America, local rivals such as MercadoLibre had already cornered much of the market by the time the auction site made its play, and so eBay never took off in South America.

Expansion can come in at least three different forms that can naturally work together:
- **Geographical expansion**
  This involves a product or brand launch in a new region. *Example*: The live podcast app Clubhouse expanded to Europe after operating in the United States only for six months.
- **Customer segment expansion**
  Here, you open your scale-up to new customer segments. *Example*: The UK-based neobank Revolut launched its successful Revolut Business and Revolut Junior services expanding from its adult-focused retail banking platform.
- **Channel-driven expansion**
  In this case, a brand leverages more existing platforms to make its services available. *Examples*: Spotify made its app available on many smart TVs; the city scooter brand Bird worked with Google to make its scooters visible on Google Maps.

One potential danger is to launch a core product in another market or segment without having first nailed your product-market fit in your core market, as your product team would now have to iterate two products. While this may be necessary, it slows down the learning cycles.

Nevertheless, there are at least two criteria that can pave the way for early expansion. First, an expansion involving a less mature product can work if the product category is already familiar, and it isn't necessary to raise awareness about the product's value among the user base. When Netflix expanded globally, the user base was already familiar with its underlying product category (video streaming). However, if the product category is new and users have to be educated about it, a better approach may be to iterate the product with multiple rounds of user feedback until the product/market fit survey shows promising results. Second, it might make sense to expand early if the market is one where "a few winners take it all" (e.g., food delivery platforms, used goods markets). Whatever the case, the company needs to be ready to handle the additional complexity (e.g., adding native speakers of the local language to the customer service team, localizing marketing measures by the marketing team, etc.) before expanding geographically. For example, Index Venture's collection of playbooks for internationalization covers geographical expansion in depth.[130]

Typical key results here include the MVP launch in Geography X, the number of new active users in Geography Y and the acquisition, activation and retention of key results as mentioned above for new products and regions in which they are to be launched.

O5. Operational efficiency: Are your product and technology teams boosting operational efficiency?
When one European FinTech was overwhelmed by customer requests in 2018 due to its steep growth trajectory, it reestablished a smooth customer experience by investing significantly in internal back-office automation and customer-facing self-help. The chatbot of this FinTech was able to address 10% of customer inquiries at launch and 20% within one year. This equates to tens of thousands of contacts per week, with the cost of handling a single customer contact usually between USD 3–8. This type of customer-facing self-help tool can boost a scale-up's unit economics significantly.

It is also important to invest in internal automation, otherwise the back-office teams will balloon with a growing customer base. Relying on Google Sheets to keep track of payment reminders sent to customers is fine in the startup phase, but this is a recipe for disaster when scaling. It is essential to have some of the product teams focus on es-tablishing internal operational efficiency. This is vital if your company relies on supply chains, such as warehouses, logistics and procurement as in eCommerce. One way to approach this can be to build one product and technology team that is solely focused on your internal efficiency metrics and collaborates closely with the operations team.

Typical key results here include measuring internal efficiency wheth-er by tracking the percentage of digitized customer records, reducing the number of product-related complaints and contacts per quarter, increasing back-office throughput time, improving the delivery experi-ence NPS or a combination of these.

The following section moves on from OKRs into some of the best prac-tices we have found to scale up a product function.

Organizational chart and roles

Practice 25: Defining the roles & responsibilities for a product function

When growing from a startup to a scale-up, product organization is one of the functions that will change the most. To pave the way for a smooth growth trajectory, a product organization ideally has three building blocks in place: cross-functional product and technology teams, a do-main structure that ensures a maximum of technical independence be-tween the teams and "collectives" for knowledge sharing and people development.

1. **Cross-functional product teams**
   Cross-functional product teams are now the industry standard for tech startups. Such cross-functional teams usually consist of 6–7 engineers along with one engineering manager, one designer and one user researcher, led by one product owner. The product own-ers need to be proficient on at least four levels. First, they need to have a basic technical understanding. While they do not need to be able to code, they should understand technical terms and be able to challenge engineers. Second, they should be proficient in financial analysis, such as customer lifetime value, ARPU, cost of sales, CAC

and contribution margin. Strong empathy and an understanding of the customer to create user-centric products and knowledge of market and industry trends and competition are the other two components for success.[131] Often resourceful and inquisitive entrepreneurs with product skills are the best candidates. The team usually also has a product designer with skills both in interaction and visual design. While everyone is ideally physically co-located (or virtually well connected), it often works best for the team to have their own autonomy in terms of the agile methods they use (e.g., Scrum, Kanban). Depending on the metric being moved, the following roles could be added to the team: data analysts, product marketers and other specialists. The latter may have particular expertise in go-to-market strategies, marketing and sales channels, messaging and positioning of the product (see Figure 23).

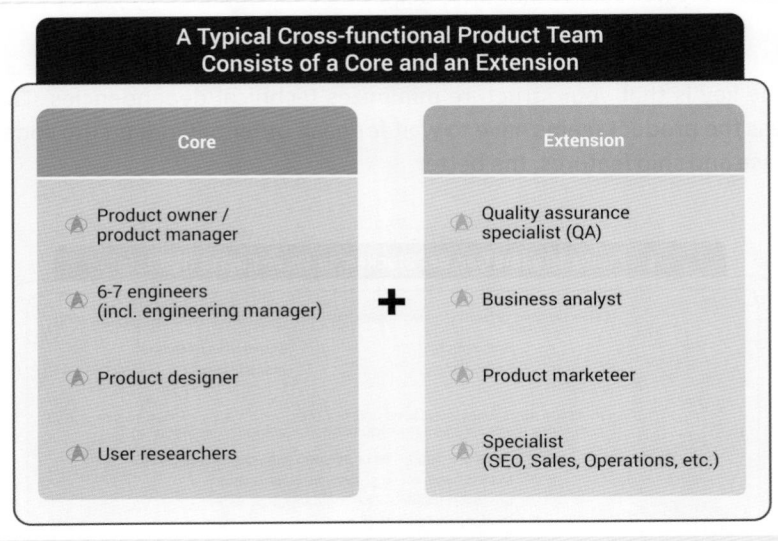

Figure 23: A Typical Cross-functional Product Team Consists of a Core and an Extension

2. **Teams, oder? with low technical dependency and high end-to-end responsibility**
   Is there a need to shift developers frequently? Are teams complaining about dependency conflicts when they want to ship features? According to Marty Cagan, these are typical signs that the product teams do not

have enough end-to-end responsibilities.[132] This is why it often makes sense to separate teams into the following categories (Figure 24):

- **Platform teams** that enable velocity and quality of other product teams with compelling internal products; the two types of platform teams are either tooling-related (e.g., self-service APIs, internal tools, knowledge) or product-related (i.e., product functions relevant for multiple teams, e.g., payment processing). All other product teams are their customers, and these teams should be present at the sprint reviews of other product teams to ensure core platform consistency and stability (all the more so in a multi-country setup).
- **Experience teams (or "program teams")** that develop apps and the user interface (i.e., features exposed to users and customers). These teams are often organized according to (customer) segments/the customer journey, specific product interfaces or geography, but they always have as much end-to-end responsibility as possible.
- **Growth teams** that drive acquisition, activation, engagement and monetization (in the B2C case).

The key is that your structure minimizes technical dependencies. The less the product teams have to wait for each other to work on the codebase and ship features, the better.

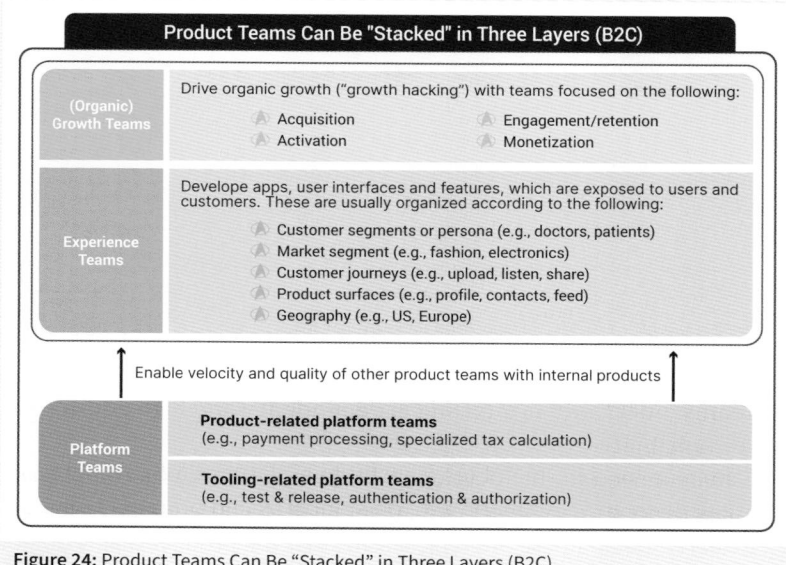

Figure 24: Product Teams Can Be "Stacked" in Three Layers (B2C)

See in Figures 25 and 26 two typical organizational blueprints of a FinTech and a marketplace startup where a platform, experience and growth logic have been deployed.

Organizational Chart: Product Function (FinTech)

Domains	Tooling Platform	Banking Platform	Payment	Bank Products	Risk Management	Organic Growth
	CI/CD	General ledger	International payment schemes	Credits & savings	Anti Money Laundering (AML)	Acquisition
Product Teams	Monitoring	Core customer data	Interbank	Crypto	Anti-fraud	Activation
	A/B testing	Authentification	Cards	Shared accounts	Know Your Customer (KYC)	Engagement & retention

Organizational Chart: Product Function (Marketplace)

Domains	Tooling Platform	Marketplace Platform	Buyer Side	Supplier Side	Organic Growth
	CI/CD	Core engine	Patients' portal	Doctors' portal	Acquisition
Product Teams	Monitoring	Authentification & authorization	Patient acquisition	Doctor acquisition	Activation
	A/B testing	Payment systems	Add-on products (patients)	Add-on products (doctors)	Engagement & retention

Figures 25 & 26: Organizational Chart: Product Function (FinTech) and Organizational Chart: Product Function (Marketplace)

3. **Professional "collectives" for knowledge sharing and people development**

   As the different professional collectives ("Chapters" or "Communities of Practice") are dispersed across various product teams, it is essential to have some structure to facilitate functional knowledge exchange and learning. Professional collectives will also aim to create a sense of belonging for their members, constitute a platform for collaboration, clarification and alignment (e.g., on standards and processes) and act as a center of gravity for functional employer branding and hiring. They are the central hub for organizing coaching, certifications and career development. These collectives typically include the various engineering communities (e.g., iOS, Android, front-end and back-end), product managers, designers, user researchers, data and QA/DevOps. One way to enable knowledge sharing is through separate company messenger channels and organizing monthly or bi-weekly best-practice sharing with "5 minutes of fame" for everyone who wants insights. Collectives in scale-ups often organize regular practice days, bar camps and people development conferences (Figure 27).

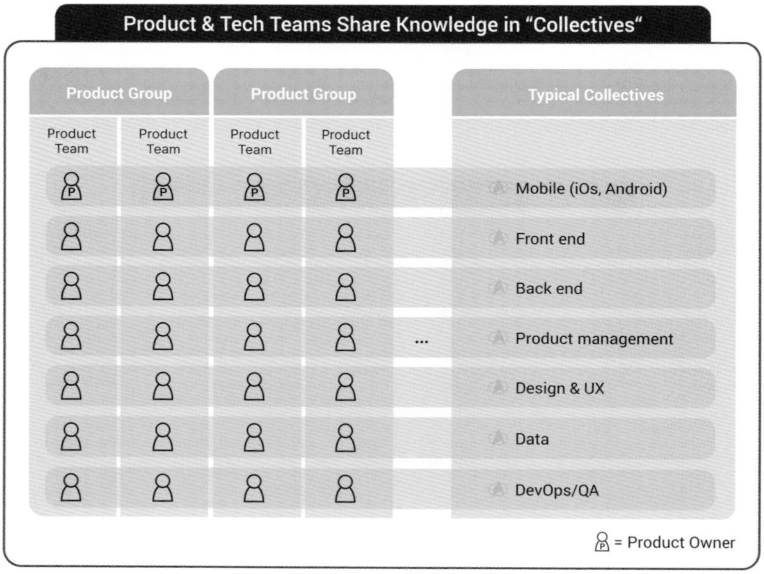

Figure 27: Product & Tech Teams Share Knowledge in "Collectives"

Practice 26: Scaling the right product roles at the right time

Scaling product organization comprises three approximate phases:
- **Early startup (1–3 product teams)**
  Here, the founder is the Chief Product Officer, as they know the customers and the product best. A good point to hire the first product

managers is when the development team reaches 5–7 FTEs at the latest. Once three product teams are up and running, the head of product is the lynchpin that oversees the startup's roadmap and makes trade-off decisions between new features for the developers. Ideally, interaction designers and user researchers are also deployed to speed up learning loops during this phase.

- **Early growth phase (3–10 product teams)**
  It is now too complex for one person to maintain a detailed overview of all development activities. This is often the point when it pays off to build groups of product teams that are overseen by senior product leaders and delegate decisions. Building and shipping fast is the key here, and stakeholder management matters less. Once they have more than three product teams, many startups employ a senior product leader (e.g., Head of Product). For 10+ teams, it is often helpful to upgrade to a VP, a director of product or even a chief product officer, along with several group product managers. Ramping up a product analytics team here to monitor the progress of key results, develop real-time dashboards, etc. is relevant, too.
- **Late growth phase (10+ product teams)**
  This is the latest time to hire a Chief Product Officer, which many companies fall victim to doing too late. This leader should be able to look at least 18 months ahead to define the future state of the product organization. They should own the product strategy, build the team, establish the product development processes, build a product culture, and foster a culture of rapid testing, continuous learning and cross-functional collaboration.[133] In this phase, internal tooling platforms that speed up developer productivity need to become a central pillar of the product and technology functions. This is also the time to empower teams even further. It is essential to lead the product groups based on product initiatives (rather than features) and focus on the outcomes that align with the stakeholders. This phase will often call for a product operations team comprised of 1–2 FTEs to streamline operations and reporting, including automated reporting to executives and product teams; report on progress, capacity, costs, outcomes and product engagement metrics; standardize product processes running across teams (e.g., setting goals); and run critical product meetings for strategy development and release management.[134]

Now that the organizational structure is in place, let us turn to the product management practices that facilitate the smooth transition to a scale-up. The key practices revolve around "Product vision and direction," "Product development process" and "Getting the basics right."

Product vision & direction

Practice 27: Developing a clear product vision and deriving your roadmap from it

Elon Musk founded Tesla "to help expedite the move from a mine-and-burn hydrocarbon economy toward a solar electric economy." He sketched out his (product) masterplan in 2006 as follows:[135]
- Build a sports car
- Use that money to build an affordable car
- Use that money to build an even more affordable car
- While doing the above, provide zero-emission electric power generation options

When the team behind Google Calendar created its product vision, it settled on four simple themes:
- A product that is fast, visually appealing and fun to use
- Adding information to the calendar should be child's play
- It should be more than boxes on a screen (reminders, invitations, etc.)
- It should be easy to share so you can see your whole life in one place

While Google Calendar is an example of a product vision in a multi-product company, the Tesla purpose and master plan *is* the product vision. Most growth companies still are a one-product company: think early Airbnb or Uber. In such companies, the product vision often equals the company "vision" (which is close to business ambition and purpose – see chapter on "North Star").

To establish the direction for your operational teams, it is best to try to break the overall purpose down into themes. Take SpaceX as an example.[136] The company's purpose is to "turn humanity into a multi-planetary species." Elon Musk estimates the current cost per person to fly to Mars at USD 10 billion, and he contends that this needs to be lowered to

somewhere around USD 200,000 (or the price of a house). Some themes he and his teams have identified in order to achieve this include:
- Full spacecraft reusability
- Refueling in orbit
- The right propellant
- Propellant production on Mars

As author Christian Strunk puts it, a product vision describes "the future state of a product that a company or team desires to achieve."[137] A good product vision articulates the *purpose for which* the product exists, rather than a detailed plan on *how* to reach the goal. In most cases, the product vision focuses on a time horizon of 3–5 years, which minimizes the focus on legacy elements and does not enter the realm of wild speculation. A good vision gives direction to your product teams, aligns all stakeholders toward a common goal, enables prioritization of the roadmap and hopefully inspires the team. Filling out a "product vision board" (see Figure 28) with a focus on vision, target group, needs, product and business goal is a good way to get started with creating the first draft of the product vision.

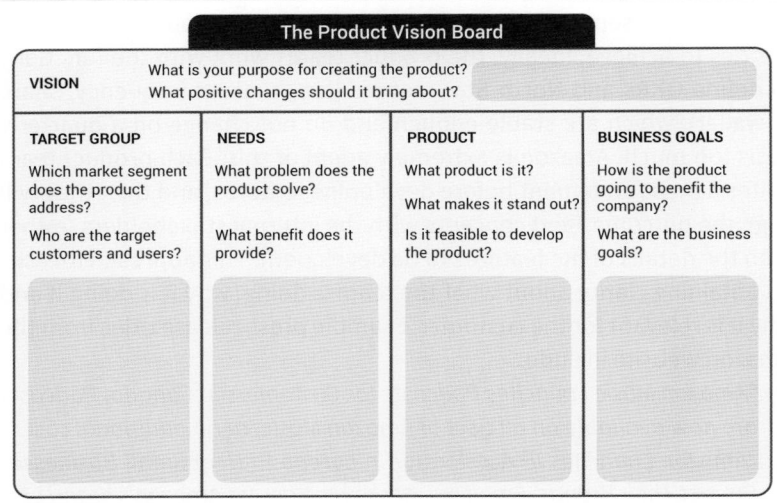

Figure 28: The Product Vision Board
Source: Roman Pichler[138]

Practice 28: Focusing your product organization on outcomes, not just designing a "feature factory"

As Melissa Perri succinctly puts it in her book, *Escaping the Build Trap*, "Products are a vehicle of value." If your product teams are only pushed to become a feature factory, they may fall short on their primary focus, which is to improve customers' lives and help them achieve their goals. This is a question of output versus outcome. *Harvard Business Review* author Deb Mills-Scofield frames this compellingly as output is what is produced for a specific type of customer (e.g., car seats for babies), while the outcome is the difference made by the output (i.e., keeping the child safe in the car).[139] A product function in a scale-up needs to combine a reliable factory that can ship the right features at the right time with missionaries who care deeply about the outcomes they achieve in their customers' eyes.

One way of creating a strong focus on outcomes in your product function is to use internal press releases as a way of working backward to align outcomes rather than aligning features with stakeholders. Failing to align stakeholders on a shared perspective for mid-term success is one of the key pitfalls here. Sometimes the product and the business functions develop separate perspectives on the joint output and outcome metrics to achieve. Ideally, the product teams work with the functions to define OKRs and North Star metrics (e.g., reorder frequency, share of wallet), which are stable enough and do not change on a quarterly basis too much. Amazon is extremely adept at this. Each product team writes a press statement before developing features, and then they will align the outcomes and concepts with the internal stakeholders (rather than the details of the features to be developed). This approach focuses on obtaining clarity about what the team is doing, why it is doing it and why it is relevant for the customer. Example press release titles from the Amazon website include:

- *"Amazon Music Launches Podcasts for Customers in Canada: Podcasts are now available on all tiers of Amazon Music, at no additional cost."*
- *"Amazon Launches IP Accelerator in Europe to Help Small Businesses Protect Their Brands: Small businesses can access Amazon's brand protection tools months before their trademark registration is issued."*

This internal press statement process has several rules as set out by Andrea Marchiotto:[140]

- Refer to a **future point in time** where success has been achieved and true success can be observed (often after launch).
- Elaborate **why the launch was important**, with a focus on the customers (or other key stakeholders). In what way did we enhance the customer experience?
- Set a **stretch goal**. State measurable results, including operational, market share or financial goals (e.g., increase the trademark applications of SMB partners by 30%; win 8% of the market share for podcast platforms in Canada).
- Describe the **principles that led to success**. This could include decisions made at critical junctures or design principles.
- Find **your passion** for the product while writing it.

Other approaches that may inspire a more outcome-focused product function include scoping **product initiatives rather than single features**. Such initiatives consist of several features that are connected by overarching themes (e.g., expanding into the UK property market by launching a competing home-selling platform, developing a remote visit app for doctors to go live on an appointment booking platform or creating a "shared spaces" social banking feature). Some companies will frame an initiative around a goal and options to be explored. For an online training company for marketing professionals, an initiative could be to "increase the content in key areas of the website." The related goal would be to "acquire more unique users while retaining existing ones, leading to a potential revenue increase of USD 2,000,000 per year." The options to explore here (i.e., the problems to solve) may include introducing easier and faster ways for teachers to create courses, establishing feedback loops for teachers on areas of interest for students and reaching out to new teachers to create relevant content.[141] The social network XING invented a good "bottom-up," internal alignment framework ("Auftragsklärung") which constitutes one way of aligning on both outcomes and features.[142]

Practice 29: Investing in the core product while pushing adjacent opportunities and venture bets

As Jeff Gothelf puts it, "Phase 2" is the mythical future world where those "things we didn't get to" in Phase 1 go to die.[143] Many product teams see refining existing products as less sexy than entering new markets, designing new features or targeting new customer segments. While product and geographical expansion are indeed essential for sustained growth, the refinement of the core experience is crucial for retaining customers once you have found your product-market fit. LinkedIn founder Reid Hofmann recommends the following approach on balancing the tension between the two:[144]

- **Invest 70% of time and resources on iterating the existing product-market fit with the core product**
  In LinkedIn's case, this would be anything from streamlining the profile pages to introducing new recruiter tools. One way to keep product and technology teams focused on the core experience is to deploy a "ninja support" model: one front-end or back-end colleague in each team who works to resolve all product-issue-related requests driven by customer complaints for one quarter (e.g., a micro-service is not working, a code is generating an error, or an open-source update has caused a crash – "level 3 support"). The response time should be a matter of hours here. This type of support assists customers *and* creates a stronger sense of ownership for engineers, which gives them more incentives to avoid product-driven customer issues in the first place.
- **Spend 20% of time and resources on expansion into new regions or product lines**
  This is essential, as the initial market segment will usually not be sufficient to capture a large share of the addressable market.
- **Reserve the final 10% for venture bets**
  Some of these more risky developments will pay off over a time horizon of one to five years. Amazon's auction bidding platform is an example of a failed bet, while Amazon's launch of Cloud Service was a successful bet (generating a substantial amount of Amazon's overall profits now). Netflix adopts a similar approach. They invest 10% of their resources in venture bets. In 2010, this was Netflix Originals (now part of the core service), while in 2020, it was interactive stories – movies or series where the user could actively guide the story – and the Netflix VR experience.

Product development process

Practice 30: Creating a crystal-clear picture of your target customers

"zTypes" refer to the seven "personas" around which European eCom-merce fashion scale-up Zalando based its business.[145] With names such as "Hip Poppers," "Street Snobs," "Fresh Families" and "Cultured Elites," each type encompasses a typical customer in one of the segments that the company targets. Zalando designs and buys clothes for these per-sonas and structures campaigns with separate landing pages and mes-sages to target each (e.g., "Don't change your body, change your jeans"). See Figure 29 for more details.

Personas are a strong way to instill a customer-centric mindset in a scale-up. Alan Cooper describes these personas as "archetypes of user" or semi-fictional characters based on a current (or ideal) customer. These work to align everyone in the company on what the experience should be for a specific group of customers.[146] It also helps the product teams make decisions on features. Defining a persona typically calls for a name, a job title, a representative photo, a quote on their needs and goals, some frustrations and pain points and (potentially) their level of knowledge in the relevant domain.[147] The best practice is to use 1:1 inter-views and surveys to create the personas and iterate them several times.

In B2B businesses, buyers are not always the same people as your us-ers. While the customer relationship management software suite may be sold to the tech team, it could end up being used by customer ser-vice. Here, it is often helpful to develop a persona for both the buyer and the user.

If there is no intent to create personas, clear customer segmentation is often the minimum required to steer marketing campaigns and product development. This tends to be done according to one or more of the fol-lowing parameters:
- **Demographic:** Segmentation according to age, gender, income, edu-cational level, etc. (e.g., parents with children under six years)
- **Geographic:** Segmentation according to country or region (e.g., par-ents living in Central Europe, young urbanites living in Berlin)

- **Psychographic:** Segmentation according to opinions, values, interests, beliefs, motivations, lifestyle, activities (e.g., fathers active on social media, single mothers who support the living wage)
- **Behavioral:** Segmentation according to observable behavior (e.g., an app for parents who share pictures of their children at least twice a week)
- **Needs-based:** Segmentation according to a common interest, such as visual monitoring of a space in real-time (e.g., parents monitoring babies, shop owners monitoring their property, pet owners watching their dogs)
- **Customer type:** Segmentation according to institutional structure (e.g., major corporation, small business, freelancer, startup, etc.)

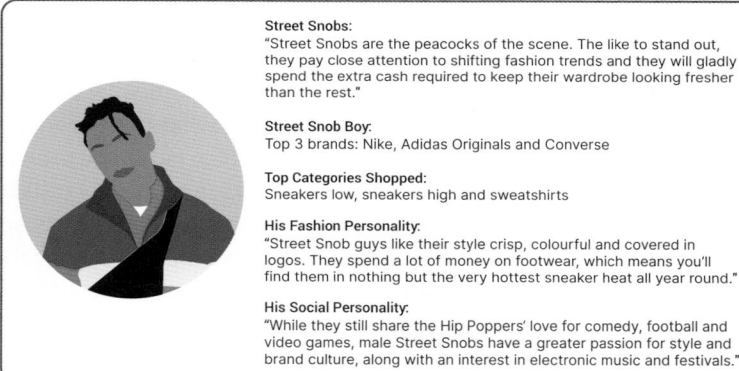

Figure 29: Customer Segmentation: Street Snobs
Source: Zalando[148]

Practice 31: Aligning your product value proposition with the underserved needs of your customers

Taxi customers often complain about rude drivers, dirty cars, cost confusion and late arrivals. Uber's business plan for hailing a taxi with a smartphone changed this. The app shows the driver's name along with a photo and a rating, an upfront cost estimate and a map pinpointing the taxi's current location. Uber identified its customers' exact unmet needs and met them – and continues doing so today. To reach this level of understanding, many product teams map the unmet needs of their customers alongside features that would resolve them. The Kano model can be used to define the types of unmet needs that should be addressed (Figure 30):[149]

- **"Must-have needs":** These are your table stakes (i.e., meeting them does not create any additional customer satisfaction, but they are required to play in the respective market). *Neobank example:* the ability to pay by smartphone.
- **"Want needs":** This refers to features that increase customer satisfaction in proportion to performance. *Neobank example:* the ability to open a bank account in minutes rather than days.
- **"Delighter needs":** These are features that exceed customer expectations. Their absence does not cause a loss in satisfaction, as they are not expected but can make the product "stickier." *Neobank example:* integrated shift planning tool for B2B customers.

This approach is detailed in the Lean Product Playbook of Dan Olson in more depth. We encourage every startup builder to read it.

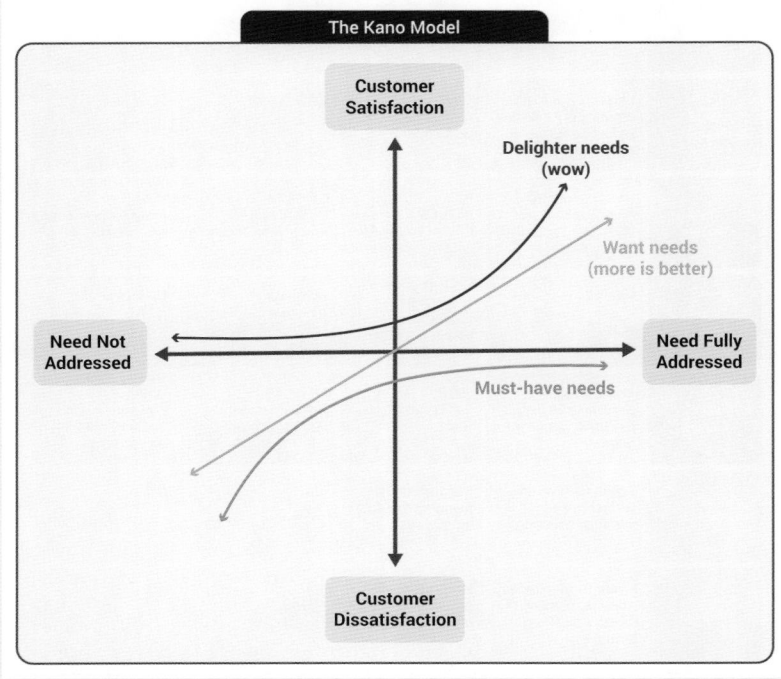

Figure 30: The Kano Model
Source: Adopted from Noriaki Kano and the Lean Product Playbook[150]

What works best here is to create a table, like the one (Figure 31), listing the type of need, the specific unmet need, and a comparison of the features that your company offers versus the competition. The table shows examples of value dimensions of a hypothetical neobank catering to small businesses and compares these dimensions to two competitors.

Type	Unmet Need	Our Features & Services (e.g., mobile first neobank)	Features & Services of Competitor 1 ("Internet bank of the 90s")	Features & Services of Competitor 2 ("incumbent bank")
Must-have	I want to be able to pay with my mobile.	YES (e.g., Apple Pay)	YES (e.g., Apple Pay)	YES (e.g., Apple Pay)
Must-have	I want to be sure my account cannot be accessed by an unauthorized party.	YES (e.g., 2-factor authentication)	YES (e.g., 2-factor authentication)	YES (e.g., 2-factor authentication)
Want Feature	I want to open my bank account quickly.	HIGH (digital verification in <10 minutes)	MEDIUM (digital verification but with print & mail)	LOW (only possible in bank branch)
Want Feature	I want to save time creating my monthly report to the tax authorities.	HIGH (automated report on a click)	LOW (absent)	LOW (n/a)
Want Feature	I want to enable my employees to pay bills and make purchases for my business.	HIGH (up to 5 additional cards available for employees for free)	MEDIUM (2 cards for employees available for free)	LOW (only a single user has access)
Want Feature	I want to receive a loan at the click of button.	HIGH (loan with automated risk scoring and transfer of money within 24h)	MEDIUM (link to a partner which verifies the customer again)	LOW (n/a)
Want Feature	I want to have a personalized service available whenever I need it.	HIGH 24/7 dedicated team	MEDIUM Dedicated team 9 am to 9 pm	LOW Call center w/o dedicated team 9 am to 6 pm
Delighter	I want to save time with shift and vacation planning.	Integrated shift planning tool for employees	n/a	n/a
Delighter	I want to save money when purchasing IT devices or office furniture.	Integrated procurement platform	n/a	n/a

Figure 31: Example of a FinTech Value Proposition

Note that all "Must-haves" are assigned a "Yes," as all competitors provide them. "Want features" can be rated with categories (e.g., high, medium, low), while delighters are true differentiating factors – the company is the only one or one of few to offer them.

Practice 32: Developing your roadmap as a communication tool with the right prioritization logic

The product roadmap is the key tool to communicate the product vision. It can rally and excite the team and change the lives of the customers. Often a small deviation of the product vision from the company vision translates into a large deviation on the roadmap. Hence, a crystal-clear company and product strategy (see Practice 27) with clearly defined outcomes (see Practice 24) is the prerequisite for putting up a useful roadmap.

A well-crafted roadmap is derived from key results (e.g., NPS) to themes or product initiatives (e.g., create ATM experience), which then distill several epics from the themes (e.g., easy and fast payment processes) and divide the epics into user stories. These are then delivered via sprints (e.g., "As an ATM user I want to get my card back before the cash so that I don't forget it in the ATM"). See Figures 32 and 33 for two hypothetical examples for a roadmap structure of a FinTech and an automotive app.

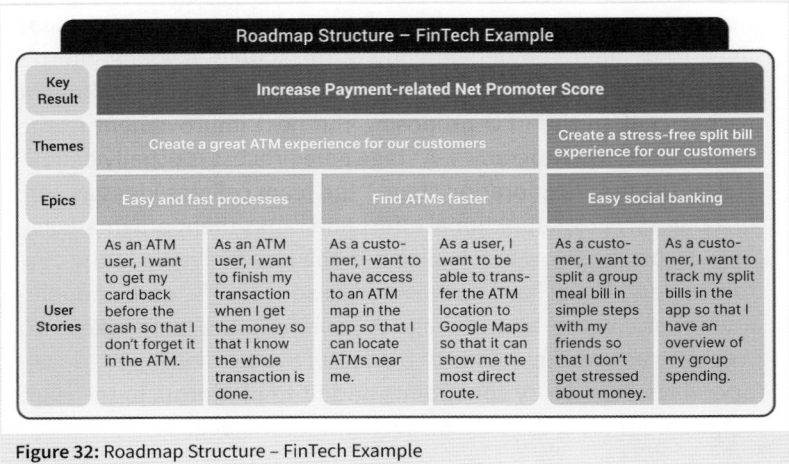

Figure 32: Roadmap Structure – FinTech Example

Roadmap Structure – iOS Car App Example

	In-time organization		In-car entertainment experience		Easy and safe communication	
Key Result	Increase the % of Daily Users of the iOS Car App					
Themes	Cover all the use cases that iOS device users want to do in their cars				Make all interactions for iOS device users voice-driven while driving	
Epics	In-time organization		In-car entertainment experience		Easy and safe communication	
User Stories	As a user and driver, I want to order my favorite coffee while I am in my car so that I save time.	As a user and driver, I want to have access to my calendar so that I know when and where my next appointment is.	As a user and driver, I want to listen to my favorite music playlist while driving so that I have fun.	As a user and driver, I want to listen to my favorite audiobook while driving so that I make better use of my time.	As a user and driver, I want to send a WhatsApp message via voice command while I am in my car so that I can find my way easily and safely.	As a user and driver, I want to ask for navigation suggestions via voice command so that I find my way easily and safely.

Figure 33: Roadmap Structure – iOS Car App Example

How do you derive this type of roadmap? Todd Lombardo and his colleagues provide excellent guidelines in their book *Product Roadmaps Relaunched*. To lead with an inspiring roadmap, the following five building blocks are key:

- **Take feature ideas from everywhere, but evaluate them independently of the source**
  Good product ideas do not originate solely within the product function. An idea funnel needs to be accessible to all stakeholders: the customers, the product colleagues, the CXOs, leaders, user researchers and junior members of the team. However, these ideas need to be filtered independently of the source. A young intern's suggestion on improvements within the conversion funnel might be better than the CEO proposing the next improvement in the in-app flow ("meritocracy"). A stage gate process is usually beneficial. In the first "exploration stage," the team collates ideas as part of a one-day cross-functional effort and ranks them pragmatically (e.g., by asking "How much juice is in the idea?" – value to the customer – and "How hard do we need to squeeze?" – ease of implementation). In the second stage ("Planning"), the team takes two weeks to assess the details of the feature to be developed (developer days, regulatory constraints and fit to platform). In the third stage ("Commit"), the actual development will begin.

- **Build the roadmap using your own prioritization logic**
  If there has been a very clear and compelling product vision, crafted themes, epics and stories deployed using the right product team structure, it should be easy for the product teams to prioritize on their own. Having difficulties with constantly shifting priorities is not a sign of a bad prioritization logic but a lack of clarity on direction. Every team needs to settle on their own prioritization logic, often combining several of the existing approaches:
  a) **Kano model**
     Prioritizes stories and related features according to "must-haves" (e.g., a windshield wiper in the car), "want needs" (an intermittent wiper that stops at intervals) and "delighters" (a rain-sensing wiper). Must-haves are usually prioritized with a mixture of performance benefits and delighters following.[151]
  b) **R.I.C.E.**
     This stands for Reach (How many users are affected by the feature?), Impact (How will each user be impacted by the feature?), Confidence (How high is our confidence on our Reach and Impact assessment?), and Effort (How many engineering weeks do we need?).
  c) **Importance vs. Satisfaction**
     Here customers state in surveys or interviews how important certain features are ("How important is it that you know when your taxi arrives?") and how satisfied they currently are with them ("How satisfied are you with the current information you have when your taxi arrives?").
  d) **Juice vs. squeeze logic:**
     This approach focuses on the effort to build a feature, along with the value it creates for the customers. This is then mapped on a 2x2 or 3x3 matrix. The value dimension can include topics like the number of times customers use the feature, the percentage of daily active users utilizing the feature and the conversion, retention and engagement of the customers who use the feature versus those who do not.
- **Estimate the development effort pragmatically**
  In agile project management, there are several estimation approaches to choose from to measure the relative effort of feature development. This is often done collaboratively via games,

such as Planning Poker on the basis of the estimated team veloc-ity. In these games, approaches for estimates can include: T-shirt sizes (S, M, L, X), story points (1 for a small feature, 3 for a medi-um feature, 8 for a large feature, etc.), John Cutler's "pragmatic approach" (1–3 hours; 1–3 weeks; 1–3 months; 1–3 quarters) and the Fibonacci sequence (1, 2, 3, 5, 8, 13, 21, 34...).[152] The key here is to get a rough estimate quickly without wasting much of the devel-oper's time with estimations. Additionally, it is necessary to break down the features into smaller chunks, so they can be put into a two-week sprint. The more pragmatic, the better. T-shirt sizes and John Cutler's approach are often sufficient.

- **A roadmap's stability needs to increase with the maturity of the company**
  Whereas monthly review cycles are usual in the early growth phase, a scale-up will eventually move to quarterly review cycles. With a clear product vision and defined themes, the roadmap should not shift substantially between quarters.
- **Consider public roadmaps as an option**
  Companies like Spotify, the UK bank Monzo or Slack publish their (high-level) roadmaps publicly.[153] This creates trust and transpar-ency with the community (Figure 34).

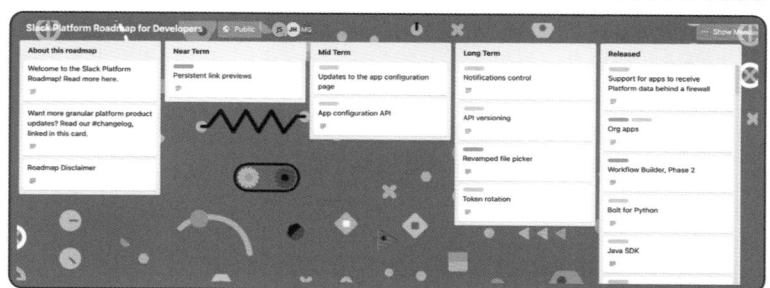

Figure 34: Slack Platform Roadmap for Developers
Source: Slack.com

Product management basics

Practice 33: Getting the brand and product design right early on

When Apple appointed Jony Ive as its first Chief Design Officer in 1992, it made the right choice. Considered Jobs' spiritual partner, Ive and his team went on to make a material impact on the company by creating the minimalist-inspired design for its products, including the iPod, iPhone, iPad, iMac, MacBook Pro, Apple Watch and iOS.[154] Designers would often have the final word in discussions, and the careful craftsmanship of Apple products has been a true business differentiator that has driven the company's growth. If an organization uses design as a core tool to solve problems, make decisions or highlight opportunities, they should consider having a designer as part of the executive team.

Simplicity is central to Apple's product design. In Ive's words: "Our goal is to try to bring calm and simplicity to incredibly complex problems so that you're not really aware of the solution, you're not aware of how hard the problem was that was eventually solved."[155] The platform InVision calls companies that anchor design at the highest level and allows them to co-shape their strategy as "Design Visionaries."[156] According to their assessment, these companies are masters of data-driven design with highly developed practices for analytics, user research and measuring the success of design efforts. This development framework can serve as a starting point to assess the current success level of your design team. The levels include "producers," "connectors," "architects," "scientists" and "visionaries." It is often helpful for markets in which design, brand and user experience matter to move the design team from "design makes our products look good" to the higher levels (Figure 35).

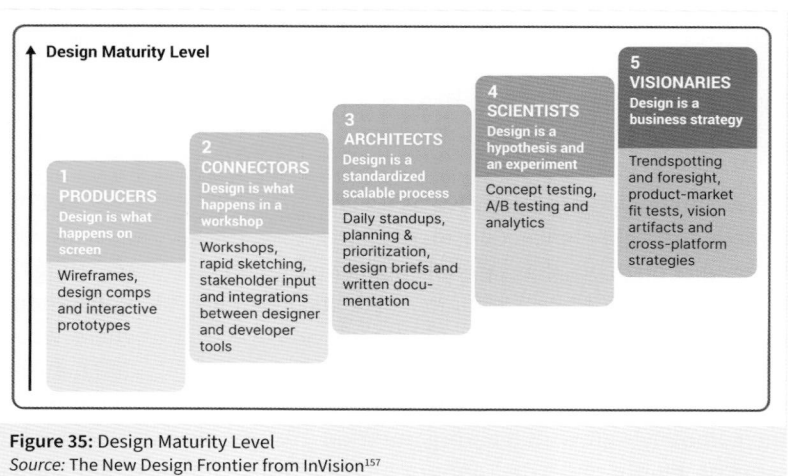

Figure 35: Design Maturity Level
Source: The New Design Frontier from InVision[157]

To create a best-in-class design team, these building blocks are helpful:
- **Put "atomic" systems design in place to enable consistent design at scale**
  Just like atoms form different compounds and molecules, Brad Frost's Atomic Design Principles take inspiration from chemistry to design deliberate user interfaces that are composed of smaller units or building blocks.[158] By defining the smallest units and building everything on this basis, the design is able to create systems that are consistent, reusable and scalable. The five atomic design levels are: atoms, molecules, organisms, templates and pages (see Figure 36). Higher levels of design development include producing a closed-design library with all the elements of the system easily documented and accessible. This design methodology allows design teams to create prototypes more easily and consistently, which allows them to update their designs faster.[159]

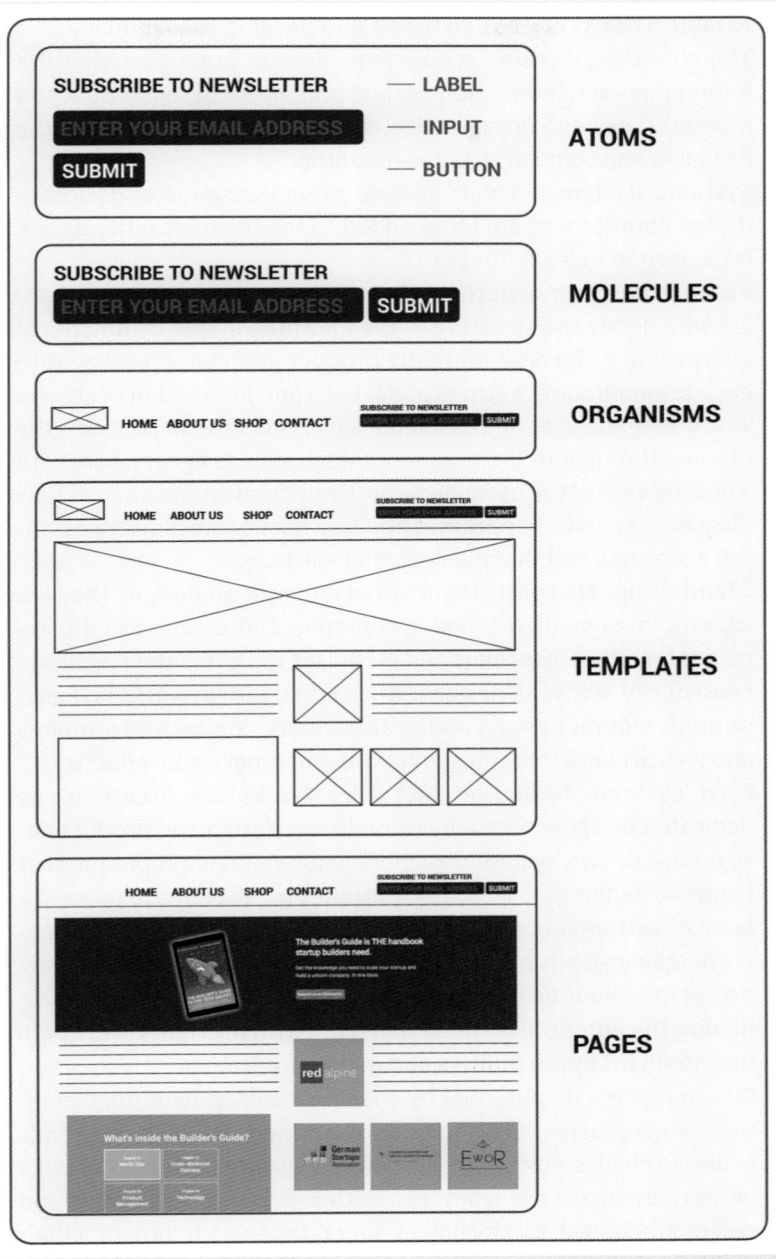

Figure 36: Five Atomic Design Level[160]
Source: Brad Frost

- **Establish the 3 core design teams and develop them quickly**
  The core design teams are systems design, product design (UX information and interaction design) and brand design (visual and motion). They should all utilize customer research to make the products and company truly user-centric.
  Systems designers create atomic design systems and closed-design libraries and are often added to the team once the design organization exceeds 10–15 FTEs.
  Product designers specialize in two fields: information design-ers who define the structure of the information and its functional interplay (e.g., by organizing the product in an intuitive way with easy-to-understand buttons and labels) and interaction designers who create the user flows enabling customers to interact with the product throughout their journey. Interaction designers work with a holistic view of the user needs, and they create items such as flow diagrams, layouts, wireframes and low-fidelity mockups to estab-lish a look and feel that the customer will love.
  Brand designers specialize in visual and motion design. They are experts in color theory and typography and create visual cam-paigns for different formats and platforms while maintaining brand consistency across all designs. While visual design works in digital or print, motion design creates animations, commercials, trailers and web artwork through animations and other visual effects.
  Each (customer-facing) product team should have access to one dedicated designer with a focus on brand design and product de-sign, one or two system designers who enable multiple product teams by defining closed-design libraries for all teams to use and a team of customer researchers (3–4 FTEs) who support the design-ers in making decisions based on customer preferences (see Prac-tice 34 for details on user research).
- **Realize the potential of the design team with the right career paths, development opportunities and mix of experience**
  Design realizes its potential by enabling development opportuni-ties, career progressions and a mix of experiences. Tools and trends in design change quickly, so it is crucial to have a broad mix of skills and experience in the team (i.e., both experienced designers and recent graduates). By starting as junior designers to broaden their abilities, the natural career progression for a designer should be the promotion to the title of senior designer and ultimately to the

title of lead designer. Lead designers work more holistically with the product managers and marketing, and they are deeply engaged in brand, product and user research.

Practice 34: Building a thriving user research engine quickly

A staggering 42% of startups fail because they tackle problems that are interesting to work on but fail to solve their customers' pain points.[161] Exploring customers' pain points in detail lies at the core of user research; it is not about explicitly asking them for solutions or features. After all, customers may be adept at describing their problems, but they are usually not good at inventing features. For example, customers would not have come up with the iPhone, the car or the personal computer. This is why exploring the "problem space" with potential customers matters so much.

Here are six key building blocks to put in place in order to conduct outstanding user research:

- **Ask questions that explore the problem space**
  Eric Migicovsky from Y Combinator defined how to explore the problem space and the underlying issues with customers with these excellent questions:[162]
  - What is the hardest thing when doing [X]? (With [X] referring to the specific problem the company aims to address, e.g., share more cooking recipes, get more women to invest in the stock market.)
  - Can you tell me about the last time you encountered that problem?
  - Why was this hard?
  - What have you done to try solving this question?
  - What don't you love about the solutions you have already tried?
- **Do it yourself**
  Ideally, every employee should have experience with customer research. Outsourcing user research tends to put up barriers that hinder direct insights from customers with regard to improving features, processes and experiences. This is no replacement for hearing a pain point directly from a customer.
- **Do it regularly**
  It often pays off to hold regular (e.g., biweekly) user research circles – your "purring UX engine" – to test product ideas and

prototypes. The key is to make it a recurring meeting in the calendar, so the product teams can simply walk into the UX sessions during the feature design phase. Otherwise, user research runs the risk of falling into the time-constrained "pre-launch stress phase."

- **Encourage and enable each product team to do user research**
  Each product team ideally has one user researcher or shares one between two teams. User research should be a central practice for all members of the product team (including engineers). This includes holding UX sessions in the morning to define 3–5 hypotheses to improve the product, then working on them during the day and closing the loop in the evening with another round of research. There are few other ways for engineers and product managers to bring about an improved user experience within one day. In the later growth stage, there is some benefit of central user research teams with specialized members, such as data analysts or focus group experts.

- **Try to reach "convergent validity" quickly**
  Use several user input sources (e.g., surveys and interviews) to triangulate the "truth" and finish your research once this knowledge converges. Your aim should be to learn within the shortest time frame.

- **Deploy the right user research methods for the right product stage**
  The best methods to use depend on the product phase your team is in. Are you currently exploring new hypotheses and user pain points for product design? Then, it is helpful to consider the following: qualitative research from both internal and external sources, user interviews and conversations with customer service agents for common customer wishes and pain points. **If the startup is in its launch phase**, methods usually include regular surveys, user flow or user behavior data, paper prototyping and (retroactive) analytics. **If the startup is looking to polish an existing product** with a proven product-market fit, user analytics at scale is often the key. This could include A/B testing for use optimization to test small-scale and low-risk improvements to your product, while surveys can provide information about UX. Google has a strong library of user research methods ready to be explored.[163]

Typical testing methods include:
- **A/B testing**: In "discovery" A/B testing, 1% of the current customer base is presented with the live-data prototype while the other 99% receive the existing product.
- **Invite-only testing**: If the beta version of a product is being tested, it can be made accessible to testers by invite only. For a company that is either more risk-averse or lacks traffic, invite-only testing can offer an alternative to A/B testing, although it lacks some of its predictive power.
- **Customer discovery program/reference customers**: These are existing model customers who have agreed to be part of a beta testing cohort. This group of people cares about the company, so they can test new features and give open and honest feedback.[164]
- **Data analytics**: Data helps to understand user behavior. Central metrics include click paths, active users, conversion rates, retention, time to close, load time and NPS.
- **Paper tests**: This is about pitching the solution to customers (e.g., with a slide deck or landing page that explains features). If customers are interested, they are directed to a waiting list. This form of testing is especially interesting for early-stage startups that wish to receive customer feedback to support their early fundraising or companies that want to extend their product lines but test ideas before building.
- **Wizard of Oz testing**: Customers are offered what seems to be a finished product or feature, while the back-office is actually still being run manually. For example, users are presented with the ability to refer their friends for a discount. Instead of building a fully-fledged and automated discount service, only the front-end components are built, and then the system will manually credit users who refer their friends. Once the feature fit has been validated, the complete back end can be built.

Below is an overview of typical user research methods (Figure 37).

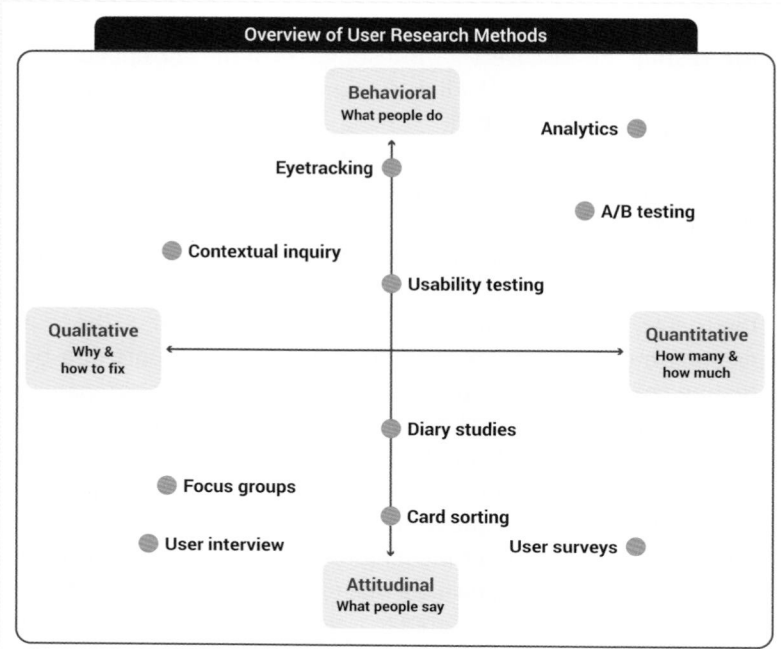

Figure 37: Overview of User Research Methods
Source: Constantin Diessenbacher, <u>Minimizing risk through User Research</u>, 2020[165]

Practice 35: Implementing best-in-class product management tools

Product tools are critical for creating high-performing product organizations. Typical categories include:[166]

- **Prototyping tools**
  To master early visualization and iterative optimization of a user interface. It helps enormously to gather feedback from everyone involved in the project (above all from users), as this enables concepts to be amended easily. Tools like Adobe XD, Figma and Sketch can help with creating and collaborating on a prototype. Other useful tools to design every step of the product experience include Framer, Principle and Premiere.
- **Roadmapping tools**
  To keep everyone on the team informed and coordinated. One possible tool for this is Product Plan, which is an easy way to plan and

communicate strategies and offer roadmap templates and links to direct communication with stakeholders. Tools like Monday and Product Board are also beneficial, as they can make it easier to understand what target users need and unify everyone from around the product roadmap.

- **Prioritizing tools**
  To guide and prioritize the team and their tasks – from wireframe to hard launch. Useful tools include Task Management, Prod-Pad and Jira.
- **Effective sprint planning tools**
  To be able to maintain a constant, efficient production schedule. Flexible tools like Agilean and Asana help to keep sprint plans, launch dates, backlogs and related communication organized and in one place.
- **Data management tools**
  To develop structures, practices and procedures to regulate and supervise data lifecycle. Airtable, Google Sheets and Coda can support this process.

Recommended publications:

- Marty Cagan (2018). *Inspired: How to Create Tech Products Customers Love.*
- Nir Eyal (2014). *Hooked: How to Build Habit-Forming Products.*
- Martin Eriksson (2017). Nate Walkingshaw, and Richard Banfield, *Product Leadership: How Top Product Managers Launch Awesome Products and Build Successful Teams.*
- Dan Olson (2015). *The Lean Product Playbook: How to Innovate with Minimum Viable Products and Rapid Customer Feedback.*
- Jeff Patton (2014). *User Story Mapping: Discover the Whole Story, Build the Right Product.*
- Melissa Perri (2018). *Escaping the Build Trap: How Effective Product Management Creates Real Value.*
- Roman Pichler (2016*). Product Strategy and Product Roadmap Practices for the Digital Age.*
- Eric Ries (2011). *The Lean Startup: How Constant Innovation Creates Radically Successful Businesses.*
- Index Venture playbooks on internationalization, *"Expanding into Europe"*, https://web.archive.org/web/20210521212205/https://www.indexventures.com/expanding-intoeurope, and *"Destination USA*

https://web.archive.org/web/20210521205055/https://www.index-ventures.com/resources/destinationusa/quick-guide/."

- *Google Venture's library for user research methods,* https://web.archive.org/web/20210521211620/https://library.gv.com/gv-guide-to-uxresearch-for-Start-upsb6d0c8ac81b3?gi=ab6cac09de79.

Watch our video on the seven key pitfalls to avoid in your product function by scanning the QR code or following this link: https://youtube/AxnVnO7VtY8.

How to set up a product team that can scale? Watch our video by scanning the QR code or following this link: https://youtube/hIoraAzdNjE.

Definitions

- **Agile**: an interactive approach adopted from software development for project management that focuses on iterative improvements made through working in small increments and requires self-organized collaboration between cross-functional teams.

- **Activation**: motivating a new or existing inactive user to engage more deeply in a product or service, which advances them to the next stage of their user lifecycle.
- **Average Revenue per User (ARPU)**: average revenue generated per user, which is calculated by taking the total revenue divided by the average number of users or subscribers during a given time period.
- **Churn**: a measure of the rate at which customers/users stop interacting or transacting with a product or service.
- **Customer value**: a measure of a product or service's worth to the consumer – this is usually measured by the degree customers buy or use a product.
- **Customer journey**: all the key interactions a customer can have with a company, product or service – usually framed in statements like "I want to close an account."
- **Cohort**: a group of individuals who share common characteristics, such as signing up for a service in a given time period (e.g., in January).
- **Epic**: a large body of product development work that can be segmented into smaller tasks (called user stories) based on the needs of the end-users. Epics serve to organize work by breaking it down into deliverable pieces that contribute to one strategic objective.
- **User story**: a small, self-contained piece of development work that has been written informally from a user's perspective and designed to contribute to a specific product goal (see Epic).
- **Features**: a term that describes what a product does, what characteristics it has or what functionality it has for end users.
- **Function**: an internal organization that oversees and is accountable for a key company activity (e.g., Sales, Finance, R&D, Supply Chain).
- **Funnel conversion rate**: the percentage of users that successfully pass through all steps of a process intended to guide them to take a particular action (e.g., sign up to a mailing list, purchase an item, create an account).
- **Growth hacking**: a collection of tactics to rapidly grow a business in a scalable, repeatable and sustainable way that puts growth above everything else (adopted from Sean Ellis).

- **Lifetime Value (LTV)**: a metric that evaluates what a customer is worth to a company across the length of their entire relationship with the company.
- **Minimum Viable Product (MVP)**: a version of a product that has been built with just enough features to attract early adopters who can then provide feedback and validate learning for future product development.
- **North Star Metric**: the primary metric a company uses to measure its growth.
- **OKRs (Objectives & Key Results)**: a method for goal-setting, internal alignment and providing transparency that provides a framework for defining goals (objectives) and evaluating progress toward achieving those goals (key results).
- **Platform**: an (internal) product that enables new products, services and operating models by making resources, information and capabilities available. This is typically done through either direct access by end-users or APIs.
- **Planning Poker (also called Scrum Poker)**: a gamified, consensus-based planning technique for estimating the relative size of development goals in product and software development. It works by having every team member anonymously estimate the number of story points or days needed for a particular development goal using a deck of playing cards. The cards are then simultaneously revealed and the estimations are discussed until a consensus is reached.
- **Product management**: the practice of developing, launching and continually supporting and improving a product, with particular attention paid to end users' needs and uses of it.
- **Product roadmap**: a summary of the vision, direction and delivery plan for a product that helps to align a team or company in coordinating their work and defining their goals – this is not a pure list of features.
- **Product-market fit**: According to Marc Andreesen this is "being in a good market with a product that can satisfy that market" and is often defined as ">40% of customers would be disappointed if the product is taken away."[167]
- **Product**: an item or service, either virtual or physical, that is provided to customers/end users.

- **Retention hook**: often habitual triggers, actions and rewards built into a product that encourage users to return to the product to use it over and over again.
- **Retention**: the process of measuring the loyalty of existing users and designing and implementing a course of action to prevent the loss of users.
- **Team velocity**: the amount of work a team can deliver during a single sprint in a scrum session, which is measured by the number of user story points delivered at the end of the sprint.
- **Unit economics**: a particular business model's revenues and costs per individual unit item that creates value for the company and demonstrates how much value is derived from each unit. For example, it can be calculated by dividing the customer lifetime value by customer acquisition costs.
- **Viral coefficient**: percentage of the number of new customers generated by a single existing customer through referrals.

6   Technology Excellence

Creating scalable and secure tech platforms for future growth

With Christoph Richter

Note: The Builder's Guide *assumes a product-led model where autonomous product and technology teams led by product owners address customer-focused goals (e.g., acquisition, conversion). Under this model, software developers tend to be deployed in cross-functional product and tech teams and work collaboratively to achieve customer-centric goals (see Chapter 5). With technology function setups and practices evolving rapidly in tech scale-ups, this chapter reflects on the state of the art of building technology functions at the time of writing.*

Key pitfalls to avoid for scale-up builders   !

- **Failing to drive enough independence in the tech teams**
  Whereas with manual deployment pipelines a lot of scripts and yaml files might work in smaller engineering organizations, things will break when scaling. Trying to minimize the cognitive load for every team by setting up teams as independently as possible so that they don't have to wait for each other when touching the code base is key here. The most common approach to solve this is by establishing an internal development platform team to take over a lot of the heavy lifting for the individual teams and improve the overall developer experience (see Practices 36 and 38).

- **Unconsciously building technical debt**
  While a company is always building technical debt to a certain degree, not making a conscious choice about whether to "hack" solutions fast or to invest substantial time for developing to scale is a pitfall easy to fall into. Documenting decisions that lead to technical debt properly for later revisions incentivizes software engineers to develop the code more cleanly from the outset and helps to prioritize it on the roadmap later on. Furthermore, the Boy Scout rule should always be applied that whenever someone touches the code, they should leave it in a better shape than it was found (see Practice 43).

- **Dying in beauty by building the "can-do-everything" platform**
  There is also the opposite pitfall of trying to build a perfect tech platform from the start. Many big tech companies have started off with a
  monolithic structure and were able to run them, to a certain degree,
  until today. Sometimes scaling is needed later on. For example, the
  product may evolve so fast that it is almost impossible to build the "can-
  do-everything platform" from the start. Therefore, it is important to
  consciously plan for rewrites and refactorings.
- **Ignoring security for too long**
  Some teams ignore investing in information security until it is too late,
  causing customer data to become compromised. The minimum standard is to perform regular external penetration testing ("red team"), having an internal "blue team" to test and remedy security weaknesses and
  holding regular employee training on social engineering (e.g., phishing
  and securing against employee fraud; see Practices 36 and 45).
- **Fencing the technology organization and hiding its performance**
  Some technology teams are not transparent enough with their objectives and key results. Every stakeholder should understand the key
  challenges of building technology, which is why identifying and transparently tracking a few essential technical OKRs is important. This might
  include uptime, deployment frequency per developer per week, change
  failure rate, bugs in production, etc. (see Practice 39).
- **Insufficiently aligning on internal technical standards**
  Technology teams can be at risk of letting their technology stack grow in
  an uncontrolled manner. While it is indeed essential to provide individual developer teams with as much autonomy as possible, some standardization is necessary – as it saves time for developers. Standardization
  may include API style, format, documentation and an easy-to-access
  catalogue of services. It is also important to communicate standards so
  clearly that it would be difficult to not follow them (see Practice 41).
- **Building a zoo of service**
  Micro-services are fashionable, yet some companies overdo it by building dozens or hundreds of services without cataloguing them properly. A
  limited number of services (in the lower 10s) with standardized and well-
  documented APIs are key here (see Practice 43).

- **Thinking that you are a very special snowflake when considering to buy or develop**
  In particular, inexperienced product or technical leaders sometimes believe that they need to develop software in house instead of buying it because their requirements are so unique. This may lead to developers investing time into tools or features that do not add enough to the company's competitive advantage. If users can be delighted directly, this is often a strong argument to build. If this cannot be done, it is best to consider open-source software or paying for managed service.

One key task of technology functions is usually creating a scalable, secure tech platform for future growth. The technology function needs to focus on ensuring the product and technology teams are productive in terms of speed of software delivery, guaranteeing technological platform performance and reliability with the right technology architecture choices, assuring the quality of the code used and mitigating security risks.

This is our formula for technology-supported growth (Figure 38):

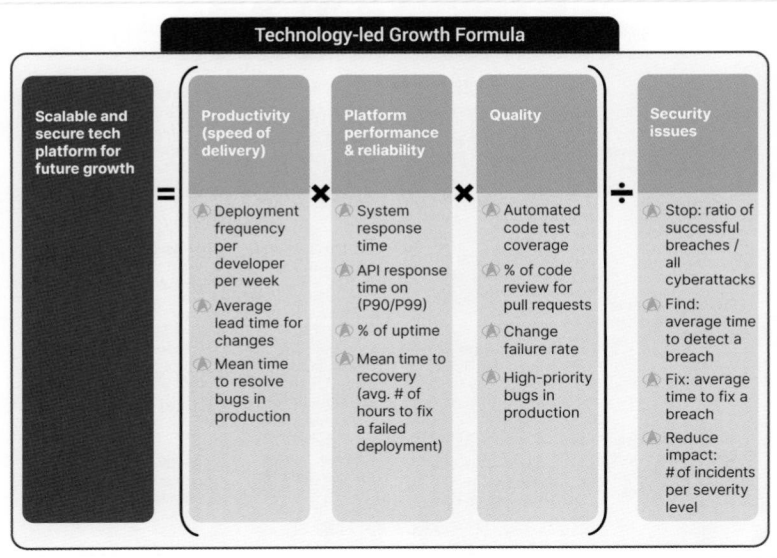

Figure 38: Technology-led Growth Formula

This formula can be turned into objectives and key results (OKRs). The next practice offers an example of a list of technology OKRs for a typical FinTech.

Practice 36: Establishing the right technology OKRs

It is important to consider the context, including level of ambition and available resources, to create a set of technology OKRs (Figure 39).

Typical Technology OKRs for a *FinTech* Scale-up

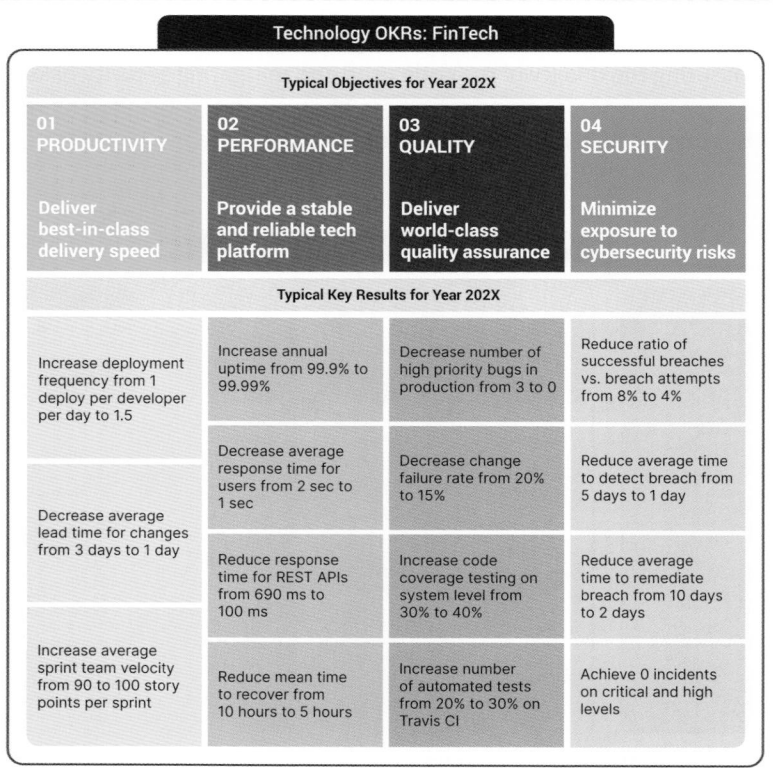

Figure 39: Technology OKRs – FinTech

Now let's take a look at each objective and the key results in more detail.

O1. Productivity: Are you deploying software fast enough?

Etsy, one of the most recognized eCommerce sites for handmade goods, struggled with slow code deployments and siloed ways of working that impeded collaboration between teams. In its early days, Etsy managed just two deployments per week, each taking several hours to complete, which would often result in faults, the temporary shutdown of the site and a loss of revenue. The fundamental issue here was a division between the developers writing the code and the operations teams responsible for its deployment and maintenance. When Chad Dickerson, then CTO of Yahoo, joined Etsy in 2008, he quickly moved to transition Etsy to a "DevOps" way of working. Development Operations refers to a set of practices that brings software development (Dev) and IT operations (Ops) closer together with the ultimate goal of speeding up the development of quality software. This shift empowered developer teams to take ownership of the code's quality, rather than leave the issues to be resolved by other teams. Dickerson's strategy led to a significant uptick in performance, and Etsy now deploys code 30 times faster than it did prior to its DevOps transition.[168]

One key objective for any scale-up technology team is to ensure a high level of developer productivity (i.e., the ability to deploy features to customers as rapidly as possible with minimum developer time required). Typical drivers for high deployment productivity include deploying a scalable software architecture so that teams can work independently on a technical level and in a DevOps environment to facilitate automated code testing and shipping. This reduces the cognitive load for each team and enables them to spend as much of their time as possible on value-creating tasks.

A typical key result here for measuring productivity is the deployment frequency, with high-performing companies being able to deploy software to users several times a day.[169] One way to measure this is through "code deploys" per day, per developer (i.e., how often working code can be moved from the internal developer environment to either the "staging environment" – where code is tested – or the "production environment" – which makes the software available for customers. The lead is typically important for the timing of changes, which is the time that elapses from when a card on a Kanban board is added to the backlog until the feature is shipped to the customer. This includes the time required to design, build, test and deploy a feature, as well as all downtime in between. The mean amount of time to resolve an issue in production is another way to measure developer productivity.

O2. Platform reliability & performance: Is your technology platform available to customers and is it fast enough?

On February 28, 2017, a team of cloud developers at Amazon Web Services in North Virginia tried to debug a slow billing system. One young team member, who was working beyond his authority, entered an incorrect command that caused multiple servers to go offline, including one responsible for the metadata of all AWS customers in that region. It took four hours to put the servers back online, and time services provided by Slack, Medium, Trello, Capital One, Atlassian and Amazon itself were all affected (Alexa devices stopped responding temporarily to voice commands, for example).[170] During the downtime, the impacted web-based applications, services and IoT devices were unable to access key data stored on Amazon's S3 cloud storage service. In other words, they were like restaurants that were left without functioning kitchens for a few hours. Once the S3 service was back online, applications, services and devices that relied on it were once again able to start processing requests made through their client-side interfaces.

It is essential to ensure technology platforms continue to be available to customers without latency, even at peak demand. A drop in availability often results in a decline in business performance. According to Google, ~30% more customers stop using a website if the time required for a mobile page to load increases from 1 to 3 seconds (see Figure 40). Amazon reported a 1% drop in sales for 100 ms of additional loading time.[171] In other words, every millisecond in page loading times matters to increase conversion rates.

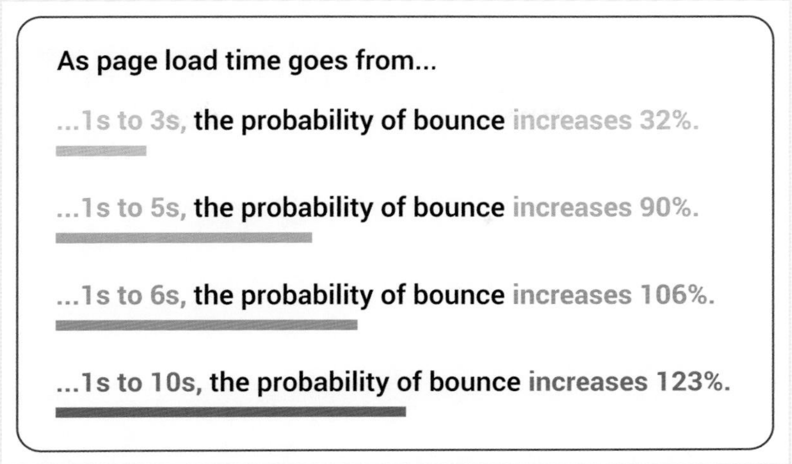

As page load time goes from...

...1s to 3s, **the probability of bounce** increases 32%.

...1s to 5s, **the probability of bounce** increases 90%.

...1s to 6s, **the probability of bounce** increases 106%.

...1s to 10s, **the probability of bounce** increases 123%.

Figure 40: Page Load Time and Business Performance
Source: Google/ SOASTA Research, 2017

A typical key result here is the uptime percentage. For example, retailers and business banks aim to achieve "four 9s" availability, meaning customers can access their services at a rate of at least 99.99 percent over the year – this target level can lead to up to 53 minutes of unplanned downtime per year.[172] In 2020, 80% of companies demanded mission-critical system reliability of at least 99.99% (see Figure 41 for more details).[173] Other key results include load speed to first user experience and API response time or the time gap between the start and end of a process or request (e.g., logging in to a user account). The "mean time to recover" (MTTR) – the time required to recover a service after an unplanned outage or service impairment – is also crucial, with best-in-class companies needing less than 1 hour.[174]

Uptime Percentage	Approximate Offline Time per Year	Typical Target Applied in Industries
99.9%	8h 45 min	This level is not acceptable for most scale-ups.
99.99%	~53 min	eCommerce (e.g., Etsy, Argos, IKEA), social media (e.g., LinkedIn, Skype, Tumblr), cloud service providers (e.g., AWS, Microsoft Azure) and banking services (e.g., FinTechs, Barclays, Citibank)
99.999%	~5 min	Mobile network operators
99.9999%	~30 sec	Air traffic controlled communication and financial trading systems
99.99999%	≤~3 sec	Global positioning system and communication satellites

Figure 41: Uptime Percentage
Sources: AWS, uptime.is, Feedzai Techblog, uptime.com, Google Cloud, itnonline.com, mapyourtech.com, Wired, cu-2.com, Cisco, Wikipedia, itilnews.com, Redhat, Idexgroup, IBM.

O3. Quality: Are you deploying quality code with minimal bugs?

At 9:30 am on August 1, 2012, the Knight Capital Group, a major US global financial service provider, realized something was seriously wrong. The market was being flooded with an unusually high number of orders to buy stock. Despite the frantic efforts of Knight Capital's developer teams to stop it, the company unintentionally bought 150 different stocks worth USD 7 billion in just 45 minutes. A few days previously, they had updated their high-speed algorithmic "SMARS" routers, which send orders to the market. However, when the code was being deployed, a developer failed to copy the new code over to one of the eight SMARS servers. With no four-eye principle in place, there was no one to review the code and spot the error. Knight Capital did not have the means to pay for these shares, so it tried to have the trades canceled. This move was rejected by the Securities and Exchange Commission. Knight Capital ended up losing USD 440 million and was eventually sold a year later.[175]

There are many ways a code deployment can go wrong without proper quality assurance. Knight Capital had no proper peer code review in place, deployed the code manually without automated testing to back it up and incorrectly classified error messages, which prevented alerts from being reviewed in time. DevOps procedures are specifically designed to prevent errors like these. This is particularly relevant for environments with pressing real-time customer needs, such as high-speed trading, access to accounts, business-to-business services for live customer service and customer identification. Building automated testing into the DevOps practices is an important step (see Practice 41).

A typical key result here includes the change failure rate or the percentage of deployments that lead to a degraded service when they are deployed or released into the production environment. These deployments usually require remediation (e.g., roll-back, hotfix or patch). An excellent change failure rate is between 0% and 15%.[176] Other key results include the current number of known high-priority bugs in production or the percentage of automated code test coverage. Tests are usually run at the unit level (i.e., code tests written by developers for the newly developed code), integration level (i.e., tests to assess the stability and performance of code when interacting with other components in the system) and as end-to-end system tests (i.e., tests on a full software product, such as a mobile app, to ensure all integrated components behave as anticipated).

O4. Security: Are you minimizing security risks while facilitating the business?

Code Spaces, an SaaS startup based in Coventry (UK), had its world turned upside down by a DDoS attack back in 2014 when cybercriminals gained access to its Amazon Web Services control panel. After refusing to pay the hacker's demands, Code Spaces lost the majority of its data and configurations along with all its backups. This led the company to nosedive into insolvency. Its greatest error? Putting all its data in one place without (multiple) remote backups.[177]

According to the IBM Cost of Data Breach Report 2020, every data breach costs the global technology sector USD 5 million on average. Typical root causes for malicious data breaches include compromised credentials, cloud misconfiguration, vulnerabilities in third-party software, phishing and physical security compromises.[178] When assessing security risks, the typical dimensions to focus on are: data, people, infrastructure and (web) applications. See Figure 42 for more details:

ASSETS	THREATS	CONTROLS
DATA	Data breach Misuse or manipulation of information Corruption of data	Data protection (e.g., encryption) Data recovery capability Boundary defense
PEOPLE	Identity theft "Man in the middle" Social engineering Abuse of authorization	Controlled access Account monitoring Security skills and training Background screening Awareness and social control
INFRASTRUCTURE	Denial of service Manipulation of hardware Botnets Network intrusion (malware)	Control of privileged access Monitoring of audit logs Malware defenses Network controls (configuration and ports) Inventory Secure configuration Continuous vulnerability assessment
APPLICATIONS	Manipulation of software Unauthorized installation of software Misuse of information systems Denial of service	Email and web-browser protections Application software security Inventory Secure configuration Continuous vulnerability assessment

Figure 42: Security Risks
Sources: McKinsey report "Perspectives on transforming cybersecurity," 2019; European Union Agency for Network and Information Security; The SANS Institute[179]

Social engineering (e.g., directing employees to fake login sites to harvest passwords) and web-based attacks on databases and web applications are the most common cybersecurity threats faced by small companies.[180] To understand technical web application risks, OWASP (the Open Web Application Security Project) has compiled the top 10 risks, including:[181]

- **Injection flaws**: hostile data is sent to a company's systems, leading false commands to be issued or data to be accessed without proper authorization.
- **Broken authentication**: non-watertight user authentication processes are exploited to hack keys, passwords or session tokens and assume the identity of users with access to internal systems.
- **Cross-site scripting (XSS)**: untrusted data is added to a webpage without proper validation, allowing attackers to redirect users to malicious sites or hijack user sessions.
- **Security misconfiguration**: internal services and databases are accessed due to a number of reasons (e.g., insecure default configurations, open cloud storage or misconfigured HTTP headers). This may result in the exposure of sensitive data (healthcare, financial, etc.).

Practice 45 outlines these malicious acts and how to mitigate them in more detail. See Figure 43 to get an idea of the typical security components a scale-up will need.

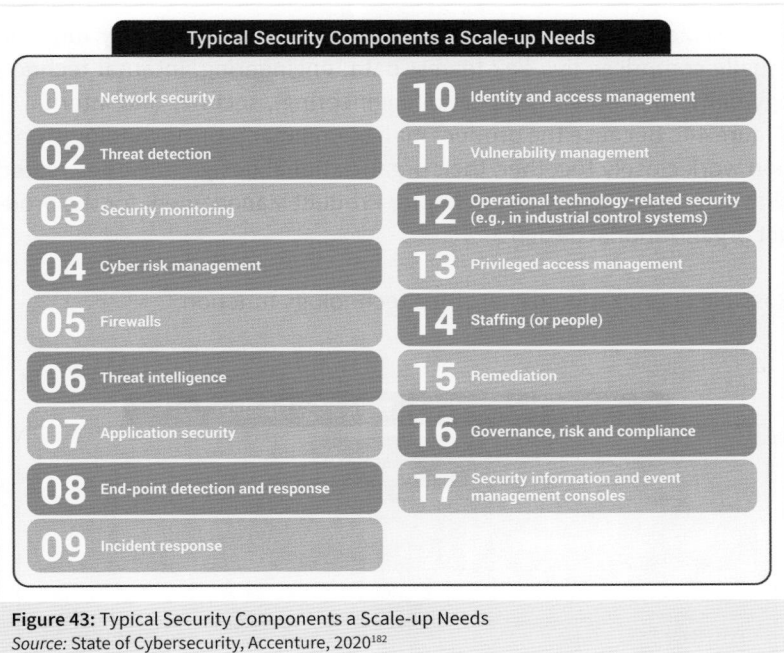

Figure 43: Typical Security Components a Scale-up Needs
Source: State of Cybersecurity, Accenture, 2020[182]

It is reasonable to expect a security team to stop as many attacks as possible, find and fix breaches quickly and reduce the impact of the breach. This is why the **typical key results** here for measuring the security team's performance include the ratio of prevented vs. successful cyberattack breaches, the average time to detect a security breach (less than one day is good) and the mean time to fix the breach (aim for fewer than 15 days).[183] According to the Accenture Cybersecurity Report 2020, security leaders report one moderate incident every 13 months and one critical incident every 22 months on average.

Organzational charts and roles

Practice 37: Defining the roles & responsibilities for a technology function

For a scale-up with a live software product, the technology function usually comprises five key teams: data, engineering, internal technology platform (sometimes part of engineering), security and internal IT (Figure 44). Because the product management and the technology function work closely together, their organizational design must be created with each other in mind (see chapter Product Management for the product organizational designs).

Possible organizational chart for a technology function

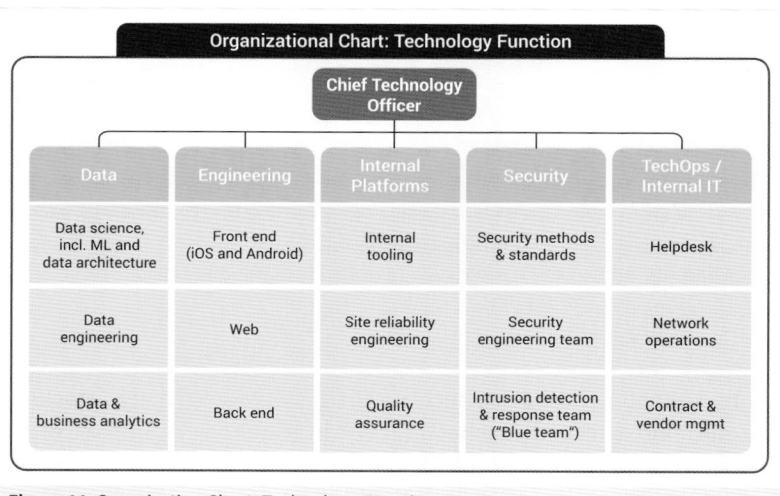

Figure 44: Organization Chart: Technology Function

- **Data teams**

    In the early 1900s, it was common to have a chief electricity officer on the executive team to ensure the central functions of the company were safely and reliably supplied with electricity. Today, many teams should also have the ability to perform advanced data analytics and set up real-time performance monitoring (e.g., dashboard) on their own. This is where data teams with three specialist roles step in.[184]

- **Data analysts** are statisticians that interpret data and are often re- sponsible for data cleaning and visualization, modeling data and building dashboards. They do not need extensive expertise in cod- ing. Typical technical skills include SQL, NoSQL, XML, Hive, Pig, Ha- doop and Spark.[185]
- **Data engineers** are strong coders and software engineers with a background in statistics, and they are often deployed on data-based product development, such as recommendation engines, using machine learning algorithms or new data analytic tools. Typical technical skills include Hadoop, Java, Python, Spark, AWS, SQL, Hive, Scala, Kafka, and NoSQL.[186]
- **Data scientists** have their fingers on the pulse of the latest research in the field to test and evolve machine learning models. They some- times also work on data architecture, setting up central data ware- houses, defining schemas and ensuring integrity and consistency across different data sources. All three roles have overlap, and an expert may specialize in one while being adept in the other two.

A scale-up could employ a central setup where a close-knit data group oversees the data architecture, database integrity and cen- tral data analytic tools and deploys data analysts in key functions to support data-focused projects (e.g., building up real-time dash- boards). Ideally, they work with business analysts in each function. Under this setup, the data team often seeks to "democratize" access to data analytic capabilities by providing analysis tools and training for data-heavy functions such as supply chain, marketing or product. Other possible setups of the data team include consulting, centers of excellence and a decentralization model in which data colleagues become part of the business teams.[187]

- **Engineering teams**
One possible organizing principle when establishing an engineering team is to divide the team members between the front end and back end. The front-end developers focus on building the application and website interfaces with which the end-user interacts. The back-end developers focus on building the underlying data and model infra- structure (e.g., defining how data is saved to the database, devel- oping APIs, establishing security standards, integrating third-party services) that determines what the software is capable of. While the exact setup depends on the scale-up's business needs, applications and programming languages, most will have several or all of these

teams: mobile/native app development for Apple (iOS) and Android with languages such as Java, Swift and Kotlin; web application development with PHP, JavaScript, HTML/CSS, Ruby and Python; and back-end application development with Java, Ruby, Python and PHP. It is very common for developers to work as part of a cross-functional product and tech team (see Practice 25).

- **Platform teams**
  As the engineering team grows, so does the importance of maintaining productivity and retaining talent. This includes designing and implementing internal tools, such as continuous integration, server configuration management, deployment automation and management. The team can measure its success in terms of how many "thank-yous" it receives from the developer teams in exchange for designing (cloud) deployment processes or enabling cloud self-service for product teams. They often own the provision process to ensure all controls and audits are in place. A special form of the (cloud) platform team pioneered by Google is "Site Reliability Engineering." After defining an "error budget" (the acceptable amount of downtime), the SRE team's key responsibility is to reject suboptimal code.[188] With internal tooling and quality assurance (QA) overlapping as more automated tests become available, QA teams are sometimes part of this group (or with engineering). These teams make sure the product works the way it should from a technical perspective, even during (unexpected) peaks. They enable the product and technology teams to test on the unit and module level and write automated system-level tests, but they should not be deployed to fix bad code.

- **Security teams**
  A security group in a scale-up often fulfills at least three roles. The first is to define security methods and standards (e.g., coding guidelines, the frequency and extent of independent penetration testing, certification standards). These standards are often implemented by a security engineering team. The second role is a "blue team," which configures and runs software and hardware, deploys patches, secures the network and makes the operating system resilient against cyberattacks (with passwords, encryption, firewalls, etc.). They also take care of digital forensics, malware analysis and threat intelligence and may involve cybersecurity training for employees. Finally, a "red team" is there to drive system penetration tests – conducting mobile, web app or network "pentesting" such as social engineering

tests (sending fake phishing emails to employees to extract log-in credentials) by checking virus scanners or trying to physically gain access to the building – and detect vulnerabilities. These duties are often outsourced to a security consultancy boutique or major providers, such as Deloitte, Capgemini or McAfee. If a company grows to more than 1,000 FTE and is regularly at risk of security incidents, it may be worth establishing a security operations center (SOC). The European Union Agency for Cybersecurity (ENISA) has published a guide on how to do this.[189]

In some cases, it may be worthwhile to integrate the security teams into the cross-functional product and technology teams. This "DevSecOps" approach means integrating cybersecurity architects and engineers in the product development teams in every phase of the software development lifecycle, from design through integration, testing and deployment to software delivery.[190]

- **TechOps/internal IT teams**
  This team resembles the "help desks" relied on by major corporations. They often procure notebooks, telephones and mobile network contracts, as well as run a help desk with service tickets to support larger issues (e.g., with office software). Additionally, they will administer passwords and printer authorizations and re-negotiate terms with IT contractors and vendor managers. Sometimes this team will take responsibility for the task of customizing internal tools, which might involve some development work (e.g., setting up Jira, connecting APIs, implementing integrations with third-party software, etc.).

When a startup enters the scale-up stage, the technology function needs to be led by a senior leader (e.g., CTO or VP of Technology) who fulfills several responsibilities: hiring top developer talent and creating a fun and satisfying work environment (high retention rate); leading major buy, build and partner decisions regarding technology; shipping quality products to markets quickly and creating a scalable technology architecture with no major technical debt; and serving as an external "evangelist" and a spokesperson with developers, partners and customers.[191]

Practice 38: Scaling the right technology roles at the right time

The steps involved in building a scalable technology platform vary greatly depending on the business model and tech stack. The following principles may be of use when creating a scalable, secure technology platform:

- **Build a monolith quickly during the startup phase**
  A monolithic structure for a technology platform is often a good way to get off the ground quickly and launch an MVP product. During this phase, it is critical to document all key architecture decisions that possibly need to be revisited later. By consciously making such decisions, developers tend to write code more cleanly with better documentation from the outset.
- **Build a modular architecture around the monolith with well-chosen services**
  It is of the essence here not to grow a "zoo of services" in the hundreds. The services should also be truly stateless, with carefully designed APIs, and ideally mapped to the domain logic (e.g., if you are a matching platform, one service should be the matching algorithm).
- **Settle on a target architecture that is good enough for now during the startup phase**
  This might include building a simple gateway and connecting new services and an existing monolith to that gateway. Over time, it is often advisable to move more and more functionality out of the monolith. The main driver should be that each of your teams has full control over the service they are building – which is not the case if they are working on a part of the monolith.
- **Deploy internal developer platforms as in-house tools to boost efficiency in the early growth phase**
  Too many scripts and configuration files will not scale with a rapidly growing tech team. Teams are starting to be blocked by reaching out to the few experts that still know everything in-and-out. Deployments might take longer. Establishing an internal platform team early on is one way out. This team's customers are the developer teams. The main task of this team should be to lower the cognitive load for each team in the organization (e.g., by standardizing deployment strategies) so that the teams can focus on what they should do.

- **Build key "collectives" for cooperation and knowledge sharing in the early growth phase**
  These collectives support the exchange of knowledge and your engineers' career development. They usually include iOS, Android, back-end and DevOps/QA and can be created as soon as each group consists of more than 10 employees.

Now that the organizational structure is in place, let's turn to the technology function practices required to facilitate the smooth transition to a scale-up. The key practices revolve around agile development, development operations (DevOps), scalable (cloud) infrastructure, security and data architecture.

Your way of agile development

Practice 39: Creating your own version of agile development

After having seen many software projects run out of time and go over budget – often with unsatisfactory results for customers – a group of software developers published the "Agile Manifesto" back in 2001. It was based on four key principles:[192]
- Individuals and interactions over processes and tools
- Working software over comprehensive documentation
- Customer collaboration over contract negotiation
- Response to change over following a plan

Delivering software faster and better was the group's intention. The manifesto was an alternative to the "waterfall approach," where software is planned for months or even years in advance, meaning that the customer's requirements had often changed by the time it was finally released. Reducing cost and time risks in software development through faster learning cycles and shipping in smaller increments is at the heart of this approach, and it usually results in:
- the ability to change the scope of software products faster
- a lower risk of shipping functionalities that do not work
- quicker feedback from customers, allowing the product development to be amended

In essence, agile development speeds up the build-measure-learn cycle as defined by Eric Ries (Figure 45):[193]

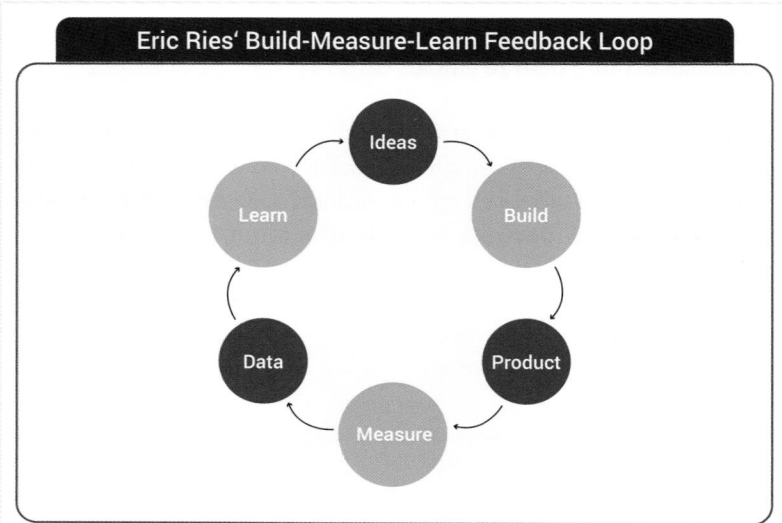

Figure 45: Eric Ries' Build-Measure-Learn Feedback Loop
Source: Eric Ries, The Lean Startup: How Today's Entrepreneurs Use Continuous Innovation to Create Radically Successful Businesses, 2011[194]

There is no one-size-fits-all approach to agile development, every company needs to develop its own approach based on the agile development principles. These include:

- **Delivering software to satisfy the customer**
  Shipping working software that is valuable for customers is the key measurement of success.
- **Delivering working software continuously**
  Shipping frequently is essential, which is why many companies work in one-week or two-week sprints based on a rank-ordered backlog.
- **Being open to change requests**
  Giving key stakeholders the ability to offer feedback on product development regularly (i.e., quarterly at the minimum) helps to create a competitive advantage in the customers' eyes.

- **Working in a cross-functional way**
  A cross-functional team that includes a product owner and stake-holders from business functions consolidates the best experiences.
- **Facilitating self-organization**
  One route to success is to give teams the autonomy to choose methods and ways of working and provide maximum clarity on purpose and outcome goals to be achieved ("aligned direction").
- **Being attentive to technical excellence and good design**
  Finding defects early on is a key element here (e.g., by deploying code reviews in which one programmer checks the code of another developer).
- **Ensuring regular feedback and reflection**
  The team reflects on how to become more effective at regular intervals, then adjusts its behavior accordingly.

To implement these principles, teams can choose between several agile methods. The Agile Alliance has put together a solid overview of agile practices from areas such as extreme programming, scrum and lean software development (Figure 46).[195]

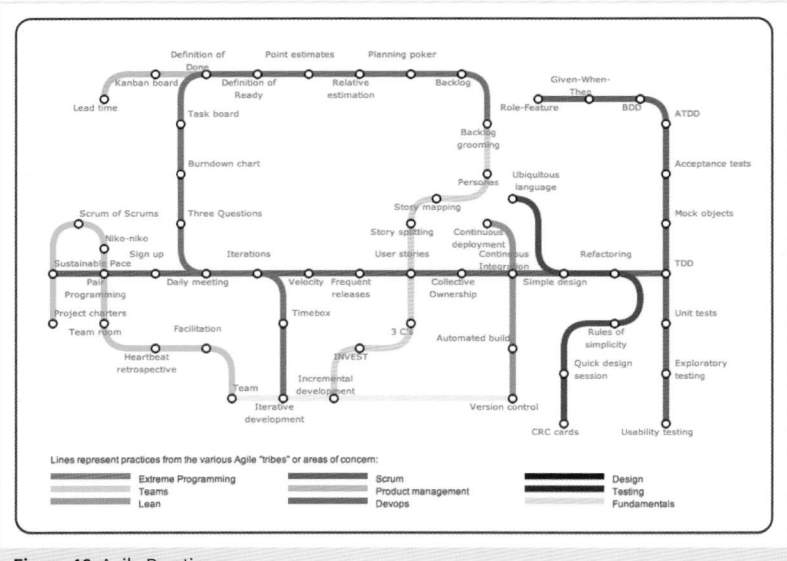

Figure 46: Agile Practices
Source: Agile Alliance, Subway Map to Agile Maps[196]

Some of these practices include:

- **Scrum**
  This is a time-boxed project management approach for frequent and incremental software delivery and is the most popular agile methodology. At the start of a sprint the team takes user stories from the product backlog and puts them into the sprint backlog, before estimating the effort involved in each story (often with story points). The goal of each sprint is to create an "increment" or a piece of work that adds further functionality to the product. During the sprint, the team holds a time-boxed daily scrum meeting (a "standup"). A burndown chart helps to track story point progress against time (see the graph in Figure 47), and quality assurance testing is performed during the sprint. The sprint is closed via a sprint review meeting. From time to time, the team reflects on its process in a "retrospective," which is a structured meeting to reflect on learnings and distill improvement suggestions for further sprints. There is often a "scrum master," who helps the team with the scrum process and increases its productivity.

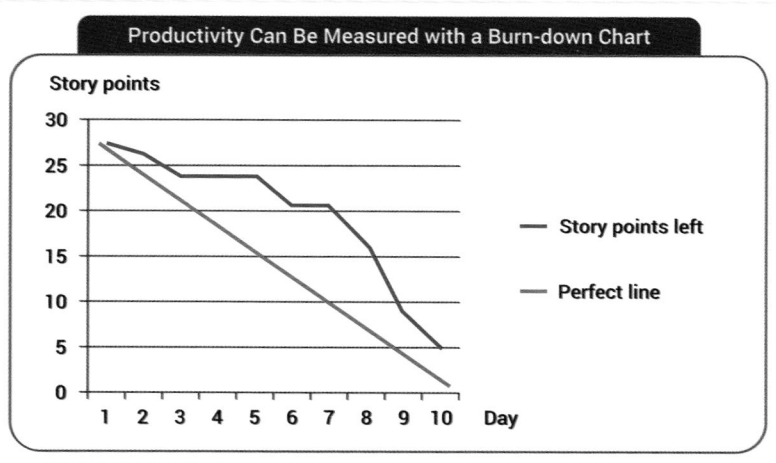

Figure 47: Productivity Can Be Measured with a Burn-down Chart

- **Kanban**

  Kanban is a system to visualize work and does not have the level of process prescription that scrum does. It often works best for smaller development teams due to the reduced complexity. At its core, there is a Kanban board consisting of different columns (see Figure 48). Possible columns include the backlog (items to be potentially worked on), ready (items selected from the backlog and ready for development), development (items that a developer has started working on), testing (items being tested for errors) and system deployed (items deployed to the production environment). Workflow transparency is one element here that fosters collaboration and team productivity. Work is labeled on cards and added to the different columns. Many teams use a paper-based board for this, as the limited physical space helps keep writing short and there is an element of enhanced commitment when a team member moves a card during a team meeting from one column to the next. The usual workflow is to move the card from left to right across different columns. Many teams define a "work in progress" (WIP) limit, which states the maximum number of cards for each column (below: four for "ready," three for "development," two for "testing"). This is relevant, as it keeps the team focused on closing work items. There is often a tendency to start new work items rather than finishing a previous one. However, this negatively affects context switching and overall productivity.

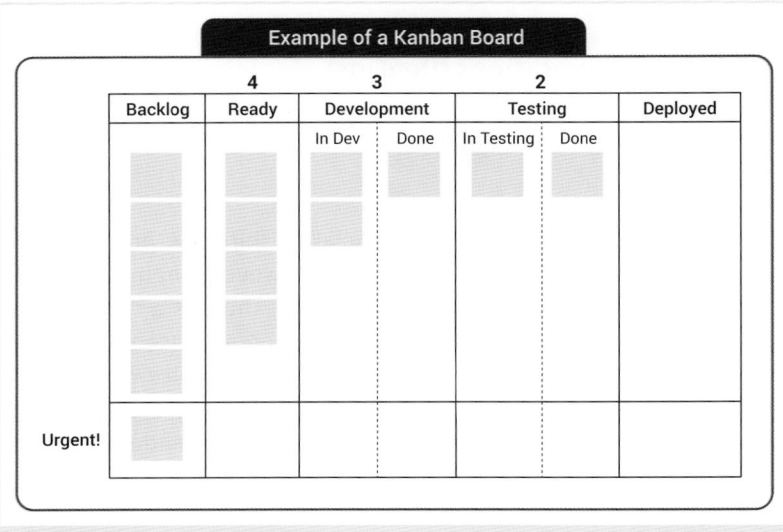

Figure 48: Example of a Kanban Board

- **Extreme programming (XP)**
  This form of agile advocates taking a few best programming practices to the extreme. This includes code reviews, which can be done
  in "real time" by programming in pairs, unit testing of all code, a very
  high degree of code simplicity and continuous integration and deployment of code through automated testing, including test-driven
  development. XP is based on the principles of communication, simplicity, feedback, courage and respect. The approach is relevant especially for dynamically changing software requirements.[197]

It is important to note that the agile approach can differ between teams
depending on the type of work, their seniority and how well they know
each other. It can also change over time for the same team. It may be
worthwhile to start with a relatively clearly defined standard approach
for each new developer team. This could go as far as precisely defining
the daily procedures, all regular meetings and the style of tickets, as this
reduces complexity from the outset. Over time, the team members will
become familiar with each other and can alter the approach to fit their
specific needs.

For further reading on these practices, see Pat Kua's *Flavours of Agile,*[198]
Johana Rothman's *Create Your Successful Agile Project* and Dan Olson's
Lean Product Playbook.

Development operations (DevOps)

Practice 40: Establishing lean software development principles

To build a unicorn company, it is crucial to ship new products and
features out faster than the competitors. However, when scaling and
adding new people to the technology teams, there is a risk that the
number of deployments per day actually decreases (see Figure 49).
There are myriad reasons for this: increasingly complex cloud architectures, tightly coupled monolithic applications starting to matter
and increasing amount of manual code testing as dependencies in the
code base rise.

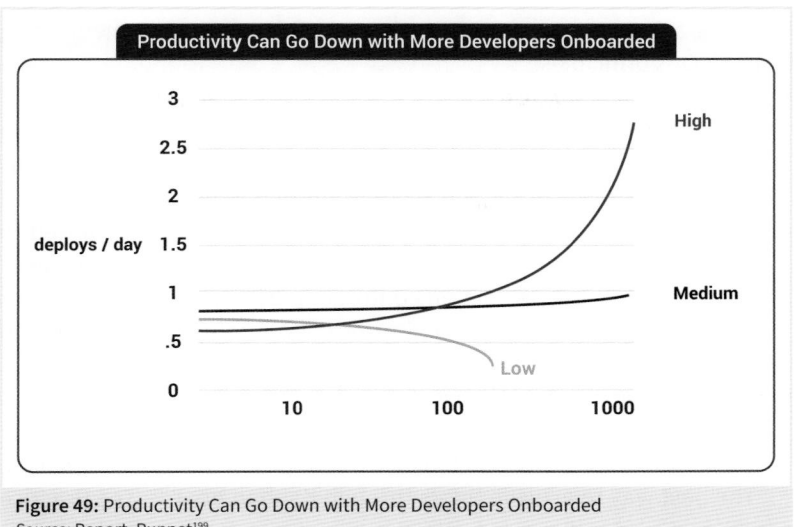

Figure 49: Productivity Can Go Down with More Developers Onboarded
Source: Report, Puppet[199]

DevOps and lean product practices are the key to keeping deployment frequency high and ensuring reliable scaling of technology platforms. DevOps brings code development and product operations closer together. In other words, a team that builds the code should also run it. DevOps focus on automating infrastructure, code testing, workflows and performance testing to boost productivity and collaboration. In this sense, it is more of a practice or mindset than a specific role or team.[200]

A 2019 report by DORA (DevOps Research and Assessment, a Google company) found that DevOps allowed elite tech teams to deploy code over 200 times more frequently. These teams were also more than 100x faster in their lead time from commitment to deployment, had a ~2,600x faster mean time to recover from downtime and a 7x lower change failure rate.[201] This makes a big difference, as low performers took between one and six months to bring code from commitment to deployment, while top performers deployed an average of four times per day with a change lead time of just 24 hours.

Here are a few management principles to follow when implementing lean DevOps principles:[202]

- **Work in small batches**
  Have developers write code in small chunks that can be deployed in 1–2 weeks or less, rather than one large piece of software. This results in shorter leads and feedback cycles.[203] Ideally, automated testing should be performed on this code before it is forwarded to peer developers for review. Review developers should check minor code changes using a version control depository and give feedback to the developers, who can deploy the code within hours (rather than weeks or months).

- **Visually keep track of the workflow**
  Both engineers and managers should have a clear overview of the workflow at all times, including obstacles for a successful sprint. The best way to achieve this is through Kanban boards (see Practice 39) and lead indicators to measure progress, such as story points visualized with burn-down charts, defects, lead times and team cycle times.

- **Get regular feedback from customers**
  Sometimes, sprint teams do not obtain feedback from customers enough (especially engineers). Ensuring a constant stream of user feedback (e.g., with usage, activation and retention metrics) is as critical as being personally involved in user research, such as interviews or observing users with a feature. Some companies organize UX cycles with a customer insight session in the morning to define 3–5 hypotheses for improving the product and then work on them over the day and close the loop in the evening with another round of research. There are few things more exciting for engineers and product managers than to see an improved user experience within one day.

- **Establish a light change process that empowers team experimentation and quality deployment**
  Cumbersome (formal) change management processes can put the brakes on rapid software deployment. A study by DORA has found no evidence of more formal approval processes (e.g., via Change Advisory Boards) leading to lower change fail rates.[204] What they surely do is to make software development slower with reduced deployment frequencies and increased lead times. Giving the team the option to carry out automated testing, roll back changes quickly and

conduct peer-based code reviews enables it to prevent and correct defects much faster than via formal approval processes. Therefore this continuous delivery approach (see Practice 41) balances speed with avoidance of defects.

Practice 41: Establishing technical DevOps practices for continuous delivery

Consider this: each time someone goes to YouTube, Netflix or Amazon, they are using the newest version of the site. And "new" really means *new*: the underlying software could have been updated hundreds of times that day alone, but they almost certainly will not have noticed. Continuous delivery allows developers to make minor improvements to features, fix bugs, change configurations and even perform experiments – all to the benefit of users – as soon as they are ready. The result: faster feedback cycles and quicker improvements.[205]

Whereas in the past, the standard was to deploy code on a monthly, quarterly or even bi-annual basis, today modern software companies aim to deploy code daily (known as "continuous delivery"). The key advantages here are faster cycle times, more frequent deployment and a lower change failure rate, as code failures can be detected quickly while remaining minor and contained. The common stages are: plan, code, build, test, release, deploy, operate and monitor. Development operations, or DevOps as it is commonly known, is a methodology that emphasizes cross-functional collaboration between IT operations and software development teams. The focus is on developer enablement by combining lean management and automating development processes, resulting in major improvements in speed and accuracy. To achieve this, it is essential to separate the production environment (the code used by customers) from the staging environment for testing the code (a replica of the code used by customers). See Figure 50 for a general overview. Other technical prerequisites for daily deployments include internal self-service tooling, configuration management and automated testing.

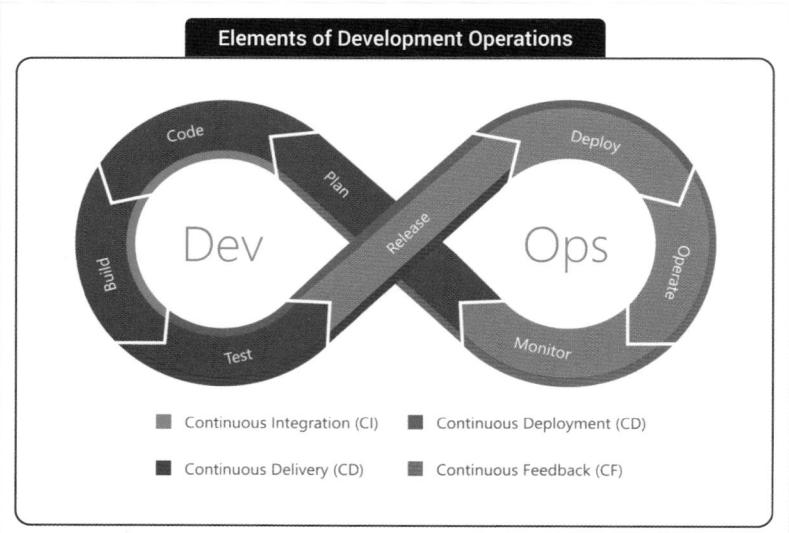

Figure 50: Elements of Development Operations
Source: The eight phases of a development pipeline[206]

- **Enable your developers with internal self-service tooling**
  Rapid deployment comes from developers – as internal clients –
  being able to rely on a suite of DevOps tools with a similar UI/UX as
  would be expected for external clients. These tools automate and
  smooth out repetitive, time-consuming tasks, giving the developers
  more time to focus on producing high-quality code with minimal friction. The internal tooling team is responsible for buying or developing and maintaining these tools, which generally covers the following
  requirements: *collaboration* (i.e., planning application requirements
  and product roadmaps with the product teams, e.g., Jira, Asana,
  Trello, Slack); *building* (i.e., writing and committing code to a shared
  repository for review, e.g., Git via GitHub or Bitbucket, SBT, Gradle);
  testing (i.e., running a continuous series of automatic error tests
  with every code change included and running deeper manual and
  automated tests in the staging environment, e.g., Jenkins, CircleCI);
  deployment (i.e., releasing the changes into the end-user environment, e.g., Spinnaker, Octopus Deploy, Ansible); and *running* (i.e.,
  orchestration of code releases, e.g., Docker, Kubernetes, performance monitoring and error reports, e.g., Prometheus).[207]

- **Ensure proper configuration management and version control**
  Configuration management refers to the process of tracking, organizing and controlling software changes, which allows anyone to identify who made changes to the code and replicate configurations across the IT infrastructure.[208] Comprehensive configuration management usually has three elements:[209] a **source repository** allows for accurate version control of all files readable by humans (e.g., test scripts, code, build scripts, deployment scripts and configuration files). This is particularly important for keeping track of all code changes (known as "commits") so that access can be controlled and code can be compared, merged and restored. The second is an **artifact repository**, which stores all machine-readable files (i.e., binaries, test data and libraries). Finally, there is a **configuration management database**, which is a data warehouse storing varied information about an organization's hardware and software assets, including device information, locations, documents, applications, services, databases and servers.[210]
- **Automate your build and test processes**
  Continuous delivery relies on automated testing to help developers detect bugs in the code within a matter of minutes.[211] The code's function is usually tested on at least four levels.
  - **Unit level tests** review basic code elements such as classes, interfaces and functions. The key here is that developers can run these tests in near-real time (e.g., less than two seconds) so that their productivity is not affected.
  - **Integration tests** – also known as module tests – check blocks of code/modules for mistakes in their interactions. They are similar to unit tests but work at a higher degree of interaction (e.g., to check if a function is interacting correctly with its input function). Both unit level and integration tests are usually performed by the product and technology teams that have written the code in the first place.
  - **System tests (or UI tests)** check if programs run flawlessly from a customer perspective. Some companies buy suites of mobile phones (e.g., with Apple and Android operating systems), build automated test applications, which download and run the different versions of the mobile app for each country 24/7, do one order or transaction both for the production and the test environment and delete the app again. If one of the apps fails, the central quality team is alerted immediately.

- **User acceptance tests** verify whether the final app/service meets business and UI/UX requirements (e.g., by checking performance, API correctness and user story criteria). The key here is that these tests are run by (internal) customers, not the developers. Sourcing them, for example, via the beta programs of the big app stores is one way to go.[212]
- **Set up real-time system performance monitoring**
  Maintaining service availability to users is the primary purpose of performance monitoring. It typically encompasses three levels: instrumentalization, monitoring and altering.
  - **Instrumentalization** refers to simply measuring the availability of the services being provided and the network health metrics (i.e., server uptime, customer response time when they request information from a digital service and CPU and memory usage). Performance measuring is often passive (metrics indicative of a properly functioning system), but it can also be active, such as by periodically probing the system to see if it is responding according to expectation levels.
  - In **monitoring**, this data is analyzed according to business metrics and the information visually presented for human use. Time-series analytics, for example, look at performance over a period of time to discover common patterns within the data, such as user behavior (e.g., logins, sign-ups, sign-outs), error frequency, error types and contextual information.
  - Finally, **alerting** makes use of automated alarms to actively notify operators of problems when metrics fall outside the acceptable range of conditions.[213] Prometheus (monitoring and altering) and Grafana (Prometheus integration for visualization) are two of the most widely used open-source tools for systems monitoring.

Practice 42: Enabling a team of doers through the right DevOps culture

Netflix has a credo that captures its culture of autonomy perfectly: "Hire smart people and get out of their way." Similarly, teams at Google have found that high psychological safety and a culture of learning matter most when setting up high-performing technology teams. The key question here: Can team members take risks without feeling insecure or embarrassed?[214] The safer they feel, the more likely they will admit their mistakes, work with each other, take on new roles and harness the power of diversity in thinking. This approach often works wonders for employee retention, too. The most desirable team environment is one of candidness, trust and no blame, with people open to listening to constructive feedback and refraining from talking behind each other's backs. This works when team members can rely on each other to deliver quality work on time and is facilitated by having roles and goals visibly and openly mapped out in team and individual OKRs. Managers also need to lead by example by admitting and sharing their own mistakes, embracing employees' input and reacting positively to questions and any instances of doubt. Mutually agreed team principles and regular team exercises (e.g., a few rounds of Google's "Just Like Me" – where people recite statements about each other, followed by "anxiety parties" – where employees write down their biggest worries and share the list with their co-workers), can help a team become close and comfortable.[215]

Ideally, this psychological safety is embedded in a culture where people learn from failure and mistakes. This culture can be developed by:

- … creating a training budget per person for certification, seminars and conferences to highlight the value of learning.
- … giving a team extra time to learn autonomously and explore ideas. For example, Google asks employees to set aside 20% of their time to explore side projects, while some companies schedule several "get things done" days per month or "hack weeks" a few times per year. This is when teams can explore new tools, technologies and ideas.
- … ensuring failure is accepted as part of the learning process, such as by engaging in blameless postmortems that recap the errors and learn from them.
- … co-locating cross-functional teams to facilitate collaboration.
- … publicly celebrating those who take risks (and potentially fail in the process). For example, Google employs monthly postmortem newsletters and postmortem reading clubs and even has a disaster roleplay scenario called "Wheel of Misfortune" in which a game master lays out a disaster scenario on stage (e.g., an outage), and two site reliability engineers try to find the root cause of the problem within 30–60 minutes in front of an audience.[216]

Scalable architecture

Practice 43: Creating a "good enough" software architecture that can evolve over time

The art of creating software architecture in a fast-growing scale-up lies in achieving a rapid go-to-market and avoiding excessive technical debt. Four principles can be of benefit here:

- **Monoliths are fine in the startup phase, as speed is key**
  Amazon's use of "OBIDOS" and LinkedIn's use of "Leo," as well as other applications from the early days of these companies had one thing in common: they were monolithic.[217] A monolith is a type of software architecture where all the components in an application – the database, the client-side application and the server-side application – are built within a single code base. When launching companies, these monoliths help to ship the first products fast. They allow for time-consuming software architecture decisions to be sidestepped, as well as the ability to avoid developing interfaces between modules. If it is necessary to pivot to another business domain (e.g., from an eCommerce shop to a marketplace), a monolithic structure is extremely beneficial, as the domain logic does not have to be redesigned from the ground up. Teams usually start off with a monolith before developing their own gateways and services outside of the architecture with the aim of gradually moving to a more service-oriented design. In the early stages, it is important to avoid dogmatic and overly complicated technological solutions that could be taken care of manually. Sending out 15 bills per month? This does not call for a sophisticated billing system. Working through a compact pipeline of prospective customers? A complex CRM is not required at this stage. Analyzing user feedback for an MVP? Advanced data science platforms are not yet a must-have. It is important to keep in mind that while monolithic architectures are often simple and facilitate a rapid roll-out for early-stage businesses, they can cause frustration. When expanding on the application's features, every minor code amendment requires the application to be rebuilt and deployed in full.
- **Conscious and well-documented decisions when building up technical debt are key**
  Every startup builds up some "technical debt," which is the additional time and resources that are lost in order to adapt (i.e., add to or

rewrite) existing code. If a team decides to program solutions that are quick to implement but have to be reworked later, they accrue technical debt. Examples include: the decision to only support two SQL databases at the beginning vs. integrating multiple database types from the outset or only allowing one type of log-in rather than allowing customers to use their Google and Facebook accounts. If technology teams add to a shared list of technical debt topics that need to be reworked later on and write technical design documents to this effect, it usually compels developers to write code more cleanly from the outset – as this saves time when revisiting the code. It is often helpful to include the following in the technical design documents: the **problem**, the **technical approach** taken, a few **implementation examples** (e.g., logic diagrams or sample code) and the **different options for technical solutions** that were considered (e.g., a longlist of open source and/or commercial software solutions). Design documents should ideally be no longer than 3–4 pages and are shared within and refined by the engineering team.

- **A service-oriented platform architecture grants ownership and control to your developer teams**
  The larger the developer team becomes, the higher the risk of interdependencies in the code base. The best practice is to set up the modules of the software product so that if one team touches an element, there is no need to tinker with another. Martin Fowler describes it as follows:[218]

> "In short, the microservice architectural style is an approach to developing a single application as a suite of small services, each running in its own process and communicating with lightweight mechanisms, often an HTTP resource API. These services are built around business capabilities and independently deployable by fully automated deployment machinery. There is a bare minimum of centralized management of these services, which may be written in different programming languages and use different data storage technologies."

This type of service orientation usually facilitates ownership and control by individual developer teams. Can your teams decide on their own tech stack and programming language? Do they have a clear understanding of the API logic? If yes, these are strong signs of a decoupled, service-oriented platform architecture.[219] Don't step into the trap of building a "zoo" of microservices (Figure 51).

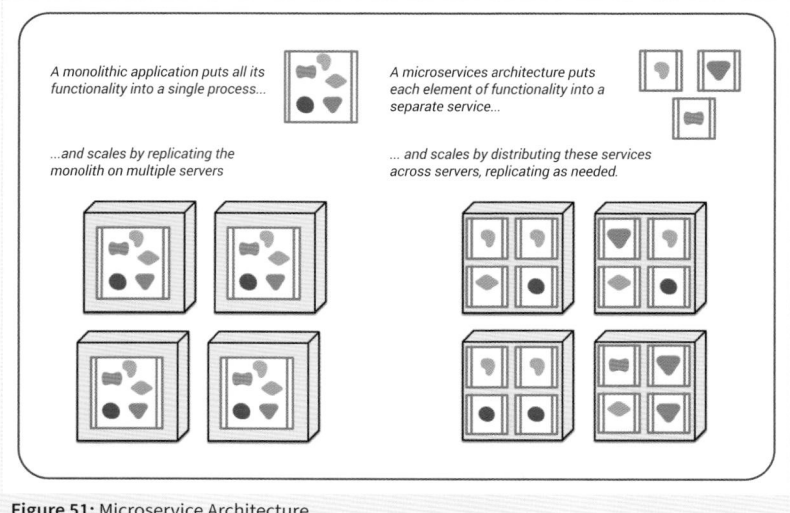

Figure 51: Microservice Architecture
Source: Martin Fowler

- **Standardize to save the time of your developer teams**
  While it is critical to grant individual developer teams as much autonomy as possible, some standardization is unavoidable. After all, reinventing the wheel over and over again helps no one. Standardization usually includes the **API style**, **format** and **documentation** along with the services developed. It may also include the following: a billing service, deployment service, authentication service or monitoring/logging service. An easy-to-access catalog of these services is essential in order to avoid duplication of work and ensure the team interfaces are used properly. Spotify, for example, used backstage.io to build a centralized and simple service catalog. By using templates in the catalog, developers can automate workflows to the point where a microservice, website or another software component can be deployed via a single click.

Practice 44: Establishing a resilient cloud architecture

For most scale-ups, the best practice is to deploy the majority of their applications in the cloud, as this enables their IT infrastructure to keep pace with rapid user growth while ensuring performance and reliability. Here, speed truly is essential. Amazon has reported a drop of 1% in sales for 100 ms of extra loading time, while Google has noted 20% fewer searches for a longer loading time of 500 ms.[220] Cloud deployment is critical for ensuring the architecture can recover from shocks quickly, whether external (e.g., a Black Friday demand peak) or internal (e.g., a developer unintentionally ramping down a server). Here are the key questions to check to see if a cloud architecture is resilient and scalable:[221]

- **Do you have a cloud technology leader with experience in scaling?**
  Many tech professionals have at least some experiences with deploying software in the cloud. Having an expert with AWS Cloud Solutions Architect or Google Cloud Architect certification on board is good but, in the scale-up phase, the difference comes from being able to rely on an experienced "Head of Site Reliability" or "Head of Cloud Platform" who can look at cloud architecture as a whole and who has already scaled up a business with several hundred developers. It may be worth it to consider hiring ex-consultants with a track record of cloud migrations for an in-house position.
- **Do you have enough redundancy built into your cloud networks?**
  Redundancy refers to the duplication of information, ensuring it is not lost when one or more system components fail (e.g., in the event of a fire in a data center).[222] This is why cloud infrastructure providers tend to operate multiple data centers in one region. For example, the AWS Europe region has a total of 18 availability zones in locations such as England (London), France (Paris), Germany (Frankfurt) and Italy (Milan). Each availability zone contains one or more data centers. AWS recommends deploying applications over three AZs to achieve optimal availability. AWS guarantees at least 99% availability for deployment in one AZ (offline for a maximum of 3 days and 15 hours per year). For two deployments in parallel, availability is at 99.99% (offline for a maximum of 53 minutes per year), and for three in parallel, availability is 99.9999% (offline for a maximum of 31 seconds).

- **Are you deploying enough auto-scaling and load-balancing resources?**
  Auto-scaling and load balancing means that applications can adjust their capacity based on the demand. If, say, a high volume of customers is accessing a website on Black Friday, it may be necessary to double the number of servers ("instances") within a few hours. Auto-scaling automatically brings more instances into play, while load balancing routes traffic to those parts of the network that remain underutilized. AWS offers automated load balancing, known as "elastic load-balancing."[223] When planning to fire up additional servers, it is essential to have properly installed applications with resolved dependencies and a short deployment time.

- **Is your infrastructure immutable and stateless?**
  Being able to quickly scale cloud infrastructure up and down depends on having "immutable components" that are replaced for every deployment rather than being constantly updated. Immutable infrastructure is a paradigm where servers cannot be modified after they are deployed. In other words, the information they contain at the moment of creation is final and unchangeable. To be able to adjust the information, new servers have to be built to replace the old ones. A simple example: a banking customer has a balance of USD 1,000 in his account. In order to add to this balance, one would have to open a new account with a new balance. To avoid having to build a new server each time, the existing server's "states" are stored not on individual servers but on a central database from which the servers update their information. This allows them to be ramped up and down quickly and with a high amount of flexibility.

- **Can you deploy infrastructure as code?**
  Deploying infrastructure as code involves writing and executing a script (e.g., to create more servers in the cloud rather than linking them together via a console). The key advantage is that it reduces errors, as configuring a network can be automatically scaled up and down. Humans are prone to errors when performing manual repetitive tasks, while machines can do them with 100% accuracy. In particular, this comes into play during an emergency. For example, a system becomes compromised and customers can no longer access their data. If an infrastructure can be deployed as a code, this may be able to restore the systems within minutes. If not, the

network teams may have to work several days without interruption to recover everything. One key question an infrastructure team needs to be able to answer is how long it will take to rebuild the infrastructure from zero. Deploying infrastructure as a code is especially relevant for businesses where every minute of downtime is critical. For example, this will matter more to a later-stage FinTech than an early-stage eCommerce business.

- **Are you using chaos engineering to test your cloud architecture's resilience?**
  As systems grow, it can be beneficial to test their resilience from time to time with simulated outages. This could be done by taking some instances offline, sending corrupted data to your systems or initiating deliberate network delays. Netflix deploys a "chaos gorilla" every few weeks that shuts down entire availability zones to test if customers can still be served from other zones. Such chaos testing tools enable the company to check microservices and data storage architecture (Netflix even published a Chaos Engineering book detailing this).[224] The logic here is to withstand turbulent conditions in a live production environment,[225] which requires effective real-time monitoring and an experienced cloud platform team.

Information security

Practice 45: Mitigating the top 10 web applications' security risks

Network, cloud and application security are three key risk categories to be managed by your security team. With web applications becoming ever more relevant, a good security team needs to have the top 10 risks on its radar at all times. The Open Web Application Security Project (OWASP) Foundation has compiled a list and updates it on an ongoing basis (see Figure 52).[226] The ranking is based on prevalence, detectability, ease of exploitation and potential technical impact. To protect web applications and online services from security risks and threats, the security teams need to run a host of specific checks and mitigation measures (Figure 52).

Top 10 Web Application Security Risks		
RANK / TOP RISK	**DEFINITION**	**MITIGATION MEASURES**
01 Injection	Untrusted data (often SQL queries) sent to an interpreter as part of a command or query	Use a safe API to avoid the use of an interpreter and provide a parameterized interface Implement whitelist server-side input validation Do not allow special characters to be used for the interpreter
02 Broken authentication	Incorrect implementation of authentication and session management	Implement multi-factor authentication Do not deploy with default credentials Implement weak-password checks and password rotation policies Limit or delay failed login attempts
03 Sensitive data exposure	Weak protection or lack of encryption for sensitive data	Encrypt all sensitive data at rest Do not store sensitive data unnecessarily Do not use caching for responses that contain sensitive data
04 XML External Entity (XXE)	Old or poorly configured XML processors that evaluate external entity references within XML documents	Use simple data formats (i.e., JSON) and avoid serialization of sensitive data Implement filtering or sanitization to prevent hostile data within XML Patch or upgrade all XML processors and libraries in use
05 Broken access control	When restrictions on what authenticated users are allowed to do are not enforced or are done poorly	Always deny by default, except on public resources Implement access control mechanisms and reuse throughout the app Disable web server directory listing and ensure file metadata and backup files are not displayed within web roots
06 Security misconfiguration	Includes insecure default configurations, incomplete configurations, unpatched operating systems and misconfigured HTTP headers	Automate the process to set up a secure environment Separate environments by using virtualization and containers Automatically test your configurations
07 Cross-site scripting (XXS)	When an application includes untrusted data in a new web page without validation	Use frameworks that automatically escape XSS by design (i.e., Ruby on Rails, React JS) Escape untrusted HTTP request data
08 Insecure deserialization	When structured (serialized) data is converted into an object without verification	Deny serialized objects from untrusted sources Use integrity checks (i.e., digital signatures) to prevent hostile object creation or data leakage Isolate and run deserializing code in low-privilege environments
09 Using components with known vulnerabilities	When components such as library and frameworks run with the same privileges as the application	Automate continuous checking for new component versions Only obtain components from trusted sources and prioritize signed packages Exchange non-maintained packages
10 Insufficient logging and monitoring	Lack of monitoring and timely responses	Log all logins, access control failures and server-side input validation failures Ensure you have an effective incident monitoring, alerting and response plan

Figure 52: Top 10 Web Application Security Risks
Source: OWASP, The Ten Most Critical Web Application Security Risks, 2017[227]

Practice 46: Integrating the key information security practices into design, development and deployment early on

Relevant security practices depend a great deal on the business model – not least how potentially valuable the company's data is to cybercriminals. A FinTech, for example, would likely need to be more diligent about cybersecurity than an eCommerce company. Whatever the sector, though, there are three security practices that are relevant to most tech scale-ups: employee awareness training against social engineering, external penetration testing and threat modeling to identify and protect your most valuable data.

- **Train employees to be resilient against social engineering**
  "Phishing" represents 53% of all cyberattacks, making it one of the most common attack vectors for small and medium enterprises.[228] Phishing refers to an email or text sent to an individual inviting them to disclose sensitive information, such as login details. Consequently, sending fake phishing emails to test the awareness of employees is one of the most relevant measures to take here. Some companies regularly send emails to their employees that resemble phishing attacks and give feedback if an employee does share sensitive information. Regular training – both during onboarding and quarterly at the minimum – can be beneficial. According to Usecure, essential training topics include awareness of email-based phishing techniques, phone-based and physical social engineering (a person calling "from IT" to ask for password information; the office of CFO calling to get a quick signature for a bank transaction that needs to go through today or the data center goes offline etc.), security at home (using approved software and mobile applications, not transferring work data to personal devices, using a VPN, etc.) and secure Internet and email use (avoiding entering sensitive data on untrusted websites, recognition and avoidance of suspicious links, multi-factor authentication, etc.).[229]
- **Hire an external security advisor to perform vulnerability checks and security penetration testing**
  Hiring an external security advisor to perform full cybersecurity screenings and reviews is like going to the dentist: regular check-ups are a cost-effective way to ensure a clean bill of health. Ideally, they are contracted to perform two services. First, they will carry out

quarterly vulnerability checks to find open ports, use of standard passwords, unpatched systems, SQL injection and weak authentication.[230] Second, they will conduct penetration tests to actively seek out passwords in network traffic, penetrate company firewalls or detect operating system and endpoint application vulnerabilities.[231] This can be complemented by an external **bounty program** inviting hackers to submit notifications about any potential security risks in return for a reward.

- **Perform threat modeling to identify and protect your most valuable data**
  It is essential to understand which data should be the most protected from cyberattacks. For a biopharmaceutical startup, this may be test results. For a FinTech, it could be the core banking system, and for an SaaS company, it may be the core feature code repository. It is crucial to protect the most vulnerable systems at all costs, with measures such as: networks protected with additional layers of security in the cloud, databases backed up in real-time and access rights with more restrictions or stronger encryption. A systematic approach is to identify the data flow of attacks for the most potentially damaging threats, prioritize them based on criteria (e.g., impact if the event actually occurs and the likelihood of occurrence) in order to determine exposure and mitigate those risks resulting in the most exposure.[232]

A good starting point from which to build up information security practices is the NIST (National Institute of Standards and Technology) cybersecurity framework (see Figure 53). The ISO 270001 cybersecurity standard is another strong framework. While some scale-ups – in their desire to stay lean – may see these standards as tedious and too resource-demanding, others will see the benefit of regularly deploying an agency to perform a maturity assessment against one of the standards in order to discover blind spots.[233]

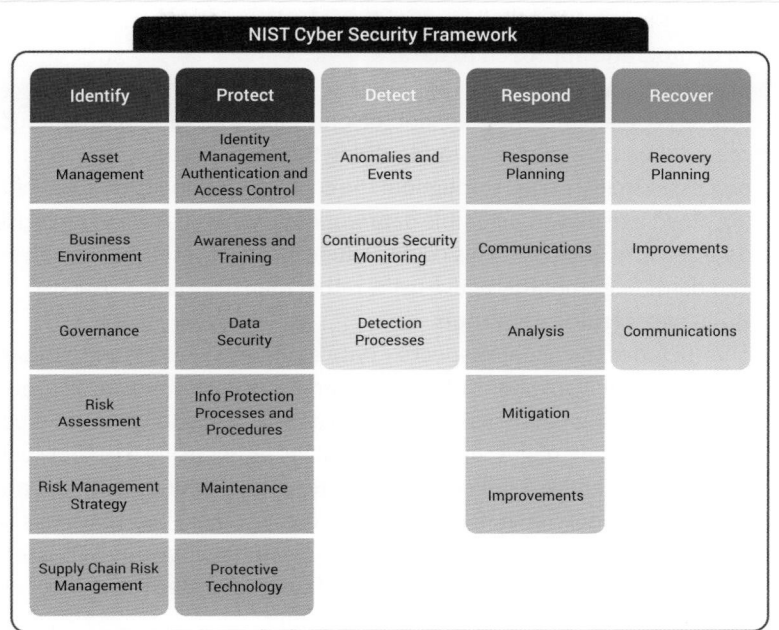

Figure 53: NIST Cyber Security Framework from US National Institute of Standards and Technology, 2018

Data management

Practice 47: Democratizing data with self-service data tools while building a scalable data architecture

Working with data has shifted from highly specialized tools and exper-tise to organization-wide participation across many roles and teams. Even just a few years ago, data engineers were essential to operate query and processing tools and served the analytics needs of the organization. Now, however, a much larger swath of the organization regularly interacts with the data platform. Because of this shift, it is essential to have a data democratization approach in place which bal-ances fully democratized data where every team has their own, slightly different definition of the company metrics in their own data silo and centralized data teams that are bottlenecks for others to self-serve with data pipelines.

With this in mind, the following building blocks are important to facilitate a democratic approach to data:

- **Standardizing data**
  SQL-savvy team members are not the only thing that will make for a successful data organization. Standardizing the tools, metrics, policies and processes that are used throughout the company is imperative for avoiding siloed and non-transferable data work outcomes, as well as high-risk data security breaches. This could include using key metrics as analysis standards (e.g., monthly active users rather than daily active users).

- **Build self-service data tools**
  This includes the usual suspects – data engineers, data scientists and analysts – but also extends to sales, marketing, customer service, etc. The lingua franca that has enabled this democratization is SQL (Structured Query Language), with users typically either using a BI tool such as Mode Analytics, Looker or even interacting directly with a data warehouse (Snowflake, BigQuery or Redshift). There are scale-ups in which up to two-thirds of the company are active monthly SQL users of the data warehouse. Regular SQL training facilitates this.

- **Creating the minimum viable data product**
  Before a central data team acts on a team's needs, it is important to avoid "overproduction." For example, streaming data in real-time may be stated as a requirement, but it may be extremely expensive and does not deliver any notably greater benefits for the business other than updating data warehouses at frequent intervals (e.g., every 30 minutes). A similar argument could be made for the capability of a company's machine learning platform. The relative benefits of having online predictive capabilities versus getting by with statically computed and offline batch predictions is something that should be framed in the context of the broader needs of the business.

- **Create scalable data infrastructures**
  The more the company grows, the more important business decisions based on accurate and (often) real-time data become. A few examples of how investment in data infrastructure can pay off include Amazon selling more than 100 million Alexa units, Netflix creating 80% of content views with machine-learning-based recommendations and Airbnb increasing its booking conversion rate by ~4% through modeling host acceptance probability. The venture capital firm Andreessen Horowitz has published an excellent overview of a modern data architecture (see Figure 54).[234]

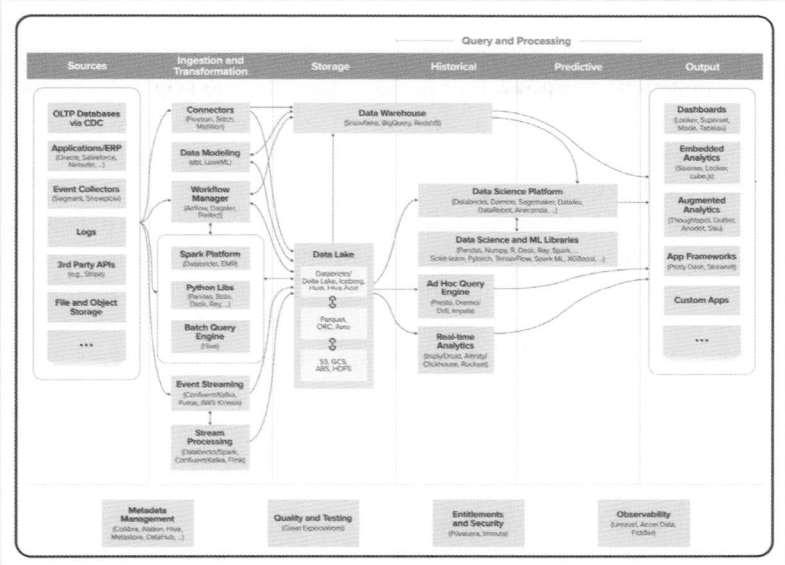

Figure 54: Modern Data Architecture
Source: Emerging Architecture for Modern Data Infrastructure, Andreessen Horowitz

According to this model, a unified data architecture ideally encompasses the following:[235]

- **Sources**

  Data generated via a range of different sources in internal ERP **systems** such as Salesforce or Oracle and delivered to external third-party APIs for myriad uses.

- **Ingestion & Transformation**

  This is the transfer of data from production **systems** (the sources of data) to a data warehouse. There are three stages: the extraction of data, the delivery of data to storage and the transformation of data for analysis. Essential components include connectors, such as Fivetran and Stitch, and workflow managers, such as Zapier and Airtable.

- **Storage**

  The storage of data in an appropriate format for querying, processing and cost optimization. There are three main types of data storage: data warehouses as the backbone of a data analytics system, where data is stored in a structured format in warehouses for rapid extraction of insights using SQL (Structured Query Language);[236] data lakes with data stored in a raw format for flexible, scalable inclusion of data intelligence within applications;[237] and the "lakehouse" concept, where data analysis is performed directly on data stored in data lakes.[238] The benefit of putting data directly into a data lake is that it can be stored in a raw format, so there is no need to decide what schema to use (unlike when storing data in a warehouse).

- **Query & Processing**
  There are two types of work performed on data stored in a data warehouse or data lake: a query, which provides the interface for deriving insights from the data, and the processing, which is the execution of queries and data models against stored data. Machine learning algorithms for identifying patterns in data sets play a role here.

- **Output**
  The insights derived from data analysis can be visualized using dashboards and data visualization tools, such as Tableau, and data models are embedded into applications and processes, such as product recommendations[239] and sentiment analysis.[240]

Recommended publications:
- Todd Barnu (2021). *The Cybersecurity Manager's Guide,* https://web.archive.org/web/20210521090839/https://www.amazon.com/Managers-Guide-Information-Security-Domain/dp/149207621X.
- Nicole Forsgren, Jez Humble, Gene Kim (2018*). Accelerate: The Science of Lean Software and DevOps: Building and Scaling High Performing Technology Organizations*.
- Johana Rothman (2017). *Create Your Successful Agile Project*.
- Matthew Skelton (2019). Manuel Pais and Ruth Malan, *Team Topologies: Organizing Business and Technology Teams for Fast Flow*.
- Nadean H. Tanner (2019). *Cybersecurity Blue Team Toolkit*.
- *Engineering Culture at Spotify* (Part 1 and Part 2), https://web.archive.org/web/20210521091325/https://www.youtube.com/watch?v=Yvfz4HGtoPc.

How to avoid the seven key pitfalls in building up a strong technology function? Watch our video by scanning the QR code or following this link: https://youtube/r2NMv7XOnV8.

How to set a direction for a technology function? Watch our video on the essential OKRs and trade-offs by scanning the QR code or following this link: https://youtube/4ryhSul4C1k.

Definitions

- **APIs (Application Programming Interface)**: a standardized computing interface that enables different applications to communicate with one another, thereby allowing the applications to share information.
- **(Product) Backlog**: a list of the new features, user stories, changes to existing features, bug fixes or infrastructure changes that a team may deliver as part of a future sprint.
- **Blue team / red team**: a cybersecurity technique for assessing an organization's security capabilities through the staging of simulated cyberattacks in which two teams face off against one another – red team using real-world cyberattack tools, behaviors and practices and blue team repelling the attack.
- **Bounce rate**: the percentage of website visits that only involved one single page view – a high bounce rate can be an indicator of poor website performance.
- **Change failure rate**: a measure of the rate of unsuccessful code deployments, measured by the ratio of deployments that resulted in a failure in production (e.g., an unusable feature in an app).

- **Cloud service providers**: this includes Amazon Web Services (AWS), a subsidiary of Amazon, which provides web-based IT infrastructure ("Cloud computing"). Alternatives are providers such as Microsoft Azure, Google Cloud Platform and Alibaba Cloud.
- **Code test coverage**: a measure of the percentage of a software's code that is validated during testing.
- **Code rewrite**: the act or result of rewriting the code for a large portion of a system with existing functionality while not reusing its source (original) code.
- **Code refactoring**: the process of systematically improving existing code without adding to its functionality. It serves to better the code's design and readability, as well as reduce the build-up of technical debt.
- **Configuration management**: a systems engineering process for maintaining consistent performance of computer systems, servers and software that leverages automated tools to manage and monitor updates.
- **Cybersecurity**: the people, processes and technology involved in the protection of systems, networks, programs, devices and electronic data from cyberattacks.
- **Deployments**: the internal process by which newly written code is uploaded to the server that hosts an application or website. It either can or cannot be noticeable to the end-user, unlike with a *software release,* which is usually noticeable to the user.
- **Development environment**: a software suite that provides developers with a workspace in which to make changes to code without the risk of causing errors in the software used by the customers.
- **Development Operations ("DevOps")**: Development Operations refers to a set of practices that brings software development (Dev) and IT operations (Ops) closer together with the ultimate goal of speeding up the development of quality software.
- **Digital forensics**: commonly used to investigate cybercrime and to troubleshoot IT operations issues.
- **Kanban**: a project management system that visualizes a project as a series of lists of tasks and tracks the progress of those tasks through to their completion, thereby focusing team members'

attention on the actual status of a project or task instead of target completion dates.

- **Latency**: a measure of the time it takes for data to be transferred between two computers on a network.
- **Monolith**: a type of software architecture where all the components in an application – the database, the client-side application and the server-side application – are built within a single code base.
- **Pentesting** ("penetration testing"): a process for testing computer systems' vulnerability to a cyberattack.
- **Production environment**: the setting in which software and products are made available for customers.
- **Quality assurance**: the process of verifying the readiness of a software product for its intended use (e.g., missing indentations, inconsistent spelling and security vulnerabilities in the code) – often done with automated code checks as well as manual testing.
- **Release**: the new version(s) of a software that contains fixes, updates and/or enhanced features; an end-user is usually aware of a release.
- **REST APIs (Representational State Transfer APIs)**: a type of API that leverages a defined set of guidelines for structuring how software communicates over the internet, which makes the integration of data from disparate applications simple and scalable.
- **Rollback, hotfix & patch**: remediation measure after unsuccessful code deployments; **rollback**: the process of restoring all transactional systems (e.g., a database) to a previous state; **hotfix**: a rapidly developed and released update of a software product; and **patch**: a temporary fix for a software product that is implemented between scheduled full releases of the product.
- **Scrum**: an agile project management framework that advocates for time-bounded periods of work – "sprints" – that often last for two weeks, carried out by small teams (typically up to 10 members) in order to speed up the delivery of software relevant for customers.
- **Social engineering**: a technique employed by cyberattackers to exploit human error to initiate and carry out cyberattacks (e.g., "phishing" – usually an email or text sent to an individual inviting them to disclose sensitive information such as login details).

- **Software engineers/developers**: IT professionals responsible for planning, designing, building, testing, deploying and maintaining software.
- **Source code**: the instructions and statements written by a programmer in a human-readable programming language.
- **Staging environment**: a replica of the product environment, which allows developers to test their products in realistic conditions before the new software goes live.
- **Story points**: a metric used in agile project management to estimate the amount of effort that will be required to build a specific feature/ piece of functionality. This metric is subjective and defined internally by a team and therefore is not comparable across teams.
- **System response time**: the amount of time that elapses between a system request being made and the request being responded to.
- **Test-driven development**: an approach to software development in which tests are defined and executed before the process of beginning to code a new feature in order to give developers a precise understanding of the new feature's requirements.
- **Uptime**: percentage of time a product or device is in an operational state (i.e., when it can be made use of by end-users).
- **Yaml files**: a data serialization language known for the ease with which it can be read by humans as a plain text file.

7   B2C Marketing Excellence

Scaling up with minimal expense and maximum customer retention

With Kelly Ford

marketing can be easily ramped up, yet quickly overemphasized. It is critical to balance this with sufficient investment in the brand while keeping the customer acquisition payback period between 6 and 24 months (see Practice 57).

- **Getting your monetization model right too late**.
  Startup leaders can be so passionate about the value of their product that they forget to price it adequately or else settle on a working monetization model too late. To avoid this error, it is critical to have "willingness to pay" conversations early on to segment deeply and develop price points accordingly (see Practice 59).

New and active customers are the initial thrust to kickstart the scale-up journey. The trick to this is to spend as efficiently as possible on measures to attract these customers – which is where the marketing & growth teams come into play. When selling directly to consumers (rather than other businesses), the key question to answer is what is the marketing team solving for? Oftentimes, it is to acquire a revenue (and customer base) with a competitive payback time for the customer acquisition costs (CAC). CAC payback time refers to the number of months it takes per customer to earn back customer acquisition costs on average. To achieve this, the marketing team usually focuses on four objectives: create fast **revenue or customer growth**, **deliver high customer retention**, make the **brand distinctive** and do all this by creating **competitive customer acquisition costs**. This is what we call our formula for marketing-supported growth (Figure 55).

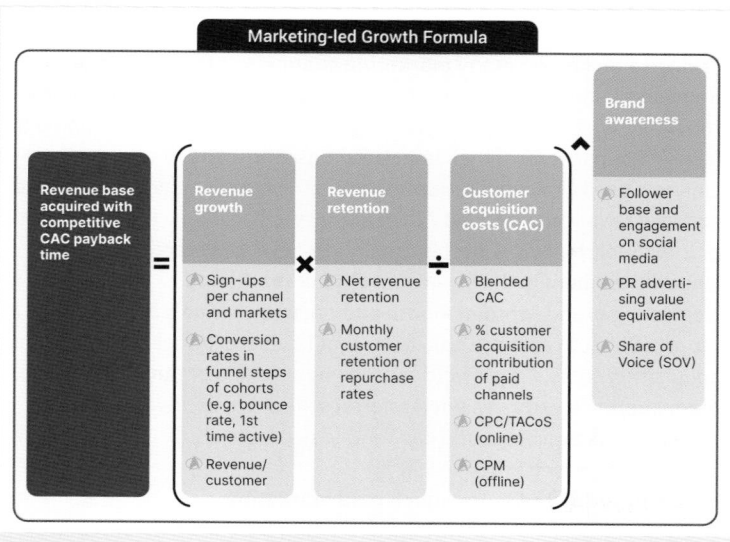

Figure 55: Marketing-led Growth Formula

The following practice will offer some inspiration for turning this formula into the right objectives and key results (OKRs) for any business context and ambitions.

OKRs

Practice 48: Establishing the right marketing OKRs

The Marketing-led Growth Formula can help construct the right objectives and key results for the marketing function. Figures 56 and 57 show example OKRs for marketing divisions in two different industries: FinTech and eCommerce.

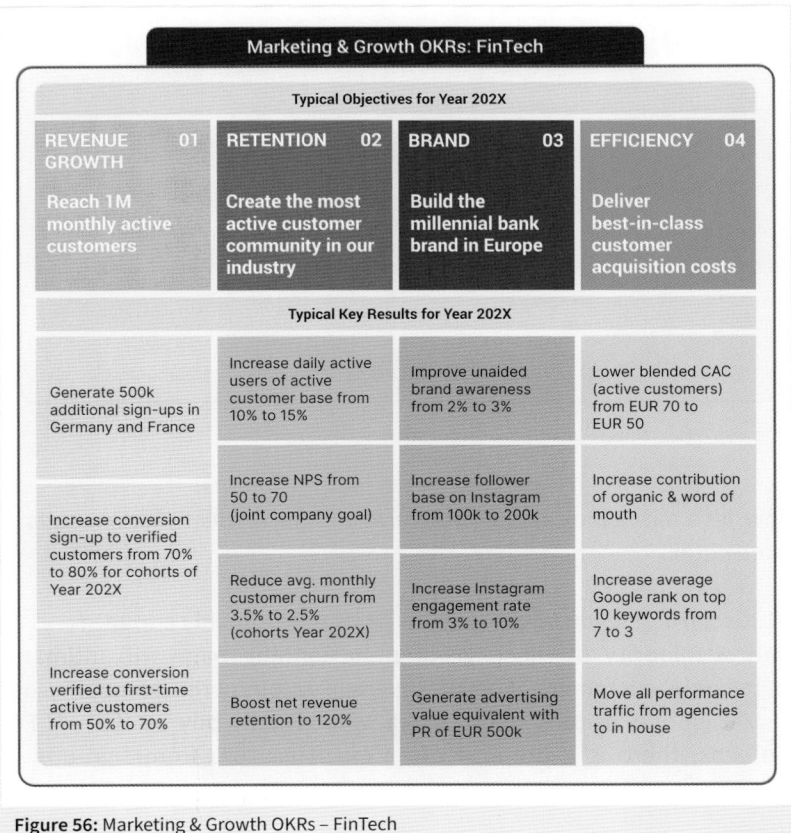

Figure 56: Marketing & Growth OKRs – FinTech

Marketing & Growth OKRs: eCommerce			
Typical Objectives for Year 202X			
REVENUE GROWTH 01	**RETENTION** 02	**BRAND** 03	**EFFICIENCY** 04
Reach 10m revenue run rate per month	Create the most loyal customer base in our industry	Build the sustainable consumer products brand in Europe	Deliver best-in-class customer acquisition costs
Typical Key Results for Year 202X			
Increase number of unique monthly website visitors from 3m to 5m	Boost net revenue retention to 120%	Increase unaided brand awareness from 2% to 3%	Reduce blended CAC from EUR 8 to EUR 5
Reduce conversion landing page ("bounce rate") from 30% to 20%		Increase follower base on Instagram from 100k to 200k	Reduce total advertising cost of sale (TACoS) on Amazon from 20% to 15%
Reduce cart abandonment rate from 20% to 15%	Increase repurchase rate from 30% to 40%	Increase Instagram share of voice from 20% to 30%	Increase return on advertising spend (ROAS) on Google Ads from 200% to 300%
Increase revenue share from owned shops ("D2C") from 30% to 50%		Deliver advertising value equivalent with PR of EUR 500k	Improve average Instagram rank on top 10 keywords from 7 to 3
Introduce 100 new stock keeping units	Increase NPS from 50 to 70	Reduce the share of plastic in production and shipping to 0	Move all performance traffic from agencies to in house

Figure 57: Marketing & Growth OKRs: eCommerce

Now, let's take a look at each objective and the respective key results in more detail.

O1. Growth: Are you acquiring new customers quickly enough?

Only a minority of those visiting the landing page will ultimately become customers. For the average eCommerce company, out of 100 unique visitors, only 1.5–5% will actually buy an item.[242] For FinTechs, there is a drop-off of as much as 90% from sign-ups to becoming monthly active customers. On their way to becoming active customers – and ideally paying – people will pass through a series of steps known as an "acquisition funnel." While the specific steps in that funnel differ from company to company, startups in the same industry often follow a similar trajectory (see Figures 58 & 59 for examples). In each step, a percentage of potential customers can drop off. The overall customer acquisition is typically measured based on revenue growth or the number of active customers for specific geographies and/or "cohorts." Cohorts refer to groups of customers that signed up, were acquired during a certain period (calendar week or month for instance) or share certain experiences (new products, events). Comparing cohorts is similar to comparing the graduating classes from a university over time and along dimensions such as income, mobility, job type, etc.

Key results for this objective typically include overall revenue targets and conversion rates (e.g., landing page bounce rates, user activation rates, first-time transactions), as measured for different cohorts.

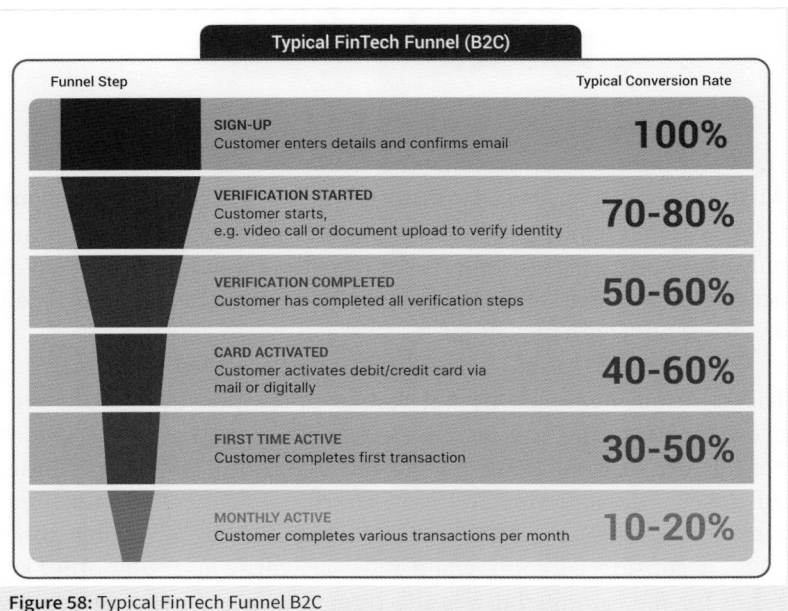

Figure 58: Typical FinTech Funnel B2C
Source: Smart Insights, E-commerce conversion rates – how do yours compare?[243]

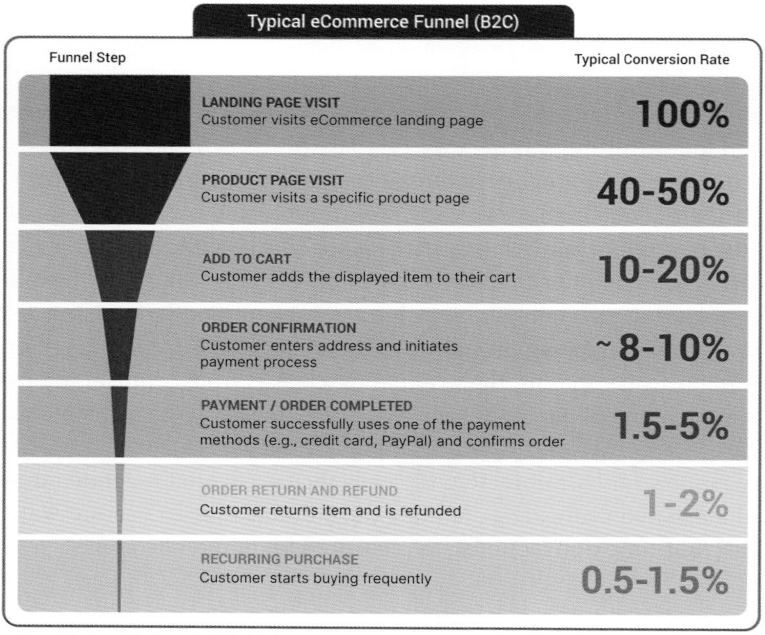

Figure 59: Typical eCommerce Funnel (B2C)
Source: Smart Insights, Shopify, Unbounce [244]

O2. Retention: Are you avoiding the "leaky bucket" scenario?
What's the one thing growth investors hate? They hate investing in long-term customer relations only to quickly lose them again. Growth is not only about acquiring customers, but it is also about retaining them. To achieve both, a marketing team needs to drive customer engagement and focus on "churn prevention."

This is often measured by net revenue retention (NRR) as a **typical key result**. Say one increases revenue among *existing* customers by 20% in comparison to the last 12 months while accounting for upsells, downgrades and hard churn (i.e., cancellation or long-term non-usage), the NRR would then be 120%. Anything above 100% is considered good, while 120+% is very good.[245] Another key result for measuring churn is the retention rate, or the percentage of active customers retained within a specific period (usually a week or month). The average repurchase rate for eCommerce firms is

20–0% of first-time buyers (order completed), with anything above 50% considered to be very good.[246]

O3. Brand: Are you creating an iconic brand?

Do your friends think you're crazy as you stay the night at a stranger's home in a foreign city? This was the key challenge Airbnb faced in its early growth phase in 2015. Their response? A massive brand investment with the campaign "Never a Stranger" to become the world's first community-driven superbrand based on bonds of trust. Focusing on creating an iconic brand is particularly helpful when a scale-up is growing beyond early adopters and attracting the "early majority" – when they shift from only attracting the young folks from Berlin or London to also include families from the countryside. Companies that have a strong brand tend to generate above-average shareholder returns, drive growth by emotionally influencing customer choice, even in commoditized markets, and attract the best talent.[247]

Typical key results to track here are: aided and unaided brand awareness surveys, share of voice (SOV) – the percentage of impressions of a brand within a time period compared to a category, follower base and engagement rates on key social media channels and NPS, representing how many customers will recommend the product or service to others.

O4. Efficiency: Are you acquiring new customers efficiently?

When the FinTech N26 pivoted its product from a credit card for young adults to a banking app for adults in 2015, the company almost tripled its customer base year-over-year for several years. The best part: the majority of new customers during that time came through friend referrals from existing consumers. N26 didn't have to pay anything for those new customers! Not every tech startup will be able to hit the jackpot with such a cheap acquisition channel. Normally, paid advertising (i.e., ads on Google, Facebook, Instagram and offline channels) goes hand in hand with unpaid ones during a growth journey. The trick is to spend the right amount. In 2017, Uber famously cut 80% of its ads without experiencing a meaningful drop in growth. eBay had a similar experience with cutting ad spending.[248] It is necessary to strike a healthy balance between paying for new customers, word-of-mouth acquisition and organic channels, such as PR and social media, in order to keep the "blended" customer acquisition costs (CAC) across these channels as low as possible. Keeping the "CAC payback period" between 6 and 24 months is often helpful here (see Practice 57).

Key results to watch here include blended CAC, which is calculated by dividing the total amount of money spent on acquisition-focused marketing by the total number of acquired customers across all channels. For example, if the daily marketing expenditure is USD 5,000 and 100 verified customers are acquired per day (with both paid and "organic" channels), the blended CAC will be USD 50 per customer. Note that a blended CAC can't just be magically scaled. To achieve a USD 50 blended CAC, there might be zero costs for 50% organic and USD 100 in costs for 50% paid channels. However, throwing another USD 100 into paid marketing will only get one, not two, new customers. It is surprising how many executives and even investors fail with this logic.

Other key results to watch include cost per conversion, cost per click, average search engine ranks for top keywords and return on advertising spend (ROAS). ROAS compares the gross profit generated by an ad campaign with the advertising budget that was spent on it (although dangerously often revenue is used instead of profit!). If an eCommerce scale-up is working with a desired ROAS of 200%, every dollar spent on advertising generates USD 2 gross profit.[249] When selling on Amazon Marketplace, the total advertising cost of sale (TACoS) is the metric that needs to be watched. It can measure the advertising spent on Amazon relative to the total revenue generated (including organic sales). Additionally, it is important to track how many customers are acquired via paid vs. organic channels (organic vs. paid "contribution").

Organizational chart and roles

Practice 49: Defining the roles & responsibilities for a marketing function

When scaling up, the marketing team fulfils the key function of plotting a growth pathway. The marketing leadership team should consist of:
- a numbers-driven **performance marketeer** for whom buying ads and optimizing search ranks is second nature;

- a creative director who greases the wheels of the **content factory** and has a penchant for visuals and cross-format campaigns;
- a **specialist for organic (i.e., unpaid) channels** who can read the figures and see whether investing in social media, partnerships, articles, site content or email marketing is the better bet;
- a **marketing intelligence leader** whose superpower is to delve into databases to find information that supports decision-making;
- a **brand expert** who is responsible for creating a consistent tone of voice and coordinates offline campaigns;
- a **PR expert** who proactively builds a network of trusted journalists and can manage PR crises; and
- a leader for the **growth hacking teams** that use data, analytics and quantitative goals to align and drive growth initiatives (often involving multiple divisions).

This group is backed up by the product marketing teams, which will co-ordinate marketing projects. Note that if the CMO is a numbers-driven person, one of their leaders should specialize in brand development (and vice versa). Figure 60 is the organizational structure of a typical B2C marketing division.

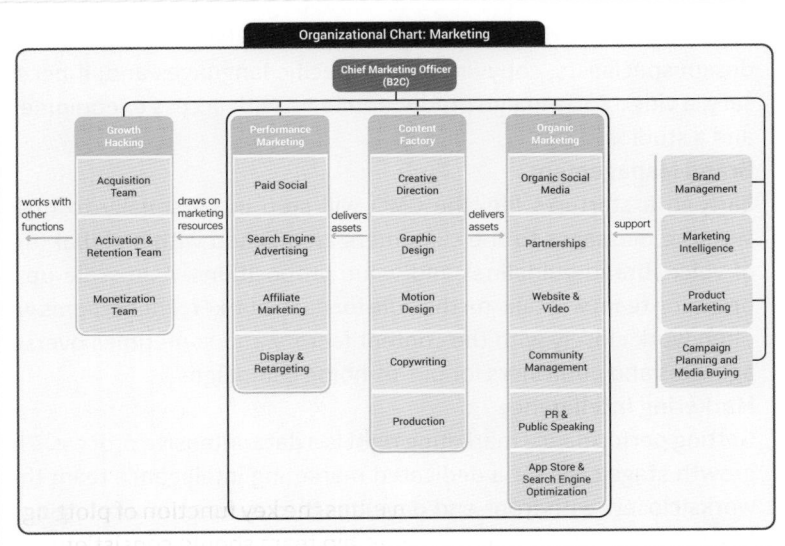

Figure 60: Organizational Chart: Marketing

Organizational blueprint of a typical B2C marketing division

Let's dig a little deeper into what each of these functions does.

- **Performance Marketing**
  This team acquires new customers by buying ads on relevant online and offline channels – whether directly or through an agency – while keeping marketing expenses efficient. The team should specialize in the channels most relevant to the company (e.g., paid search, paid social, affiliate, display).

- **Organic Marketing**
  Here, organic acquisition means sign-ups without any directly attributable source of paid marketing. This includes: recommendations from a friend, social media posts on the company's LinkedIn channel, articles in the press or Google searches with a click on an organic and non-paid listing. As PR is a key role for the overall company, this role sometimes reports directly to the CMO (if product PR is key) or CEO (if corporate communications are key). The SEO/ASO teams are usually part of this group, too.

- **Content Factory**
  This team often features designers and content experts. They create marketing assets, including charts, graphs, images, videos and ads for the performance and organic marketing teams. They are usually led by a creative director along with graphic designers and motion design specialists, copywriters for specific languages and, if necessary, a video & campaign production team with access to equipment and a studio.

- **Brand Management**
  Early in a startup's life, the CMO will step in personally to make sure the messages to the customers are aligned with a global tone of voice, brand guidelines and value propositions. As a scale-up, a branding team will take on this role for each market. These teams will often work closely with the content factory and sometimes oversee agencies and publishers for out-of-home campaigns.

- **Marketing Intelligence**
  Getting performance marketing right is a data-intensive process. The growth stage calls for a dedicated marketing intelligence team that works closely with front-end developers to oversee marketing analytics, track customer activities, apply the results to campaigns and

ensure all ads are technically adequate. The marketing intelligence team also pursues complex data queries on brand health, growth and conversion, and they are often seen as the "right hand" and primary advisor to the CMO. Sometimes this support can come from a dedicated team in a centralized data science function to ensure data consistency across teams. Over time, though, it is preferable for this person to be directly reporting into the marketing team.

- **Product Marketing**
  Some growth companies have a product marketing team to manage product launches, ongoing customer engagement and retention initiatives. This team often serves as the interface to the respective product teams and coordinates cross-functional task forces to drive conversion through the customer acquisition funnel or usage frequency retention through customer engagement activities.

- **Growth Hacking Teams**
  Most scale-ups need a cross-functional team whose sole focus is on driving growth. It usually involves an analytical cross-functional team testing new ideas to drive growth through the customer acquisition funnel in an iterate-learn-scale model (see Practice 8).

Practice 50: Scaling the right marketing roles at the right time

Startup marketing teams are populated by generalists. However, a scale-up calls for specialization, and there's a sequence that can be followed to make it easier for everyone to achieve a smooth transition. First, the performance marketing team has to specialize in channels that drive growth, for example, by hiring a dedicated Amazon ad or Google SEA expert. Second, it is necessary to hire a PR expert with trusted media contacts in key markets and have them align all internal and external corporate communication (see Practice 7). Third, organic teams need to be encouraged to branch out to different channels (e.g., organic social media and partnerships). Fourth, a content factory has to be put in place with dedicated designers, copywriters and, later on, a creative director. Fifth, data analytics experts need to be brought on board who are 100% dedicated to the marketing efforts. Sixth, while a startup can get away with the CMO driving brand consistency, in a scale-up, there needs to be dedicated brand experts, including people to oversee a consistent global tone of voice and campaign planning. And seventh, expanding beyond the core market (e.g., from the US to Germany and Spain) calls for additional language skills in the team and additional market intelligence that exposes distinct needs of each market. Another thing to note is that many companies will add product marketing experts in the later growth stages.

Now that the organizational structure is in place, let's turn to the marketing and growth practices to facilitate the smooth transition from startup to scale-up. There are five types of practices: get the marketing basics in place, deliver on organic and viral marketing, deliver on paid online marketing, deliver on offline marketing and nail monetization.

Marketing basics

Practice 51: Establishing a single source of truth for key marketing and growth KPIs

Often a scale-up's marketing KPIs can be the least understood figures in the company. On the contrary, *every* leader in a company should have a strong grasp of the 2–3 key growth metrics. Questions to ask here include: Does the eCommerce revenue reflect the gross merchandising value (incl. third-party sales), and does it exclude returns? Is it including or excluding VAT? Do the weekly customer acquisition costs refer to cost per sign-up or cost per customer verified? Do monthly active users include customers who have paid for a service but are otherwise inactive? It's all about the details here. In addition, ONE source of truth is key (e.g., a common SQL query). Nothing is a bigger waste of time than having multiple departments referring to what they think is the same metric while ending up with different results.

Practice 52: Bridging the gap between marketing quants and creative brains

There can be a natural tension between brand artists focused on slick, on-brand visuals and performance marketeers making decisions based on quant metrics. The challenge and opportunity is for them to work together to find a happy medium – beautiful and distinctly branded content that still drives performance metrics. Sometimes, a well-designed brand campaign may simply not perform as well as an unpolished, ten-second smartphone video that makes the customer smile – and the designers involved need to understand that. A sprint team needs to be set up with performance, brand, content and marketing intelligence colleagues with an ambitious project goal (e.g., 10,000 new premium customers within two months following the launch of a new product). This can push a company's creatives to appreciate quantitative performance in addition to strong branding.

Practice 53: Equipping your teams with the right marketing and growth tools

Google Sheets should be ditched in favor of specialist productivity tools for the scaling marketing teams. Here are a few examples: paid social (Nanigans, Facebook Power Editor), programmatic management and SEA (TradeDesk, Choice Streams, Rocket Fuel, Simpli.fi), affiliate marketing (CJ Affiliate, VigLink), display retargeting (AdRoll, ReTargeter, MixRank), organic social media (Sprout Social, Wyng, Woobox), SEO (Moz, SEMRush, Screaming Frog), CRM (HubSpot, Mailchimp, Marketo), website analytics (Kissmetrics, Google Analytics, Woopra), brand management (Brandwatch), community management (Sociality, Swat, Hootsuite), content creation and curation (Canva, Feedly, Scoop.it) and video hosting (Wistia, Vimeo).

Practice 54: Finding your product-channel fit quickly and maintaining it

The mantra "less is more" applies well to channels where focus and depth can provide efficiency while keeping things relatively simple. In fact, many major tech companies have built up their initial user base by up to 80% through just one channel. LinkedIn used viral emails, HubSpot relied on content marketing, TripAdvisor used search engines and Zynga harnessed Facebook. It is best to identify 1–2 channels that drive the North Star metric (e.g., monthly active users, gross merchandising volume) and double down on them. Brian Balfour suggests a pragmatic way for selecting channels by starting with a long list of 7–10 growth channels focused on organic, word-of-mouth, paid online and offline (see Figure 61).[250] Eventually, each channel on the longlist should be rated according to these factors (questions adopted from Brian Balfour):

- **Targeting**: How close to your target audience can you get through this channel? Facebook ads can be very targeted, while PR is often not.
- **Costs**: What is the likely cost per conversion? Are there any upfront costs? Cost-per-conversion data can be sourced from benchmark providers, such as Wordstream or Unbounce.[251]
- **Input time**: How much time do you need to get the first experiment up and running? Google ads usually have a low input time, while content marketing can take weeks or months.
- **Output time**: How long will it take to see the results of your experiments? Facebook ads will take days, whereas SEO is a matter of months.
- **Control**: Can you switch the channel on and off fast? Facebook ads can be turned on and off quickly, while a TV campaign needs to be booked weeks in advance.
- **Scale**: Is the channel scalable in terms of time and resources? This can be assessed using dedicated tools for that channel (see Practice 3) and by speaking to other relevant startups or by simply searching publicly available numbers including likes and views.

Marketing Channel Overview

ORGANIC	VIRAL & WORD OF MOUTH	PAID ONLINE	OFFLINE
SEO Drive up organic rankings for specific keywords on search engines which drive quality and quantity traffic to your website	**FRIEND REFERRAL PROGRAMS** Incentivize customers to recommend your product to others	**AFFILIATE ADVERTISING** Give out a commission for partners who successfully create leads for your product online	**TV** Run ads on television
PR Gain favorable press coverage in your target media	**ONLINE VIDEO** Production and presentation of video material	**INFLUENCER CAMPAIGNS** Partner with influencers (Instagram, TikTok etc.) who run campaigns for your products and services	**PRINT** Place ads in print media, e.g. newspapers, magazines
(GUEST) BLOGGING Publish blog content on issues relevant to your customers on your owned online sites or on relevant platforms (e.g. Medium)	**CROWDFUNDING** Rally a community around a crowdfunding campaign		**BILLBOARDS** Place ads on outdoor billboards
APP STORE OPTIMIZATION Optimize app visibility within the app stores and increase app conversion rates	**COMMUNITY BUILDING / ENGAGEMENT** Foster a community between customers and enable them to interact (e.g. discussion forums)	**NATIVE CONTENT ADS** Run ads that fit the publication or site's usual editorial style and tone	**RADIO** Run ads via radio
FREE TOOLS Provide free online tools (e.g. Google Alerts, Talkwalker Alerts)	**CONTESTS, GIVEAWAYS, GAMES, QUIZZES** Give away prizes, hold contests, quizzes in your community	**RE-TARGETING** Re-target customers with ads that left your sales funnel without completing it	**EVENTS** Host or speak at (industry-specific) events
DIRECT MESSAGING VIA EMAIL OR IN-APP PUSH ("CUSTOMER RELATIONSHIP MANAGEMENT") Contact existing or potential customers via email or in-app push	**VIRALITY HACKS ON SOCIAL MEDIA PLATFORMS (E.G. INSTAGRAM, FACEBOOK, YOUTUBE, TIKTOK)** Launch (interactive) campaigns on growth-driving social media platforms	**BLOGS AND PODCASTS SPONSORSHIPS** Become sponsor of e.g. a podcast or a podcast episode	**STORES** Open and maintain stores that represent your brand
WEBINARS Hold webinars on relevant topics for your customers			**FIELD SALES** Contact customers outdoors (door to door)
STRATEGIC PARTNERSHIPS Co-brand with a partner to raise the profile of your campaign or acquire additional customers.	**EMBEDDABLE WIDGETS** Embed content, especially viral content (e.g. Twitter feed) about your product, into your website	**PROGAMMATIC ADVERTISTING** Bid for ads on Google, Facebook, Bing, YouTube, Instagram, TikTok etc.	**POS DISPLAY** Set up POS displays that communicate your brand
EBOOKS Publish (free) ebooks			

Figure 61: Marketing Channel Overview

Organic and viral marketing

Practice 55: Leveraging the power of organic conversions to drive down customer acquisition costs

Paid marketing can become an addiction, particularly with the injection of growth capital. It is easy to get started and may even feel like it is worthwhile at the beginning. However, ultimately, it leads to more and more money being spent and often fails to produce lasting results. In other words, it is best to avoid feeding this beast too much. There is a better way through making early investments and continuously investing in organic and word-of-mouth marketing. Organic marketing is about growing the customer base naturally using internal measures rather than paying for expensive campaigns. There are at least four levers to pull here.

- **First lever: A great product**
  The most obvious starting point is to build a killer product that people love and talk about. There is no way around this one.
- **Second lever: Customer Relationship Management**
  Collecting the contact data of potential and existing customers (e.g., through a signup for a newsletter) is the basis for this. CRM can be used as a tool to distribute differentiating messages via newsletter or as an in-app push. For example, Medium gives users an overview of the day or week's latest flood of articles while delivering the digest in a minimalistic, clear design and layout. Although viewed partly as outdated, email marketing still matters for both B2B and B2C: 59% of marketing professionals state that email is the channel with the biggest ROI.[252]
- **Third lever: Word-of-mouth loops**
  A referral bonus can be the key to a functioning referral scheme. Existing customers should be given a simple option to share a link to the app or product that is connected to a promise for a discount on a future purchase. Uber grew its customer base using a customizable referral message, which made it more approachable for new users. It also gave a free ride as a reward not only to the new customers but also to existing customers that make the referral.[253]

Branded "edgy" campaigns that get people talking are another effective technique. The aim is for people to spontaneously tell a friend: "Did you see that cool campaign?" Integrating network effects and community-sharing into the product's functionality works, too. A FinTech example of this is instant money transfers between users of the same product. In the eCommerce world, it could be providing quick ways to share favorite items with friends in exchange for feedback.

- **Fourth lever: Great content**
  If the style of your content marketing is right, it can attract customers through (almost) free organic channels. One way to deliver great content marketing is to work the content marketing pyramid[254] from top to bottom. A major statement, such as an e-book or a whitepaper, can be the starting point. Tien Tzuo, the founder of Zuora, published *Subscribed* as a starting block for his company's content. This flagship content piece can then serve as the basis for more (and more frequent) blog posts, podcasts, and presentations. The bottom of the pyramid is populated by promotional daily or weekly micro-content, such as tweets fed by the major content pieces. An alternative way is to have the content factory produce a steady flow of smaller pieces of content (articles, reviews, quizzes, case studies, etc.). The content factory should lay out a content calendar, which is the roadmap for target publication dates (per channel), and be in close sync with the PR team. For every piece of content, the language/market fit should be kept in mind. Headlines and descriptions should be written in the language and tone that is best understood by the customers. Upworthy, a media site for "positive storytelling," does this by generating up to 25 headlines for each story, which are then tested among specific groups/regions on social media before deciding which headline is right for the website.[255]

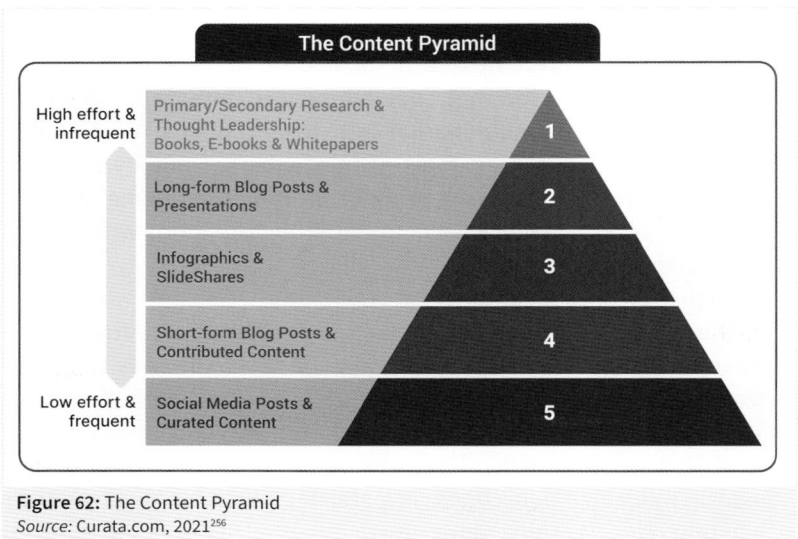

Figure 62: The Content Pyramid
Source: Curata.com, 2021[256]

Organic marketing takes time to produce meaningful results – that's why it is so essential to start early.

Practice 56: Getting your PR machine up with trust

Eva Büchner, at the time the managing director of the startup refund .me, claimed in an open letter to Ryanair CEO Michael O'Leary that the airline's aircraft were delayed due to irresponsible practices involving employees. Ryanair responded with an open letter of its own, thus giving refund.me free publicity for weeks on end. This is what is known as a PR stunt – a smart trick employed by one party to encourage another party to play their game. Generally speaking, a PR stunt is not used to outwit or exploit the other player; the aim is to create a strong basis of trust that will enable the company to weather a crisis later on. A good PR team should focus on creating long-term relationships with prominent journalists and other influential figures. In doing so, the team helps to unearth and tell the most exciting and most interesting stories about the company's founders and the company itself, and to increase the social significance of the firm while immunizing it against attacks. Ideally, the PR team should comprise journalists or communication professionals with good networks who work together directly with the CXOs and senior management. The team is there to identify narratives, figures, dates and facts that are either already firmly in the public eye or that will be of interest to the public, and to then steer these figures, dates and facts toward the correct channels. The aim: to ensure a high level of attention and acceptance of the interpretations proffered in the target groups. Furthermore, a good PR team should be doing its research, at the latest, as its responsibilities grow beyond the development phase and maintaining mailing lists:

- **Coordinating messages**
  To guarantee consistent external communication, the team has to make sure it is involved in all key internal processes and decisions at an early stage; otherwise, it runs the risk of propagating incorrect information among the public or being surprised by an inquiry – both come at the cost of trust. Depending on the current situation, key messages and words should be coordinated in writing and orally with the founders and/or management board on an ongoing basis. In addition, this should be used as the basis for setting up a consistent press area on the website that provides texts, images, videos, founder information (including quotes), names and photos of experts who speak on behalf of the company.

- **Initiating PR within a company**
  Employees are not fond of finding out important information about their company in the media. If, on the other hand, they are the first to be informed – and are informed well – they will become the firm's ambassadors. This information can be provided via email, newsletter, messenger service, intranet or knowledge database, though it may be better to first inform the managers, who then speak to their individual teams. Other options include a townhall or an all-hands meeting. The point is that employees are kept up to date sooner and in more detail than the rest of the world.

- **Building trust**
  This applies first and foremost to the employees; like the rest of the world, they will not trust the PR team until they experience the internal communication service for a while. The team should have between five and seven usable contacts from the world of journalism for each market as well as a varied list of trade journalists and their areas of expertise. Personal relationships are essential, which is why it is important to court certain journalists from time to time with exclusive stories or information – and to keep them informed about the company's background and the branch as a whole.

- **Preparing well for a crisis**
  The team should have a crisis PR agency on standby 24/7, regularly work through crisis scenarios along with the relevant solutions, update the company's reporting chains on an ongoing basis, pursue communication for the purpose of crisis prevention, and – if it comes to it – take to the 'war room' in order to weather any storms that arise.
- **Setting up PR performance management**
  The team should measure and demonstrate its success, e.g. via an ongoing media resonance analysis. Only by doing so can internal value and a power base be created to serve its prominent role. Added to this is the share of voice for certain hashtags on social media platforms as well as projections as to the advertising value equivalent, or the amount of revenue attributed to an article. Landau Media, Meltwater and Mediatoolkit all offer suitable tools for this.

Paid online marketing

Practice 57: Harnessing the six key hacks for buying online ads efficiently

The most important thing to get right when it comes to online ads is the "CAC payback period." The right payback period is often between 6 and 24 months and depends on at least four factors:

- **Recurring revenues**
  The more recurring revenue you can expect, the longer your payback can be (e.g., FinTechs often can afford 1–2 years payback time and eCommerce enablers like Shopify can afford even longer, while businesses with few recurring revenues like Parship will likely stay closer to 6 months).
- **Launch phase**
  A new market or product launch often requires higher acquisition investments (e.g., accepting a longer payback time for 24–30 months is often right in the first "launch months" if it is shortened afterward).
- **Industry competitiveness**
  The more competitive an industry with new players driving up paid customer acquisition, the more emphasis should be placed on non-paid channels, such as word-of-mouth and organic, or trust-building channels, such as PR, and the shorter the CAC payback period should be.

- **Data basis**
  The stronger the (historic) data basis is, the more that can be spent as predicting payback time gets better.

Six hacks for allocating online ad budgets:

- **Hack one: Smart bidding strategies must align with the company's objectives**
  The most common bidding strategies are target cost per acquisition, target return on advertising spend (ROAS) and conversion value (which optimizes for sales revenue or profit margins). When running a brand campaign for which the focus is not on conversion rates, a good metric to use is Cost per Thousand Viewed Impressions (vCPM – viewable Cost per Mille). Want to dominate impressions for specific keyword searches (e.g., "bank account")? The target impression share should be the main bidding strategy. When going for a "target impression share," bids are (automatically) set with the goal of showing an ad close to the top of the page.

- **Hack two: Smart bidding should be enabled with tracking and attribution**
  Tracking allows for the ability to see which online ads are leading to conversions (e.g., website visits, verified customers, first-time buyers or retail sales). Tracking logic can include anything from "last click" – where the ad the customer saw last is given full credit for conversion – to "position-based attribution," which gives ads a certain weighting (e.g., 40% weight for the 1st ad clicked on, 40% for the last and 20% for the rest). As attribution tracking isn't perfect, a good verification mechanism is to simply ask some customers how they heard about the company or product (e.g., via a popup window on the homepage / in the app).

- **Hack three: Quality scores should be used to boost your campaigns**
  Quality is usually measured based on click rates, ad relevance and landing page experience. If ads are clicked on very often, get many comments or likes and the bounce rate of the landing page is low, the quality scores skyrocket. It is important to note that increasing quality scores can come with concrete financial implications. For instance, Google may place a company's high-quality score ad at a higher rank than a competitor who outbids them on CPC. Google uses a score of 1–10, where 6 is average and 8–9 is very good.

- **Hack four: A/B tests should be used to evaluate copies and creative assets**
  Creative assets such as text, picture and video can pull customers in. In order to understand what works for the customers, each asset needs to be tested using A/B tests. There are at least five themes to test when designing assets:
  - **Clickbait**: An unbelievable or disturbing headline, such as "3 reasons why most startups fail."
  - **Explainer**: A longer descriptive story delivered in a step-by-step manner.
  - **Testimonial**: A customer describes authentically his or her positive experience with the product or service.
  - **USP**: A list of unique selling points, which are value-driving for the potential customers.
  - **Conversion**: Very reduced content with a focus on transactional information and a strong call to action.
- **Hack five: Retargeting is key**
  On average, 96% of people who visit a website "bounce" before buying any products or doing what the marketing team wants them to do.[257] Retargeting gives a company more chances to address those visitors again. With retargeted ads on Facebook, a company can achieve on average a CTR that is ten times higher than the CTR of regular display ads.[258] For a retargeting campaign to work, it needs to be super-focused and super-specific. That means there needs to be a detailed breakdown of individual customer groups (e.g., people who look at product category A vs. product category B) and then target each group with quality content that builds on their existing relationship with a product.
- **Hack six: 10% of the paid-ads budget should be allocated to a special task force of "growth hackers," which try unconventional or new channels**
  They should be the best functional experts within the marketing team and come together in a cross-functional team to experiment. With simple A/B testing of versions of campaigns, landing pages and the like, growth hackers can make a massive difference (see Practice 8).

Offline marketing

Practice 58: Leveraging the power of offline marketing in the digital age

Offline marketing still matters today, particularly for B2C scale-ups beyond their early growth phase. This includes billboards, TV and radio ads, as well as nontraditional media, such as projecting a logo onto a downtown building ("guerilla" marketing). Successful examples include HelloFresh's radio branding campaign, the N26 #nobullshit branding campaign and Lean Cuisine's famous art wall of scales in NYC where women could define the measure by which they wanted to be "weighed" (e.g., being back in college by 55).

How should offline marketing be approached? One (or a maximum of two) offline channel should be chosen to test a campaign in a specific region along with a control city. Enough money should be spent to reach a meaningful share of voice over a reasonable time period. The data team should model the expected trajectory and constantly monitor the campaign's progress. Tracking the source of increased customer traffic to link back to the offline campaign is essential for this. A pop-up window for every 50th person visiting the site asking where they heard the offer is one way to do it. Other ways of tracking and measuring offline campaigns include dedicated landing pages, email addresses (specific to the poster, flyer or billboard) and discount codes specific to the offline activity. A more sophisticated version is an attribution model (e.g., marketing mix modeling, multi-touch attribution), which quantifies the additional revenue created by each offline channel (e.g., TV, radio, billboard). When evaluating the effectiveness of offline campaigns, the standard approach is to measure cost per thousand views (CPM) and the return on advertising spend (ROAS). Nontraditional media – or guerrilla marketing – can run the risk of being perceived as vanity projects that raise legal and implementation issues, and they are hard to measure in terms of success. They only offer true value if the campaign goes viral or the press picks it up in a positive way.

Monetization

Practice 59: Nailing your monetization strategy to drive revenue

Startup leaders can be so passionate about their products that they forget about monetization. However, price is one of the best measures of value. Charge too much, and a company will miss out on customers; charge too little, and they will make less money than they could have. As Omar Mohout puts it, "The optimal price provides the maximum revenue – not the highest margin or the largest number of customers."[259] In essence, there are two ways to tackle pricing. The first is "cost plus," which involves working out the full cost of delivering a product and charging a margin on top. The second is "value-based pricing," which revolves around an understanding of the value created by a product for the customer (e.g., savings per year) and then splitting this value accordingly. As one guideline, it is worthwhile for (B2B) startups to explore the value-based pricing option, as this often results in more revenue than the "cost plus" variant. For more details on this, see a great talk by Kevin Hale from Y Combinator.[260]

Here are some starting points for how to experiment with monetization and to find "product-market-price" fit:
- **Have the "willingness-to-pay" conversations early**
  This is a way to tell early on if there is an opportunity to monetize a product and if this will support a feature prioritization. The key questions to ask the customers are:[261]
    - "At what price does this product start to become a good deal?" – When optimizing for growth with a pricing strategy, this is the price point.
    - "At what price does this product start to become expensive, but you would still consider buying it?" – In this price area, the pricing often fits the true value of the product best.
    - "At what price does this product start to become so expensive that you would never consider buying it?" – This is the price that can be charged in the future.

Ideally, this process will use features to create a ranking system. When starting with ten features, a subset (e.g., six) is first created for the customers to name the feature that they believe to be of most value and the one to which they attribute the least value. Afterward, the customers are shown another set of features and made to repeat the process. This allows for the creation of both a ranking system and a prioritization of the features. For more details on these methods, check out the book "Monetizing Innovation" on the essentials reading list. It is often helpful to plot the results as a "price sensitivity meter," as shown in Figure 63. This can be done for each market (USD 5 may be too cheap in the United States but too high in India, for example).

- **Segment deeply and price accordingly**
  Depending on the customers' needs, water can be priced very differently. As Madhavan Ramanujam puts it: "If water is in a fountain, it's free, if you put it in a bottle in a supermarket shelf, it's USD 2, if you put gas in, it's USD 2.50, if you put it in a minibar, it's USD 5."[262] If a customer wants a phone with all the latest features, Apple may charge them more than USD 1000 for the privilege; if their priority is to have a reliable and working phone, they can pick up an older iPhone model for a steep discount. Is there a customer desire for absolute silence in

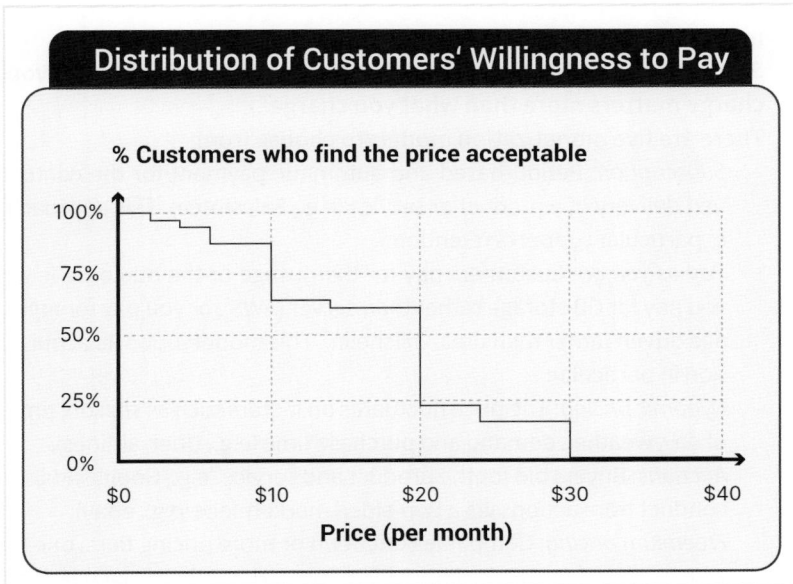

Figure 63: Distribution of Customers' Willingness to Pay

the car? Uber has introduced a feature to request this from the driver, but it is only guaranteed in Uber Black and Uber Black SUV premium rides. These are examples of segmentation according to user needs and pricing accordingly. Grouping customers according to their willingness to pay is usually a good way to segment a customer base into 3–4 groups. Typical segments include customers who want the optimal product, those who want it as soon as possible, those who just want the normal version and those who are very price sensitive.[263]

- **Speak value, not (only) features**
An SaaS company focusing on supporting warehouse and supply chain operations with automated picking and shipping workflows can also provide support to its sales team with a tool to calculate the savings for its customers. During the sales pitch, the team explores – together with potential buyers – relevant data (e.g., the number of hours spent manually picking from shelves or the number of shipping errors incurred). From this, the team can calculate the annual savings for the customers. What is a better basis for a price negotiation? For B2C companies, it is essential to be crystal clear about the 1–2 primary elements of value (e.g., saving on time/hassle, reducing personal risks) and put these at the forefront of a company's communications. See the North Star chapter for more details.

- **Settle on a monetization model that fits your objectives ("How you charge matters more than what you charge")**
There are five monetization models to choose from:
  - *Subscription*: Period-based and automatic payment for the continued delivery of a product or service (e.g., Salesforce). This approach in particular supports retention.
  - *Pay as you go*: Customers pay for their usage or the outcome (e.g., you pay for GB storage rather than server (AWS), or you pay for mileage driven rather than tires – Michelin). This model supports acquisition in particular.
  - *Dynamic pricing*: The price fluctuates on factors such as season, time of day, weather, demand and purchase time (e.g., Uber, airlines).
  - *Auctions*: Buyers bid for the product and service (e.g., Google Ads) or conduct transactions via a two-sided marketplace (e.g., eBay).
  - *Freemium pricing*: Companies offer two or more pricing tiers, one of which is free (e.g., LinkedIn and Dropbox). Here, there is a need for a strong upsell hook, as companies that use this model often give away up to 80% of their product's value. The premium features

should be important enough for sufficient customers to upgrade (e.g., Dropbox's premium storage feature, Adobe's premium plan allowing users to alter PDFs).

- **Consider pricing thresholds in B2C**
  Demand sensitivity curves are nonlinear and are based on pricing thresholds. Demand often drops significantly if a company exceeds price hurdles such as USD 19.90 or USD 29.90. However, it can be worthwhile to remain close to these thresholds (i.e., a price increase from USD 18.90 to USD 19.90 will often lead to revenue increases despite a minor reduction in demand). This discussion needs to be done for each market separately as thresholds in foreign currencies may be exceeded.

Growth hacking

Practice 60: Establishing cross-functional growth hacking teams for activation, retention and monetization

Once Dropbox reached 100k users, its growth engine went into overdrive. Within two years its customer base grew by 3900%. What had happened? Dropbox had implemented one of the most famous growth hacks in business history: a two-sided gamified referral system. They offered additional storage to both referring and referred users during the sign-up flow for recommending Dropbox. Growth hacking usually involves a cross-functional team that runs a series of experiments to drive growth through the customer acquisition funnel in an iterate-learn-scale model. A typical approach is to have a team of marketers, product managers, interaction designers, front-end developers and data analysts develop, test and scale different versions of the landing pages, product value propositions or customer referral programs. Success is then measured through simple A/B testing.

The classic example for a successful growth hack is Hotmail's "P.S. I love you" campaign, which contained a link to sign up for its free online email service. Another growth hacking success story: in the early days of Airbnb, the company leveraged Craigslist to post its own accommodation listings. This differs from strategies like Gmail, which was originally invite-only (like the social media app Clubhouse), and these strategies can be effective when they create hype around the product and a fear of missing out. Still, growth hacking is not about finding just ONE silver bullet; the idea is to test new ideas in order to drive growth week in and week out. Some companies have different growth hacking teams for customer acquisition, activation/retention and revenue growth.

The approach usually works by first identifying the key metrics to influence (e.g., conversion of website visitors into buyers), developing ideas for experiments (e.g., better product value proposition, first-time shopper promotion, refinement of the recommendation engine), prioritizing them using an impact vs. ease of implementation matrix and measuring the effect after running the initial experiments. A mix of small-scale wins (e.g., changes to landing page) with game-changing growth hacks (e.g., Airbnb's Craigslist hack) is one successful approach. For more details, see Sean Ellis' and Morgan Brown's excellent book, *Hacking Growth*.

There are several types of growth hacks to consider:
- **Activation hacks**
  This is not only about getting customers through a company's digital door but enticing them to use the products early and regularly. Part of solving this challenge comes from having a strong understanding of activation friction. Sean Ellis sets this out in a simple equation: Desire – Friction = Conversion Rate. The first source of insight for activation friction is data along the customer acquisition funnel. Are users from organic Google searches leaving the store before paying for what they have in their cart? Are Instagram ads rather than Facebook ads leading customers to become repeat purchasers? The process of reaching this level of understanding is made easier with the use of funnel analytics from tools such as Kissmetric, Google Analytics and Adobe Omniture's SiteCatalyst. Qualitative customer interviews can complement this with the following approaches: call or email customers whenever possible, ideally with open-ended questions, such as "What is stopping you from completing your order?" or "Is there anything preventing you from performing a transaction with us today?" Some of the best answers come from those customers who are not yet active.[264] These insights can also be used to design activation experiments. If the customer says it is too difficult to use an app, it would be important to design a landing page, explanation video or

message explaining how to use it. Does the activation rate for credit cards vary by country and mailing service? In this case, the process of trying out different mailing providers and address verification methods in the sign-up flow can be worthwhile. Running 30+ experiments like this is a good starting point, and the result will often lead to solutions that can eradicate activation friction. More possible experiments that reduce activation friction include a single, social sign-on or "flipping the funnel," where customers experience the product immediately upon signing up and only register later. Bubble.io, a no-code platform for building web apps, is a perfect example. If the "Edit this page to see how it works" link is clicked on the bubble.io homepage, customers are forwarded to Bubble's demo editor tool, which can be used to explore in its entirety without login or sign-up. Gamification elements work, too, such as LinkedIn's profile progress meter. One widely (mis)used activation solution is the "trigger," which tends to be an email notification or in-app push message to complete an account creation or purchase or to announce new features. Triggers that leverage scarcity are common, such as Amazon's "Only 3 items left in stock" or Booking.com's "20 people are looking at this property now." As a rule of thumb, triggers should only be used when they provide clear customer value.

- **Retention hacks**
  Habit formation is critical for retaining customers. From religiously checking a LinkedIn feed and following Instagram prompts, to using Amazon to compare prices, a habit can help to keep the customer coming back for more. Nir Eyal describes this vividly in his book *Hooked*. How do you create this habit in the first place?
  - **First, it is necessary to identify the early retention metric.** This may be the repurchase rate within 90 days (eCommerce), the daily returning users (social media) or the number of customers actively using products (SaaS). It is crucial to make sure to pay attention to early retention metrics: What is the ONE thing that turns a trial customer into a loyal follower? Several companies understand this very well – Pinterest (at least three visits in the first two weeks), Facebook (at least 7 friends within 10 days), Slack (at least 2000 messages sent within a team) or Dropbox (save at least one file in a folder on one device).[265]

- **Second, retention and churn behavior need to be tracked.** This should be done for cohorts (e.g., through the use of sign-up months).
- **Third, there should be experiments conducted on triggers.** These should prompt customers toward actions that deliver the most value and consequently drive up the retention metric. One trigger is a "brand ambassador model," where customers are rewarded when they are active. Google's Local Guides program offers ten reward levels with different batches depending on how active the reviewer is. Recognition of achievement is another way to support habitual behavior, such as by sending a customer an email when they reach a milestone. Medium writers, for example, receive a pat on the back from the company's co-founder when an article receives 50 or 100 recommendations. Personalized communication is another effective ploy. For example, Pinterest uses machine-learning algorithms to vary the copy on Pins (see Figure 64).

- **"Resurrection" hacks**

  Resurrection experiments may take the form of emails, targeted ads to win customers back or push notifications with special offers. When Evernote realized some of their customers were failing to use their products because their apps weren't being installed, the team designed an email campaign that urged these customers to reinstall

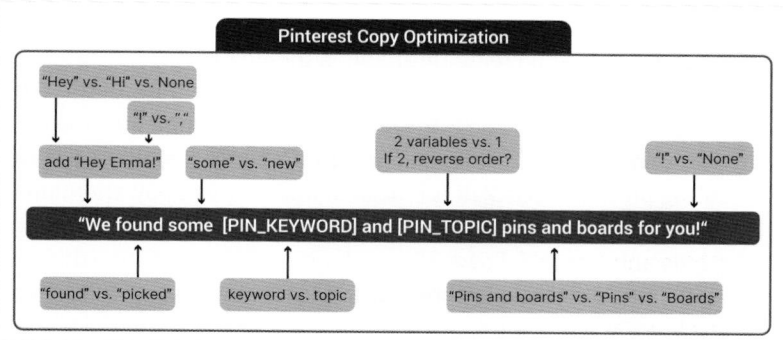

Figure 64: Pinterest Copy Optimization
Source: John Egan[266]

the apps. After encountering a similar situation, the eReading startup Kobo designed an email campaign that took an extreme, but very effective measure, of giving out a 90% discount to churning customers that were targeted for reactivation. Virgin Trains took a different and creative approach to winning back customers. They provoked disengaged users with the risky (and untrue) subject line "All seat sales cancelled forever." When the customers then opened the mail, Virgin explained that this was not the case, while taking the opportunity to showcase current sales options and promotional events.

- **Monetization hacks**
When the eCommerce shop Zappos reviewed its return policy, it took the step to dig deep into its monetization data. Interestingly, Zappos found that customers who spent the most money and generated the most profit also returned products most frequently. In fact, those customers who bought more expensive footwear had a 50% return rate. Because of this, Zappos realized that a strict returns policy would lead the company to lose major monetization potential and adapted its return policy accordingly by offering an extremely generous 365-day returns and free two-way shipping policy to drive up revenue.[267] This is a typical monetization hack – they usually are aimed to increase a customer's "lifetime value" (i.e., the amount of revenue the company earns until the customer leaves). Monetization teams often map revenue creation opportunities along the customer acquisition funnel and identify drop-off points where monetization potential is lost. This may take the form of an eCommerce page with videos that create substantially fewer sales than industry benchmarks would indicate or copies of product pages that vary widely when converted to different languages. Experiments with different subscription prices, virtual goods or in-app currency can also be worth exploring (see Practice 59).

Recommended publications:
- Sean Ellis and Morgan Brown (2017). *Hacking Growth*.
- Nir Eyal and Ryan Hoover (2013). *Hooked: How to Build Habit-Forming Products*.
- Omar Mohout (2015). *Lean Pricing: Pricing Strategies for Startups*.
- Madhavan Ramanujam and Georg Tacke (2016). *Monetizing Innovation: How Smart Companies Design the Product Around the Price*.

Watch our video on the six key pitfalls to avoid in your B2C marketing function by scanning the QR code or following this link: https://youtube/l2nLzftLF-I.

How to set up a marketing team that can scale? Watch our video by scanning the QR code or following this link: https://youtube/fBtjF3iFr6g.

Definitions

- **Brand**: both the tangible features of a product or service – cosmetic design, functionality, logo and the intangible features – the emotions, expectations and their connotations – that together create the reason for choosing the product or service.
- **Blended CAC (Customer Acquisition Cost)**: a metric measuring the total acquisition cost for a customer, which takes into account all types of marketing channels. It is calculated by dividing the total amount of money spent on acquisition-focused marketing by the total number of acquired customers across all channels.

- **Channels**: the mediums through which marketing is delivered to generate engagements with existing and potential customers (i.e., social media, email, website).
- **Cohort**: a grouping of users/customers that share certain characteristics (such as geographical location, age or mobile phone operating system), which can help to create and test targeted marketing strategies.
- **Content factory**: the people, processes and tools that are needed to create articles, videos and other media for attracting customers.
- **Conversion rate**: a measure of the rate at which users of a product or service follow a particular action after interacting with (a part of) the product or service (i.e., opening a page link or signing up to an account).
- **CPC (Cost per Click)**: a metric for measuring the cost of a digital ad; CPC measures the cost per click on the ad.
- **CPM (Cost per Thousand)**: a metric for measuring the cost of a digital ad; CPM measures the cost of reaching 1000 impressions/ visitors/ viewers.
- **Customer acquisition funnel**: the set of steps a customer follows, from the first point of engagement with the company through to the target interaction (e.g., a sale, an account creation).
- **Customer acquisition**: the use of marketing strategies and techniques to generate new customers for a business by guiding them through a funnel or set of steps from brand awareness to moment of purchase.
- **Growth hacking**: a cross-functional team effort for rapidly growing the number of users/customers for a company – this usually involves product, technology and marketing measures.
- **Marketing mix modeling**: the use of statistical analysis for predicting the effectiveness of different marketing channels and campaigns.
- **Multi-touch attribution**: a method to determine the impact of each marketing touchpoint with the customer (e.g., campaign on Facebook, ad on Google) on the conversion – it aims to allocate to each touchpoint in different channels of its "fair share" for creating a desired effect with the customer (e.g., signing-up to an app).

- **Monetization**: the process of generating cash from a product or service, which can be achieved through a range of means (i.e., charging advertisers for digital real estate on your website or charging users a subscription fee).
- **Organic marketing**: the generation of traffic to your website or business through natural and authentic engagements with prospective customers (i.e., blog posts, social media posts and other unpaid content).
- **Paid marketing**: digital advertising and media placements that target customers based on their interests and habits, which are paid for by the advertiser.
- **Performance marketing**: a form of paid marketing where the advertiser only pays for the marketing services when a specific action is completed or a goal is reached (i.e., a sale, page visit or a certain number of page impressions).
- **Revenue**: the total amount of income a company generates through the sale of products and/or services over a specified period of time, without taking into account the costs expended by the business.
- **ROAS (Return on Ad Spend)**: a metric comparing the gross profit generated by an ad campaign with the advertising budget spent on it (although dangerously often revenue is used instead of profit!).
- **Segmentation**: a key component of marketing strategies in which audiences are divided up according to a particular classification so that they can be more efficiently targeted by marketing teams.
- **TACoS (Total Advertising Cost of Sales)**: a metric for measuring the performance of advertising in a broader way by evaluating a company's advertising spending in relation to the total revenue generated by the company – often used in the Amazon ecosystem.
- **Vanity metrics**: metrics that appear impressive but do not provide insights into the performance of a company or its product(s) or service(s) and therefore are of limited business value.
- **WTP (Willingness to Pay)**: an important metric when assessing demand and pricing products/services. WTP measures the maximum price a customer would be willing to pay for a product or service.

8 B2B Sales Excellence

Creating brand advocates & pipelines full of sales opportunities

With Karan Sharma

Major pitfalls for scale-up builders to avoid   !

- **Running sales development, account management, pre-sales and product marketing in silos.**
  Many scale-ups insist on keeping their sales, marketing and customer success management teams in silos, which can result in a disjointed experience for the customer. This experience should be shaped as a continuum – from sales development to customer success.
- **Insufficient investment in customer success management.**
  Sometimes sales teams believe that if they sign contracts, the promised value will materialize on its own accord. However, customers often require support in navigating a company's product in order to fully appreciate its value. This is why a B2B startup should consider employing a customer success manager among its first 10 hires. Their job is to make the promises of the sales team come true and to identify customers who may churn early (see Practice 62).
- **Insufficient investment in hiring and retaining a world-class sales team.**
  "If you can't be with the one you love, love the one you are with." This is a poetic sentiment, but it is not one that makes for good advice when hiring a world-class sales team. More substantial ways to attract and retain a world-class sales team include creating clear career paths that start in sales development with the option to move up through the ranks, reserving an annual education budget, setting referral bonuses for hiring strong colleagues and the like (see Practices 62 and 63).

- **Separating sales development and pre-sales from account management too late.**
  Relying on a generalist sales approach is not a great way to secure unicorn status. In the early start-up phase, it is natural to have a single sales colleague responsible for creating leads, pitching the product and answering technical questions for early customers. This approach will no longer fly in the scale-up phase. A good practice is to separate sales into sales development (to generate leads), pre-sales (to provide expert technical knowledge during the sales process) and account management (as a single holistic face to the customers) (see Practice 63).
- **Designing sales commissions that do not incentivize the right sales behavior.**
  Some scale-ups do not adopt the sales commission plans early and frequently enough. Adapting the commission plan over the company's life cycle (e.g., by creating a "hunting plan" to incentivize customer acquisition in the early stages, a "customer success plan" to prevent customer churn or a "customer commitment plan" to incentivize cash flow and monetization) is one way to go (see Practice 65).
- **Not deploying the right mix of tech tools to enable sales.**
  Delays in execution can come from not giving the sales team the right sales technology toolkit. Understanding sales tech stacks that work together is of critical importance when planning to hire and sell at scale. Salespeople are quick to abandon tools that do not fit their preferences, so introducing them with care is essential (see Practices 66 and 67).
- **Not daring to optimize the pricing strategy enough.**
  If a company's pricing is public and they allow inconsistencies to creep in, it can hamper their business model. When done right, this pricing strategy could become one of the most effective levers for driving up revenue. Settling on the right pricing methodology from the outset will help a sales team to avoid having to deal with pricing objections. Embedding payment terms into a pricing model – with a focus on annual contracts and upfront payments – is a worthwhile avenue to explore.

Simply put, the sales division is the B2B starship's engine room. If a good one is built, it will get the company to where it needs to go. If corners are cut, the company won't make it outside the solar system. Often, the primary aim is to meet the total annual (recurring) revenue goals with competitive sales efficiency. To achieve this, the sales team usually needs to work toward four key objectives: increase the **total annual (recurring) revenue**, deliver high levels of **retention** while establishing a significant **market share in relevant target niches** and keep sales costs low. This is what we call our formula for sales-supported growth (Figure 65).

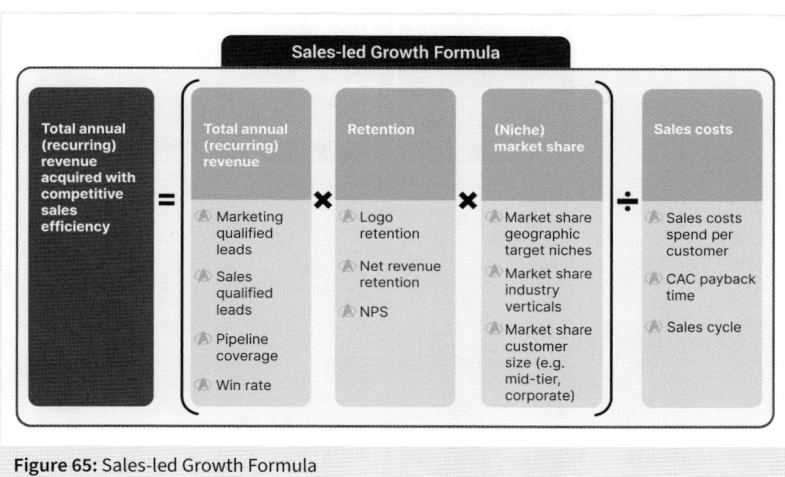

Figure 65: Sales-led Growth Formula

The sales-supported growth formula can be translated into objectives and key results (OKRs). Figure 66 shows typical objectives and key results for a B2B sales team for orientation purposes. The individual values set as targets may vary significantly. The example shown is intended to be an ambitious one.

OKRs

Practice 61: Establishing the right sales OKRs

Typical Annual Sales Objectives and Key Results for B2B Sales in Scale-ups

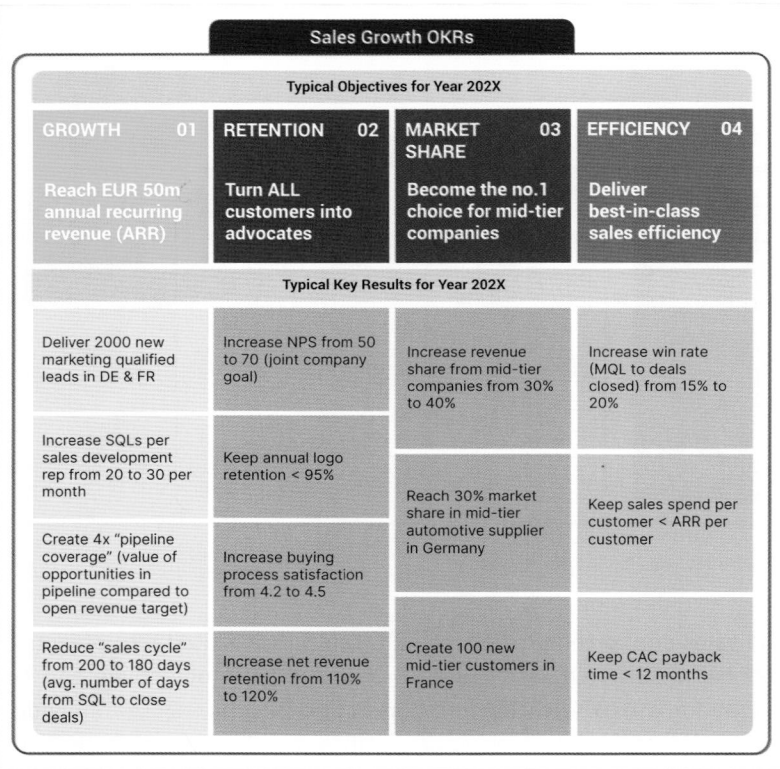

Figure 66: Sales OKRs: SaaS Company

O1. Growth: Are you delivering on your sales targets?

In the early 2000s, the SaaS company HubSpot grew its revenue by 6,000% within four years. Mark Roberge, its VP of Sales at the time, described in one word how they achieved this: science.[268] A clearly defined sales funnel, sales process steps, conversion tracking and perpetual redirection were the core drivers behind HubSpot's sales and ultimately its success. In 2020, the company had a market capitalization of USD 17bn. Science is essential when it comes to business customers. While end consumers are like satellites – quick to enter orbit and quick to leave – business customers are more like asteroids – slow-moving, but packed with resources to exploit. There are three ways to attract them:[269] via outbound outreach, such as calls, emails and LinkedIn ("spears"); with excellent content, such as whitepapers, explanatory videos and how-to guides ("nets"); and by leveraging word of mouth and relationships ("seeds"). Once there are "qualified" leads, the sales executives should shuttle these potential customers along the steps of the B2B sales customer acquisition funnel (set out in Figure 67).

Typical key results to be measured include additional leads created, primarily engaged prospects and sales-qualified leads (SQLs). MQLs are potential customers who show proactively initial interest (e.g., by providing their contact details). The marketing team or the sales development representatives will forward these details to their account management colleagues, who will try to convert them into SQLs, or potential buyers, who clearly want to find a solution to a business pain point. SQLs increase the "pipeline coverage," which measures the potential revenue that the funnel's current sales opportunities could generate in comparison to next quarter's revenue target. Many SaaS companies aim to have pipeline coverage between 3:1 and 5:1. If EUR 20 million is the goal for sales for the next quarter, the pipeline should have EUR 60–100 million in potential revenue during the previous quarter. Is the company relying on a strong brand, moving in an uncompetitive market or selling add-ons to existing customers? The pipeline coverage may then need to be lower (2:1 to 3:1). A good win rate counts, too. This often refers to the percentage of "opportunities" (i.e., customers that are in the process of evaluating the product) converted into contracts signed. For B2B tech companies, a good win rate is ~20%.[270]

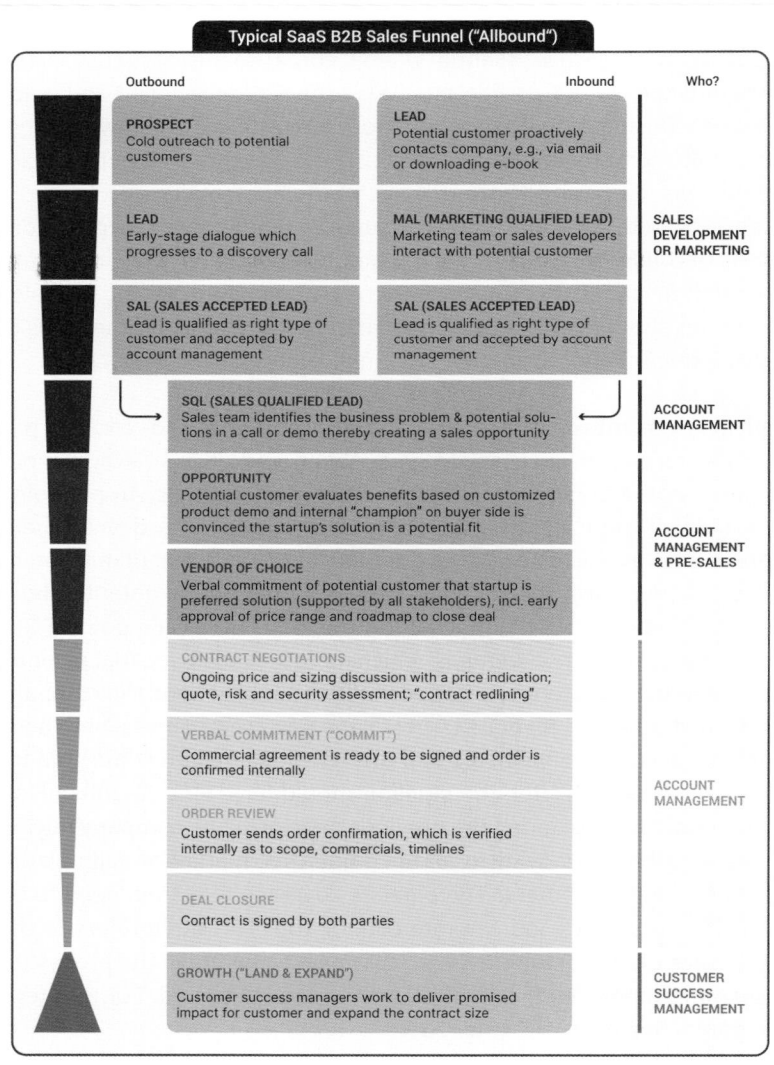

Figure 67: Typical SaaS B2B Sales Funnel ("Allbound")

O2. Retention: Do you turn customers into advocates?

After growing rapidly for several years, the SaaS startup Groove started bleeding customers just as fast, and they had an unsustainable annual customer churn of 50%. The reason: after aggressively acquiring customers, Groove didn't work to keep them on board. Customer success management turned things around: with "red flag metrics" such as first session length and login frequency for the first 30 days. Groove identified customers with a high churn risk, then offered setup guidance, shared implementation and onboarding approaches that have been considered useful for similar businesses in the past.[271] A strong sales machine that fails to focus on customer experience can lead to high churn, which is why sales teams should be measured both on short-term sales and long-term customer success. Without it, an aggressive form of sales behavior is the only thing that is left.

Typical key results here include the Net Promoter Score and a survey score on the buying experience after 90 days of contract sales. This ide-ally creates a high "logo retention" (i.e., the percentage of customers retained over a given period). A typical range is 93–99%, with larger cor-porations at the lower end and SMEs at the higher end.[272] This in turn in-creases net revenue retention (NRR), which measures the revenue made from existing customers after accounting for upselling, downgrades and churn (120% is excellent).[273]

O3. Market share: Are you nailing your niches?
Oracle alumnus Marc Benioff started Salesforce in 1999 after seeing how a booming new customer segment neglected by Oracle – startups and SMEs – had been underserved by incumbents for years. He introduced SaaS as a cheaper and more accessible option. His success with this tac-tic was huge, as indicated by a market cap that has been higher than Oracle's for years now.[274] When scaling up, finding a company's niche is critical. Think Facebook with Ivy League schools, PayPal with eBay users, Amazon with books or Zappos with shoes. Niches are usually fo-cused on country, industry vertical or company size. All niches have cus-tomers with specific pain points – and sales teams can prepare standard communications materials and product demos along the different pipe-line stages to address them. In the early growth phase, a B2B tech com-pany will often have a sweet spot in terms of deal size. A focus on annual contract values of EUR 50,000–500,000, for instance, can make the go-to-market highly efficient.

When defining the right customer segment, **typical key results** here often involve having a target market share for different segments or winning a certain number of deals in a segment (e.g., 100 new mid-tier contracts in France). To continuously monitor the market share in different regions and industry verticals is of the essence, as is shifting the focus of the sales team at the right time is important for long-term success. Has a 60% market share for CRM systems in the German automotive supplier industry been achieved? The next direction would be to have more sales colleagues target FinTech or healthcare companies. At later growth stages, companies often start to hedge their sales bets by addressing more niches (e.g., subscription service company Zoura, which sells to three: US mid-tier SaaS companies, larger B2C subscription companies like the Financial Times, and business transformation companies – Fortune 1000 companies that move into services).[275]

O4. Sales costs: Do you deliver best-in-class sales efficiency?
The business messenger Slack more than doubled its annual number of paying users between 2013 and 2017, despite its limited marketing spending and lack of a sales team.[276] While Slack founder Stewart Butterfield and his colleagues were experienced entrepreneurs and arrived just as peak email fatigue was setting in, the real secret to their sales success was a product-first sales approach.[277] This "touchless" sales strategy meant that people could buy USD 20.000 worth of Slack per year and never speak to a salesperson. From the outset of the scaling process, Slack offered a freemium product with a strong brand behind it, which quickly got it into many offices – virtually without any real sales/marketing spend. In 2020, Salesforce bought Slack for USD 27.7 billion.[278] While not every sales approach can be as efficient as this, go-to-market efficiency still matters, especially when cash is scarce.

The **typical key result** to focus on here is the sales cost spent per customer. As a rule of thumb, spending up to one euro for every euro of annually recurring revenue represents good sales efficiency for a B2B scale-up in the early growth phase.[279] Many scale-ups also set 6 to 24 months as their goal for earning back their customer acquisition costs.

Organizational chart and roles

Practice 62: Defining the roles & responsibilities for a sales function

To staff a talented B2B engine room, the team should be assembled based on these 4 building blocks:

- **"Hunters":** The sales development teams push and pull "leads" into the pipeline by reaching out to customers "cold" or by qualifying inbound leads.
- **"Closers":** The account managers that take over SQLs and try to close them together with the technical "pre-sales" teams.
- **"Farmers":** The customer success managers that try to turn customers into advocates after they have signed a contract. This is the starting point for upselling.
- **"Enablers":** The sales operations, training & qualification and sales intelligence teams that free up all other sales teams from administrative hassle, thus enabling them to focus on efficient selling.

Figure 68 is a basic organizational blueprint for B2B sales.

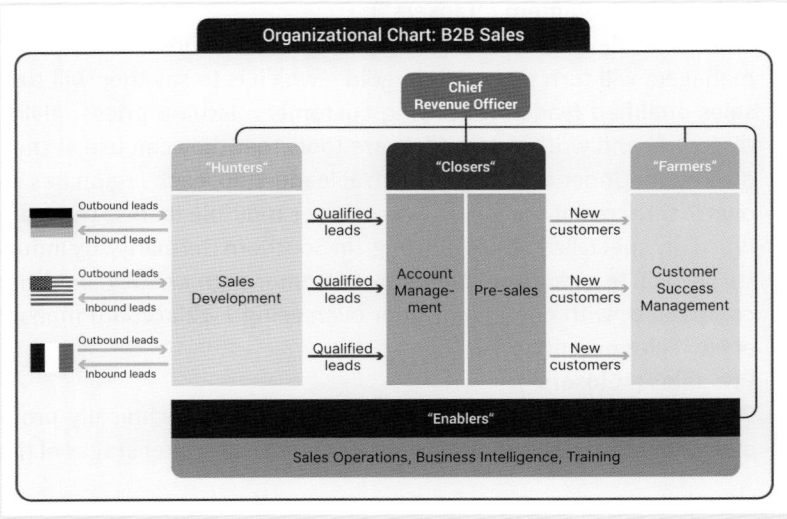

Figure 68: Organizational Blueprint of a Typical B2B Sales Division

In detail:

- **Sales development ("Hunters")**

  Sales development is about filling the top of a sales funnel. It fulfills two main purposes: the first is to source new leads, and the second is to qualify inbound leads before they are handed over to the account management. In an inbound sales track, incoming requests are picked up and qualified by the sales development representative (acting as a gatekeeper), and the requests that are deemed suitable are then forwarded to the account managers. In the outbound sales track, sales development reaches out to potential leads in the form of cold calls, emails or social media (e.g., LinkedIn). Sales development representatives build the foundation by obtaining the right contacts and reaching out to them, initiating dialog and progressing to a discovery call. Once the potential customer ("prospect") is qualified, the sales development representatives hand the contact over to account management. There are major differences between the inbound and outbound track, which is why it often makes sense to track and compensate them separately. Sales development can be the entry-level for a business and a training ground for account management. While leadership is often centrally positioned, it is common practice to set up market-based sales development teams.

- **Account management ("Closers")**

  While sales development representatives find the ore veins, account managers will turn this ore into gold – which is to say they will turn sales-qualified leads into paying customers. Issuing prices, giving discounts and writing proposals are tools that they can use at their discretion. Under a system of central leadership, each region has its own local account managers who oversee multiple teams. The team is usually specialized by region (e.g., in Southern Germany), by industry vertical (e.g., automotive) or by customer segment (e.g., mid-tier companies), with one team leader overseeing 7–12 account managers (or sales executives).

- **Pre-sales ("Closers")**

  Pre-sales (or sales engineering) teams consist of technically proficient individuals who support the sales team in the later stages of the sales funnel. Once a potential customer reaches the product demonstration stage, the pre-sales teams will apply their expert technical knowledge (e.g., if a customer wants to discuss configuration management, API access or single sign-on options). The average standard industry ratio for B2B SaaS companies is 2–3 sales colleagues for one pre-seller. Having them on board can enable a company to grow their sales team much faster, as the technical knowledge required in the account management team is lower and can be learned on the job.

- **Customer success management ("Farmers")**
  CSM acts once the contract is signed. Their job is to turn customers into advocates. They come in at least three flavors: a technical support team, which helps customers troubleshoot operational issues such as bugs or log-in issues; the professional service team, which is usually paid per day and facilitates the adoption of a product by delivering projects; and customer success managers, who are not paid by customers but work to turn them into advocates. CSMs call users regularly, observe their usage statistics and customer health scores, connect customers with each other and are the point of contact if a customer wants to upgrade. This may also include coaching and community management.

- **Sales enablement ("Enablers")**
  The enablement team supports all sales teams directly so they can focus on what matters. "Enablers" calculate sales commissions, issue contracts and purchase orders, and may also consolidate performance management and perform small-scale analytics. The training and coaching members of the team lead certifications for the pre-sales team, employee onboarding, regular refresher training sessions and training for the sales playbooks.

The sales team should be supported by a strong marketing team that delivers marketing-qualified leads (MQLs) (i.e., relevant and gated content where prospective customers leave contact data, PR, localized campaigns, events, etc.). The team should also seek to be featured in the Gartner Magic Quadrant or Forrester Wave for specific products.

Practice 63: Scaling the right sales roles at the right time

Insurance providers in the early 20th century learned that having a sales team of hunters, closers and farmers greatly increased their chance of doubling their sales.[280] While a company can rely on a team of intelligent generalists in the startup phase, the early growth phase calls for this team to become specialized. Many scale-up leaders assemble a customer success management (CSM) team far too late, despite this being the first area of specialization that should be mastered. The job of the CSM team is to deliver the business impact promised to customers and to gather case studies and reference customers that help to grow them faster. Once this team is set up, it is worth pursuing further specializations along the sales funnel. Account management and pre-sales can split to enable the hiring of sales managers who do not require in-depth technical knowledge. Bringing sales development experts and sales enablers on board allows the more senior account executives to focus on their core responsibilities – closing contracts with customers. In later growth stages, it would also be beneficial to specialize by country, customer size (e.g., corporate customers vs. small businesses) and industry vertical (e.g., automotive vs. financial). As many customer segments have vastly different use cases, the sales teams will need to adapt to their customer's specific needs (i.e., a corporate customer's requirements will differ from small business sellers when it comes to the sale of a particular product). When scaling up, the 80/20 specialization ratio is often helpful: if a secondary task takes up more than 20% of a team's working time (e.g., account executives doing technical work), it is time to specialize further.[281]

Excelling in B2B sales requires finding the right playing field, getting the basics in place, qualifying and closing leads and retaining and farming customers.

Sales playing field

Practice 64: Exploiting the right niches

"Are you starting with a big share of a small market?" is one of the questions the entrepreneur Peter Thiel asks before investing in a company. With that in mind, sales teams can look for clearly defined niches where the company can win big and become the niche-winner. Niches are identified by country, industry vertical and company size. The size of a customer base is particularly relevant: for example, selling B2B software to major corporate customers has a vastly different use case than selling to SMEs. Other companies go for regions (e.g., top 10 countries and the top 40 cities). The key is for a company to choose niches carefully and stick to them until their growth starts to plateau. It is also important to be careful when adding sales complexity. Even if a loyal, long-term customer encourages a company to sell to a corporate partner, they may have to decline because they target mid-tier companies. Maintaining niche focus is the key.

How can a niche be identified? Aaron Ross and Marylou Tyler suggest starting with these steps:[282]

1. **List market opportunities**
   It is necessary to think about the top 5–10 customers and ask questions like: Which companies feel enough pain to pay real money for a solution? Exciting, weird and compelling outlier customers can be added to understand the full breadth of the opportunity. Which market niche in terms of industry, country and customer size has worked so far and where should a company double down?
2. **Rank list items based on six dimensions**
   Aaron Ross and Marylou Tyler list in their workbook of "Predictable Revenue" six dimensions (see Figure 69) that provide great starting points for this.

DIMENSION	KEY QUESTION	EXAMPLE
POPULAR PAIN OR NEED	Is the pain point your product is solving common enough in your target niche?	Lack of sales recruiting efficiency
BUYER PERSONA	Who are the 1-2 key people in the organisations who have the buying power and who benefit directly from your solution?	Head of account management
BUYER PERSONA'S PAIN	What specific pain points does your buyer have?	Overwhelmed with time spent in interview processes due to lack of candidate filters early in the recruiting process
SOLUTION	What solution do you offer for this pain?	Gamification-based tool to assess sales candidates online at start of recruiting process
RESULTS	What are the customer's identifiable business outcomes?	20% less time spent in recruiting and better candidates
PROOF	Do you have proof that your solution works (free trials, case studies, testimonials, brand name customers, references or demos)?	Testimonials of comparable customers where the tool increases sales efficiency

Figure 69: Six Dimensions of Predictable Revenue
Source: Workbook of Aaron Ross and Marylou Tyler in "Predictable Revenue."

3. **Choose a primary opportunity to pursue**
    If time and resources are available, pick a second niche to test against it.
4. **Validate**
    Follow the 20-interview rule by Aaron Ross and Jason Lemkin. Before creating content for a new niche or writing code to change the product, it is important to interview 20 real customers to gain insights. A "paper test" can also work, which sets out to build a page on a company's website with their niche-specific value proposition and checks how many MQLs they can create with minimal outlay.
5. **Start a lead generation campaign**
    Lead generation should be done by a sales development team, and it should focus on bringing leads into the funnel. Aaron Ross,[283] former

Salesforce Director of Sales, proposed an innovative outbound lead gen approach for that team first by sending "short and sweet emails" to VP and C-level executives to get a referral to the right person in a target organization and second by having a call/conversation with those new leads and handing them over to the account managers.

Sales basics

Practice 65: Creating a commission plan that fits your growth stage

At one of the prime global SaaS companies in the world, the top seven sellers are invited for breakfast at Tiffany's in New York each year to eat and chat with the CEO. Afterward, seven ex–Miss Hawaiis enter the room carrying a small box for each top seller containing USD 5000 to be spent in the next 30 minutes at the jeweler. This type of corporate legend creates buzz in sales organizations (though we strongly encourage incentives that are more inclusive and less focused on "bro-culture"). WordStream, for example, presents various meaningful awards (e.g., the "transparency core value award") and invites employees to share their insights into their work in short personal videos. Other possibilities are to select outstanding team members to speak at webinars or host an all-hands meeting to honor first-class performers. This also taps into the potential of women in B2B sales, who often tend to surpass men, according to some studies, due to a stronger emphasis on connecting, co-shaping solutions and collaborating with potential customers.[284]

A commission plan should correspond to a company's growth stage. HubSpot did this brilliantly.[285] A startup will tend to have a **"hunting plan"** in place that focuses on rewarding customer acquisition. At HubSpot, a sales rep received USD 2 for every dollar of monthly recurring revenue (MRR) that they brought in. To prevent churn, HubSpot added a four-month clawback (i.e., if customers left before the four-month mark, the rep had to pay back the commission). When the emphasis is more on customer success and preventing churn, a **"customer success plan"** becomes essential. HubSpot saw that customer churn was most frequent directly after the expiration of the four-month clawback period, so they divided their salespeople into four quartiles representing how often and how early their customers churned. The top quartile had their commission raised by 100% and the second by 50%. The third quartile remained at USD 2 per dollar MRR. The lowest quartile only received a single dollar for every dollar they brought on. With this shift, churn dropped by 70% within six months.

When cash flow and monetization become priorities, a **"customer commitment plan"** is one way to go. For HubSpot, one key metric to get right in this phase was the advanced payment terms for new customers. Initially, the commission was USD 2 for each dollar of MRR brought in. However, later on, only 50% of the commission was paid out after the customer's first monthly payment, with the next 25% being paid out after six months and the remaining part paid after one year. In other words, if a customer signs up month to month, the sales rep would have to wait a year to receive their full commission. If they convince the customer to sign up for a year in advance, the sales rep would receive the whole commission immediately. Under this plan, the average prepayment commitment went up from 2.5 to 7 in the span of months.

Once the type of sales commission plan has been chosen according to the growth stage, a best-in-class sales commission scheme is the next step. Here are the six key elements:

1. **Get the salary-to-commission ratio right**
   How much of an employee's earnings will come from a fixed salary? How much will depend on commissions based on sales performance? While in the UK and US commissions around 50–60% of the "on-target earnings" are common, in Central Europe it is often slightly lower (e.g., 30–40%).[286] The term "on-target earnings" refers to the total annual compensation received by a sales employee if they achieve 100% of their sales goals.
2. **Make the compensation plan easy to understand**
   Salespeople need to know how much commission they will lose if they give a customer a discount. Avoiding the individual weighing of products in the commission plan helps to reduce complexity (e.g., sell product X to get a 150% commission).
3. **Use sales performance incentive funds (SPIFs) to drive unforeseen sales opportunities**
   Deploying SPIFs throughout the year is one way to react in the short term without affecting the annual compensation plan. Example: "Get a 20% higher commission on every sale of our new product extension this month." SPIFs should always be short-term, simple and without

precedent. Otherwise, employees expecting an SPIF for a certain activity may sandbag it for the time being.

4. **Design the commission curve to have a sweet spot**
   To incentivize a sales force to obtain targets rapidly, commissions should increase once a certain threshold is reached. For instance, this can be done by doubling an employee's commission for every euro above their quarterly quota (e.g., EUR 1 million MRR). Many sales organizations put the sweet spot where the commission accelerates between 100% and 150% of target earnings. Instead of capping the commission at 150%, the act of flattening the curve is often helpful to keep sales rock stars motivated. An alternative for driving retention is to introduce a seniority and performance-based tier model. With each tier, the commission percentage increases.[287]

5. **Use non-monetary "badge" incentives as motivators**
   Breakfast at Tiffany's is one thing; other rewards can include tickets to a show, a bottle of high-quality wine or membership to a "club" of high-performing sales employees. This club, like a frequent-flyer status, may offer access to cruises and family vacations, as well as exclusive training programs, meet-and-greets with the founders, a parking spot in the underground car park or even a sales cup that the monthly winner can display on their desk. These rewards should be aligned with the company's culture and inclusive for all genders, age groups and nationalities.

6. **Incentivize annual upfront payments but quarterly goals**
   Creating a commission plan that differentiates between annual payment and monthly payment deals (e.g., 7.5% for monthly and 15% for annual) is a sensible way to go. Without a plan, salespeople will have no incentive to put in the extra effort needed to close deals with annual upfront payments.

Practice 66: Enabling your sales teams with the right sales tech stack

With more than 950 options, choosing the right sales tools can be a challenge. However, the right tech stack will become necessary as a company grows. It can provide a sales team with many benefits, including enhanced productivity through automation, improved key metrics (e.g., close rates, lead velocity) and better hiring and retention. A sales technology blueprint is shown in Figure 70.[288] A good overview of the B2B tool stack is provided as well by Hubsell.

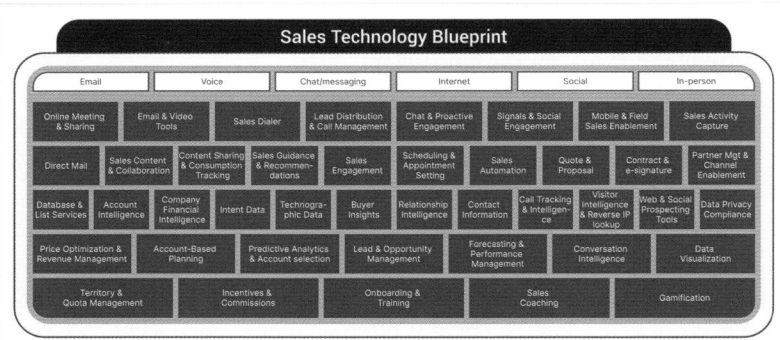

Figure 70: Sales Technology Blueprint
Source: Sales Hackers[289]

The top 5 tool categories to focus on are:

- **Lead generation and prospecting to identify, analyze and qualify promising leads.** Outbound tools usually come in three categories: data vendors, outreach solutions and a combination of the two. Data vendors either sell databases of potential customers (e.g., email lists) or perform on-demand data processing to facilitate sales development with personalized outreach. Examples of data vendors include ZoomInfo, Cognism, Vainu, LeadGenius, D&B, CDQ and Hubsell. Outreach solutions enable automated outreach and prospecting (e.g., via email or LinkedIn) and may include workflows that help a team to reach out with personalized contact sequences (e.g., email, voicemail, LinkedIn messages). Examples of workflow tools include reply.io, outreach.io, woodpecker.co, we-connect.io, hubsell.com and salesloft.com.
- **Customer relationship management (CRM) tools** are the beating heart of a sales process. Tools like Salesforce, SAP Business by Design, Microsoft Dynamics and Freshworks provide a centralized location for logging a customer's communication history and help to perform forecasting and management reporting on sales opportunities and team performance. If a company doesn't want to go with the proven flagship tools but instead prefers leaner startup solutions, they can try Pipedrive or Copper.
- **Onboarding, training and coaching sales teams** with the appropriate tool stack (e.g., Dooly, Guru).

- **Contract management, billing and accounting** to support subscription billing, tendering, invoicing, contract management and financial reporting (e.g., SORA, NetSweet, SAP Business ByDesign).
- **Customer success management** to identify any risk of churn early enough and alert teams by combining scores such as ticket volume, NPS, intensity and depth of usage of the product, with an internal tool alerting the CSM team (e.g., GainSight, ToTango).

Practice 67: Attracting and hiring a world-class sales team

Assembling a great sales team rests on five columns: first, leveraging the existing employee basis for referrals.

- **First: a referral program for new colleagues**
  A happy crew can bring in up to 50% of sales colleagues from their networks. A referral bonus of several thousand euros or dollars paid after a successful probation period is one option.
- **Second: getting the employer branding right**
  When the US state of Indiana debated introducing a law affecting the rights of LGTBQ+, Salesforce founder Marc Benioff closed the company's office in Indianapolis. This type of public statement boosts a company's reputation. Even an entertaining TikTok video by a member of senior management can help to cement a company's branding.
- **Third: going beyond the usual fishponds**
  When a company starts to develop a sales team, they may want to hire the top dogs from big sales companies that can bring large networks with them. However, when scaling up, adding more high-performers with 10+ years of experience does not bring as much ROI anymore. Now, it is time to hire young talent from other sources and train them in-house. Looking beyond industries and experience and seeking people who can understand digital buyer journeys is key here.
- **Fourth: outlining a clear career path is a booster to attract a great team**
  Business development teams are often a great way to kickstart a career and build up to an account executive position for small customers (and then enterprise customers). Another path is to assign more people management responsibilities within the business development or account management. Outlining these paths is essential during this phase.

- **Fifth: getting the hiring process right**
  A company should have an idea about its ideal sales candidate. At HubSpot, the team discovered five particular traits that allowed sales reps to interact most effectively with their B2B customers.[290] These are:
  - **Coachability:** The candidate's capacity to take in and apply coaching lessons. This can be tested during an interview with a role-playing exercise followed by self-evaluation and feedback.
  - **Curiosity and intelligence:** "Nobody has asked me that before. Now that I think about it. . ." is a perfect answer for potential customers. Sales reps who have a genuine interest in the customer and can actively listen are a great asset.
  - **Work ethic:** Behavior and energy levels during the interview and follow-ups offer insights into the candidate's work ethic. Do they want to be hired?
  - **Prior performance:** If candidates come from a large sales organization, they should have been in the top 10%. If they are from outside sales, other signs of prior success should be taken into account (e.g., excelling at sports or playing in a renowned orchestra).

Practice 68: Training and coaching a "challenger" sales team

Almost a century ago, E. K. Strong started a revolution in sales with his book *The Psychology of Selling and Advertising*. Strong claimed that selling wasn't an innate ability people were born with but a set of identifiable skills that could be learned. His manual was the precursor to modern-day sales training departments that boosted performance among sales reps. There are three types of sales techniques in use today. The **"product selling" approach**, which is considered to be a little "old school," focuses on emphasizing product features and is usually applicable only in highly commoditized markets. Another one is the **"solution selling" approach** in which sales executives diagnose customer pain points (e.g., "What keeps you up at night?") and then will attach an adapted value proposition based on that need. This relationship-focused approach often performs best with experienced salespeople who have interacted with hundreds of customers. The last one is the **"challenger"** or **"insight**

selling" approach in which the salesperson is an advisor and teacher. A typical conversation starter for this one is: "Here is what should be keeping you up at night." The challenger approach is often suitable for tech scale-ups, as they either challenge existing platforms and products or create a new product need. It is also appropriate for younger salespeople with comparatively little experience. They can leverage the insights of the company as a whole rather than being wholly dependent on their own experience. This is often the type of situation encountered when upgrading a tech startup to a scale-up. In complex B2B sales environments, one study found that almost 40% of high performers excel in "challenger sales" techniques.[291]

To assemble an effective challenger sales team, there are four building blocks that matter:

- **The right challenger story**
  It usually takes three to six months to build the story. Marketing usually leads this effort, with sales and product being closely involved. For sales, it is important to clearly map out the buyer's journey and relate each of the sales processes to a prospective buyer's step. See Practice 69 on how to develop your sales story.
- **Teach the sales managers**
  Managers should act as coaches for sales executives. The process of creating tension and constructive conflict is often something new that takes time to get used to. Companies offering challenger sales training for managers and sales reps include Challenger Inc., Corporate Visions, The RAIN Group, Richardson and Wilson Learning.
- **Training your sales executives**
  A company's sales teams need to understand how to become effective advisers and teachers. This includes **teaching** sales reps about unique perspectives on how to increase their competitiveness in their market (e.g., by reducing risk and expenses, entering new markets, or operating more efficiently). Challenger salespeople also **tailor** their message to the metrics of what individual decision-makers care about (i.e., marketing, technology or operations). They **take control** by being positively assertive without being aggressive (e.g., when refocusing on price discussions on the value of the product), and they build **tension** by challenging the customer's reasoning and subtly pushing them into the decision-making process. Training usually includes a multi-day onboarding camp with a focus on

the overall mission, tools, product and sales standards. Regular refresher training is essential, as well as periodical refresher quizzes (e.g., MindTickle). This is often supported by a learning management system (LMS) for digital training (e.g., Docebo, Kallidus, TalentLMS).

- **Coaching as additional support**
  A coach or a team manager needs to be able to work with each sales executive on refining their behavior to make them more effective. A sales rep with a low lead quantity may need coaching in prioritization to select the right leads. A sales rep who has a high number of leads but few product demo meetings may not be personalizing their approach enough. The sales team should use a consistent coaching framework, such as GROW (Goal, Reality, Options/Obstacles, Way Forward) or WOOP (Wish, Outcome, Obstacles, Plan),[292] to tackle these issues.

Practice 69: Getting your basic sales pitch in place

When Salesforce introduced its "no software" narrative in 2000, it jump-started the SaaS market and left Oracle and SAP behind. This is the blueprint for a B2B sales communications play in five acts. Successful scale-ups like Salesforce, Zuora and Drift have all used it to craft convincing sales value propositions as part of engaging pitches.[293] The five stages are:

- **Identify a major tectonic shift in the world**
  This might be the change from a single purchase to a subscription economy (Zuora) or a sharing economy (Uber or Airbnb). From mainframe computing to on-demand cloud solutions, the shift was always something Salesforce and AWS advocated for.
- **Create an enemy to rally against**
  It is necessary to drive home the point that a business can either profit from an enemy or be consumed by it. Frodo had Sauron, Harry Potter had Voldemort and Luke Skywalker had Darth Vader. Salesforce framed its "no software" story as a war against the legacy software industry rather than specific competitors. Rather than simply "purchasing a product," they invited the audience to join the war.[294]

- **Sketch out your vision of a better future**
  Note that this can be entirely independent of a company's product. For Salesforce, this vision was the 1:1 relationship with its customers and the ability to connect the "Internet of customers" with smart companies which understand them through data. Zoura painted the picture of a promising new economy based on subscriptions, with customers able to receive instant personalized fulfillment in real-time and in any location.
- **Showcase your product with all its features**
  This is how a customer will overcome the enemy. Zoura now showcases the amount of personalization that the product's customer record offers (payment history, lifetime value, customer moments, etc.) in comparison to traditional records (phone, name, etc.). Meanwhile, Salesforce now demonstrates how its customer success platform enables companies to connect with users individually via their data management platform and predictive analytics.
- **Back up your value proposition with concrete evidence**
  Salesforce is unapologetic about this. For its *dreamforce* event, the company plasters San Francisco with myriad positive quotes about their products from CEOs of Fortune 500 companies on huge billboards, while their keynotes always include customer films, stories and demos. Effective and colorful communication of central customer stories makes the B2B hero story a reality.

These five stages can also be condensed into three questions for customers to answer: "Why do I need this?," "Why do I need this now?" and "Why do I need your product?"

Qualifying and closing leads

Practice 70: Becoming rigorous with lead qualifications

Being rigorous in qualifying leads is one secret to B2B sales success. It improves sales rep productivity, forecasting accuracy and time-to-close on deals. The right qualification criteria, a disciplined pipeline and deal review process are all essential here.

The **qualification process** guides a sales team in turning potential buyers into prospects and leads. "Potential Buyers" are companies a startup has identified that are in the right regions, industries and target segment for them. "Prospects" have a pressing business need for a solution, while "Leads" are potential customers interested in their products or services. They come in two forms: marketing-qualified leads (MQLs), who provide contact details that are forwarded to your sales teams, and sales-qualified leads (SQL) (i.e., persons interested in finding a solution to their business pains).

The use of several frameworks, all with varying themes, can generate SQLs, including BANT, ANUM, CHAMP, FAINT and MEDDIC.[295] Developed by IBM, BANT (budget, authority, need, timeline) has long been the de-facto standard. In contrast, MEDDIC is especially valuable for driving up forecasting accuracy in complex B2B deals (Figure 71). The above frameworks are a good starting point, but they may not entirely fit the business case and sales reality. It is common practice to customize frameworks. HubSpot, for example, started with the BANT framework.[296]

MEDDIC

Metrics

Does our solution create tangible economic benefits compared to a competitor (e.g. return on investment within three months, 5 hours saved per person per week)?

Economic Buyer

Have you identified the decision-maker, i.e. the person with the purchasing power to close the deal?

Decision Criteria

What are the top factors used by the potential customer to make purchasing decisions (e.g. price, essential features, service levels)?

Decision Process

What are the key steps that will ultimately lead to the approval of the contract (e.g. stakeholders, timelines)?

Pain Identifier

What is the exact business pain and how does our solution alleviate it (e.g. loss of time/money, lack of compliance)?

Champion

Is there someone associated with the potential customers who can advocate for us?

GPCT

Goals

Are the business goals of the prospect company well defined ("SMART") and the implications of (not) reaching the goals clear?

Plan

Does our product really meet the customer's needs and is there a clear plan to reach the goal?

Challenges

What are the potential problems in the execution of the plan and possible workarounds (right staff, budget and infrastructure)?

Timeline

Is a date set by which the goal must be achieved?

Figure 71: MEDDIC and GPCT

Whatever framework is chosen, it is necessary to employ different meeting types to ensure that it is applied properly:

- A **bimonthly pipeline review** focuses on ensuring high "pipeline integrity" (i.e., the right number of leads at the right stage). Are there enough prospects at the top of the sales funnel to ensure the sales reps have a sufficient early-stage pipeline to achieve the monthly/quarterly sales goals?

- A **weekly deal review or sales forecast meeting** helps sales reps win deals. It also puts sales reps on the spot by focusing on questions like: What could go wrong with this deal? What happens to customers if they don't close the deal with us? What is the specific business pain? What is the business case for buying our solution? The focus should be on the middle to bottom of the sales funnel or later-stage deals. Senior management (VP of Sales, CRO) is often involved here.

Practice 71: Enabling your sales teams to close leads

The favorite song of any good salesperson? It would have to be *The Winner Takes It All*, of course. When deals are almost closed, the win rate is what counts. This is what enables "closers" (account managers and pre-sales teams) to frequently emerge victorious in competitive deals. Three elements give the "closers" the extra edge:

- **Position the product on quality-controlled B2B peer review & rating platforms**
  Once exclusive to B2C, these platforms are now firmly part of the B2B world and work to verify, check and rigorously vet reviews to ensure that there is no vendor bias or hidden agenda. The most relevant platforms are G2 Crowd, Clutch.co, Trustradius, IT Central Station, Trustpilot Business, Capterra and Gartner Peer Insights. Encouraging customers to leave a review on these sites is of the essence (some B2B companies even ask for a review directly after a successful service call).

- **Have competitive battlecards ready**
  A company will be asked how they measure up to the competition. The SaaS company Signavio puts "competitive battle cards" up the sleeves of its sales teams: one slide per competitor with a section on "What they say" (i.e., the competitor's supposed USP), and a section on "What we say," which refutes the competitor's argument.

The battle cards end with a slide that focuses the customer's attention on a signature strength of the product (which the competition doesn't have).

- **Put a discount policy in place**
Discounts are the most substantial marketing investment for the majority of companies in B2B industries.[297] It is often helpful to start with a "value-based pricing" approach, which revolves around understanding the value created by a product for a customer (e.g., savings per year) and then splitting this value accordingly (see Practice 59). A company can then provide discounts to award customer behavior that creates value for it. Forms of value-based discounting include multi-annual contracts, the provision of data to the business in order to benefit the ongoing product design and evolution of the service and case studies or testimonials to attract potential new customers. Discounts are also essential for winning tenders and are typically leveraged by large customers in markets with strong competition. Also, it is important to remember that for larger customers who have procurement teams of their own it is important to factor in a double discount: one on the list price so the deal champion is satisfied and 10–20% for the procurement team, which receives a bonus for the discount that it provides.

Retaining and "farming" customers

Practice 72: Measuring customer health to predict and prevent customer churn

Want to earn more with the existing customer base year on year even after attrition? If so, taking customer success management seriously matters. Sales are the beginning of a relationship, and customer success management deepens it. Of a company's first 10 hires, one should be a CSM specialist. After all, a great product does NOT automatically create successful customers. If a startup is approaching the growth phase and they don't have a customer success manager, they are missing out on an invaluable driver of churn prevention and advocacy for additional revenue. CSMs can help customers make the best decisions on which applications to employ on their platforms or identify ways for professional service specialists to improve customer engagement.

CSM typically consists of three primary building blocks: customer success managers, a technical support team to troubleshoot customer issues and a professional service team, which may include a variety of specialists ranging from technical architects to engagement managers. At the heart of customer success teams are the CS managers, who are dedicated to supporting individual customers (usually for free). They schedule regular meetings, invite customers to industry events, make sure the product is used to a customer's complete satisfaction and monitor customer health scores. Aiming to have approximately one CS manager per USD 2 million annual recurring revenue is often good advice, though a company may wish to over-invest in the early stages.[298]

CSMs should create customer health scores to detect churn risk (i.e., the probability that a customer will leave). These scores are usually presented as a traffic light, with green being healthy and red indicating an urgent need for action. A typical customer health score aggregates five date sources:[299]

1. **Product usage and adoption:** Are daily log-ins increasing? Is a high percentage of the features being used? How many teams and departments does your product impact?
2. **License utilization:** Are most of the licenses being utilized? Are key renewal dates coming up?
3. **Business results:** Is the customer getting the promised business value?
4. **Engagement:** Are we resolving billing issues and support questions quickly? Do we have regular customer success engagement calls? Do we have low unsubscription rates from marketing offers (e.g., newsletters)? Is our internal sponsor the same person and is he or she responsive to our communications?
5. **Advocacy:** Is the customer willing to reference and advocate for us? Is the Net Promoter Score of the customer's key users above average and increasing?

CSM prediction models need to be continuously validated. A strong model would result in at least 90% of customers having red customer health scores at the week when they leave the company. A strong model would as well only create up to 20% false alarms (i.e., renewals while on red status) (see the tool provider Totango for a best-in-class approach).

Recommended publications:

- Matt Dixon and Brent Adamson (2013). *The Challenger Sale: How to Take Control of the Customer Conversations.*
- Jacco van der Kooij and Fernando Pizarro (2018*). Blueprints for a SaaS Sales Organization.*
- Jacco van der Kooij (2018). *SaaS Sales Method for Account Executives: How to Win Customers.*
- Mark Roberge (2015). *The Sales Acceleration Formula: Using Data, Technology, and Inbound Selling to Go from $0 to $100 Million.*
- Mark Roberge (2021). *The Science of Scaling.*
- Aaron Ross and Jason Lemkin (2019). *From Impossible to Inevitable: How SaaS and Other Hyper-Growth Companies Create Predictable Revenue.*
- Aaron Ross and Marylou Tyler (2011). *Predictable Revenue: Turn Your Business into a Sales Machine with the $100 Million Best Practices of Salesforce.com.*

Watch our video on the six key pitfalls to avoid in your B2B sales function by scanning the QR code or following this link: https://youtube/XeQK6TsNHWA.

How to set a B2B sales team that can scale? Watch our video by scanning the QR code or following this link: https://youtube/P9acQ1zU6f4.

Definitions

- **Annual recurring revenue**: a metric used by subscription-based businesses for measuring the amount of revenue that will be generated on a yearly basis.
- **Challenger selling**: this sales approach emphasizes the importance of sales reps teaching, guiding, challenging and (constructively) pushing customers during the sales process based on unique insights – rather than focusing on relationship building as emphasized in the solution selling approach.
- **Churn**: a measure of the rate at which customers/users stop interacting or transacting with a product or service.
- **Commission**: additional compensation paid to salespeople based on their sales performance, which is used to incentivize sales teams.
- **CRM (Customer Relationship Management)**: the strategy, technology and processes involved in organizing interactions with prospects, leads and customers to maximize customer acquisition, retention and success.
- **Customer health**: a metric constructed by sales teams for assessing the state of a customer's attitude toward the company, which can be used in turn to evaluate the likelihood of growth, renewal or churn.

- **Customer success**: a proactive, relationship-based business strategy where a company strives to meet the goals and needs of customers that make use of the company's products or services and continuously adjusts its customer handling to ensure high rates of customer satisfaction.
- **Marketing-qualified leads (MQLs)**: a lead (prospective customer) with a certain probability of becoming a customer based on an analysis of the interactions with that company's marketing content (e.g., a visit to a price page on a website).
- **Net Promoter Score**: a measure of customer satisfaction and loyalty, ranging from −100 to +100, which is assessed by asking customers how likely they are to recommend a product/service/business to another person.
- **Net revenue retention**: a measure of the percentage of recurring revenue that is retained from one time period (monthly, annual) to the next.
- **On-target earnings**: the total annual compensation received by a sales employee if they achieve 100% of their sales goals.
- **Opportunity**: a potential customer that is in the process of evaluating the benefits of a product or service based on a customized product demo and with an internal "champion" on the buyer side who is convinced that the solution is a potential fit.
- **Pipeline coverage**: a measure of the potential value of a sales pipeline relative to the overall sales target; for example, if a sales pipeline has a potential value of USD 1 million and the overall sales target is USD 250,000, pipeline coverage is 4x.
- **Pipeline**: a visualization of where leads are within the sales cycle that can be used to estimate how many sales are expected to close during a given timeframe.
- **Product selling**: this sales approach is often pursued in response to requests for proposals and focuses on delivering quality products at a good price. It is often viewed as the more transactional and volume-based approach, with sellers differentiating primarily based on price.
- **Prospecting**: often this is the first step in a sales process. Prospecting involves the identification of and initial outreach to potential customers (prospects) by a sales team.
- **Sales cycle**: the time required from the seller's initial contact with a prospect to closing the deal (e.g., signing a contract).

- **Sales development**: the processes that form the early stages of the sales cycle: identifying, connecting with and qualifying leads.
- **Sales-accepted leads (SALs)**: a lead (prospective customer) that has satisfied the qualification criteria set out by the sales team and is accepted by the sales team as a potential customer to approach.
- **Sales-qualified leads (SQLs)**: a lead (prospective customer) with a clearly identified business problem that might be solved by the company's products and services – a sales team usually has several interactions with an SQL.
- **Solution selling**: this sales approach focuses on a deep understanding of customers' business problems and the provision of insights to solve these problems – the supplier is viewed more as a trusted advisor rather than someone who fulfills purchase orders. This approach often requires substantial expertise to understand and react flexibly to the customers' needs.

9   Service Operations Excellence

Resolving customer inquiries while delivering the wow factor

With Dr. Nicola Glusac

Key pitfalls to avoid for scale-up builders

- **Failing to put customer experience as one of the top priorities of the executive team.**
  Some operations functions focus purely on resolving customer issues caused somewhere else within the organization. The operations teams should be responsible for this, but there also needs to be an internal advocate of customer experience across all levels, thereby turning the customer experience into the lifeblood pumping through the heart of the business. Everyone in the company needs to view exceptional customer experience as one of their primary goals – on par with growth, profit, revenue and cost savings.
- **Relegating customer service to a topic of secondary importance compared to the product.**
  Some companies fail to understand that customers will make no distinction between product and service. In competitive markets in particular, where it is not possible to differentiate by product alone, service plays an increasingly pivotal role when it comes to creating an outstanding customer experience.
- **Underinvesting in the "voice of the customer."**
  Some operations teams fail to install a customer feedback routine between the customer service and the product teams. This includes quantitative analyses of top contact reasons and a daily contact spike analysis as an early warning system for operational risks.
- **Failing to install guardrails regarding measurement criteria and driving customer experience in the day-to-day business.**
  Some businesses do not measure customer experience on a sufficiently granular level. It is especially important to measure Net Promoter Scores along each customer journey (e.g., onboarding, buying product X) as something more than an overall company metric (see Practice 73).
- **Underinvesting in preventing unnecessary contacts in the first place.**
  Some service operations teams overemphasize customer service, but they insufficiently invest in solving the root causes of contacts before problems arise, as well as in pushing self-service for transactional cus-

tomer journeys (e.g., paying a bill). To remediate this, it often helps to involve operations early on in the product development process by installing a "polluter pays principle" and monitoring technical incidents in real-time (see Practices 73 and 76).

- **Investing too late in ensuring sufficient availability of customer service in times of "hypergrowth."**
Often, the customer base will grow faster than the company can recruit in-house service colleagues. Some operations teams fail to understand that sufficient availability tends to come from onboarding external contact centers (i.e., partners which often can scale faster than you). Installing a "hybrid" operating model early can pay off in these cases (see Practice 78).
- **Failing to understand the relevance of process excellence.**
Many startups treat problems with processes as "edge cases," and they do not build up their capabilities to develop smooth processes with methods like Lean Six Sigma quickly enough (see Practice 80).

Banking as a service, music as a service, transport as a service and even gaming as a service: a decade ago, it would have taken years to launch these types of consumer businesses. Today, it can be done with the touch of a button. Building a great tech product is no longer enough. To boost a growth trajectory, a company needs to excel both with its products *and* its service experience. And what is the key to delivering great service consistently? It is the service operations teams. Excellent service operations are the domain of scale-ups without a supply chain: processing 100,000+ incoming customer inquiries by chat, phone or email per week.

What is being solved for when building a service operation? A high (Service) Net Promoter Score can be delivered with best-in-class costs per customer. To achieve this, it is often helpful to work toward three key objectives: **reducing unnecessary contacts by avoiding transactional contacts** and investing in self-service wherever possible, as well as delivering a great **live service experience** while achieving a **competitive cost per contact** (Figure 72).

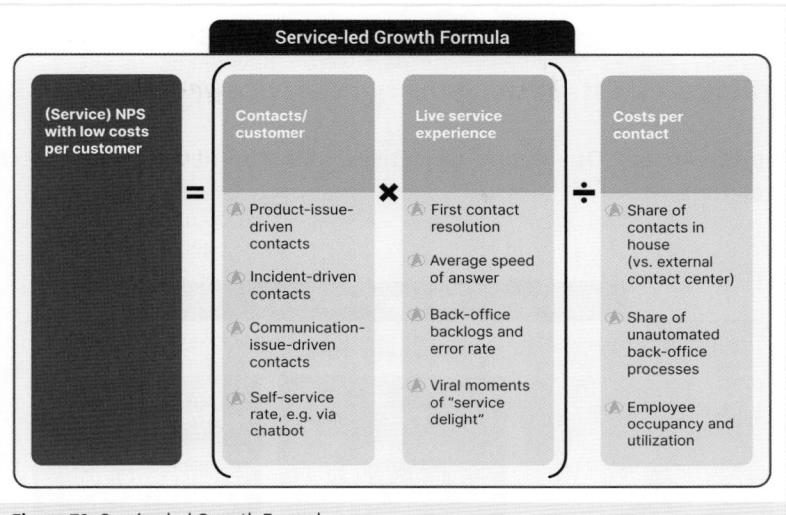

Figure 72: Service-led Growth Formula

The most important principle for the operations team is to be the strongest internal advocate for customer experience. Every leader in the company needs to have the mindset of a Chief Customer Officer, and customer experience needs to be a primary goal – on par with growth revenue, profit or cost savings. Service operations can only become a true source of a competitive advantage if customer experience objectives, like Net Promoter Score (NPS), are anchored in the top company key results. After all, companies with a strong NPS grow on average twice as much as companies with median NPS scores.[300] If startups don't advocate for this kind of thinking with all senior leaders, operations will always sit on "no news is good news" tasks with the unthankful challenge to catch problems caused by other departments.

The table in the next practice (Figure 73) shows the typical OKRs of a service operations division.

OKRs

Practice 73: Establishing the right service operations OKRs

Typical Annual Operations Objectives and Key Results for *FinTech* Scale-ups

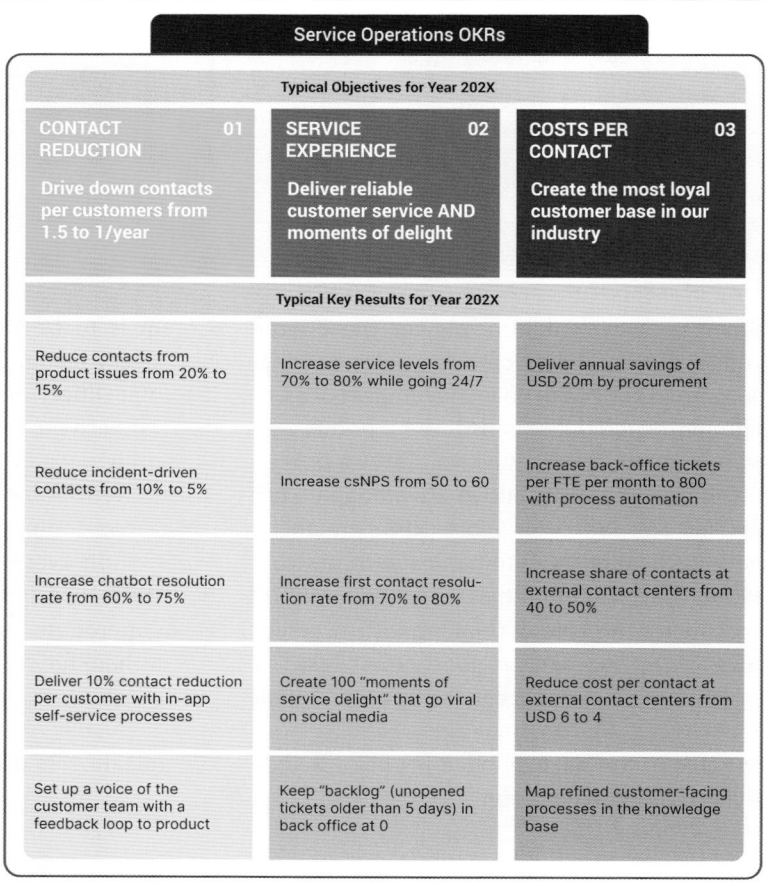

Figure 73: Service Operations OKRs: FinTech

Let's look at each objective in more detail.

O1. Contact reduction: Are you avoiding unnecessary contacts? ("Best service is no service") Nobody likes contacting Amazon when a delivery goes missing, Netflix about a monthly payment or N26 to figure out how to download an account statement. B2C customers hate having to contact a company as part of a "routine" customer journey when products or services aren't working the way they should. The more often a customer needs to contact a company, the lower their NPS will be. In one direct bank we studied, customers who contacted a company at least once within one year were 20% less satisfied and 20% more likely to stop using its services. This is common across industries. Customer loyalty scores, such as share of wallet or repurchase rates, are four times more likely to be negatively affected if the customer has to contact a company even once.[301] In other words: the best service is no service. Eliminating the root causes behind customer contact issues should be the cornerstone of a service excellence strategy. These causes tend to be linked either to the product, processes or communication.

Typical key results here include reducing the share of *product-related* contacts (e.g., a faulty payment app feature), *incident-driven* contacts (e.g., an unavailable webpage), *communication-driven* contacts (e.g., promised something on the website which is not true, misleading descriptions) and creating a high share of self-service shares (e.g., chatbot resolution rate). Together, these measures will drive down the number of live contacts per customer. As most of these contacts are issue-driven, this will not only increase NPS, but it will also drive down the costs per customer.

Note: Many of these results can only be delivered if the customer experience is anchored among the top company goals and if particular product and technology teams invest in developer capacity to drive down unnecessary contacts in the first place.

O2. Service experience: Is your live service able to resolve issues effectively? When PayPal started to hit product-market fit back in its early days, the company found itself overwhelmed with customer inquiries. Their response? They stopped answering the phone to focus on improving the product. While this might work at an early scale-up phase, the customer experience should be the focus as a startup progresses into more sustained growth phases. Failure to do so can cause a brand to be hit hard. They may even fall foul of the regulator. This is particularly relevant in so-called "emotive customer journeys," which are usually connected to a dispute, a sale or an urgent need. Say a FinTech customer lost her wallet abroad while traveling and can't access her funds. This type of situation calls for a live service team to be available to resolve the issue at hand. Or: a customer needs to claim back money due to an unauthorized payment. A stellar back-office needs to resolve the issue quickly, so the front-facing customer service team can provide a rapid answer. While the live service teams have an opportunity to delight customers in these types of situations (see Practice 80), routine journeys (e.g., downloading a bank statement) call for automation and self-service (Practice 77).

Typical key results here include "service levels" per channel (i.e., answering 80% of all calls/emails within 20 seconds on average) with 80% of the inquiries being solved in the first contact and increased Customer Service NPS or "agent satisfaction" (ASAT) levels. The speed of the back-office also matters: active open tickets older than 7 days ("backlog") is one indicator to track.

O3. Costs: Are you relentlessly driving down your costs per contact?
While an operations team needs to fuel growth by delivering a great customer experience, it should also contribute to strong unit economics by driving down the costs per contact and customer. Assembling a strong procurement team to negotiate contracts with service suppliers (e.g., external contact centers) almost always pays off. Measuring process efficiency in all operations departments and deploying operational excellence teams to refine your processes using Lean Six Sigma–style approaches is of the essence, too. **Typical key results** here include achieving annual savings via contract renegotiations, increasing the share of contacts taken by (offshore) external contact centers, driving up the utilization and occupancy in your in-house service centers and processing efficiency metrics, such as "tickets closed per full-time employee."

Organizational chart and roles

Practice 74: Defining the roles & responsibilities for a service operations function

Service operations functions can be built around a customer-facing front end (customer service), a supporting back end (back-office) and functions that enable a consistently superior customer experience (Figure 74). Customer contacts are either routed to the in-house or the external contact center. If the cases require more in-depth checks (e.g., chargebacks in a bank), they can be routed to the back-office, which resolves the issue and answers directly to the customer, or they forward their findings to the front-office. All functions should have a global footprint (i.e., they should be available and accessible for different countries and in different languages). An alternative setup would be to create relatively autonomous teams for certain customer groups with all the resources they need to resolve customer inquiries from both the front and back-office (see Practice 78).

Organizational blueprint of a typical B2C service operations division

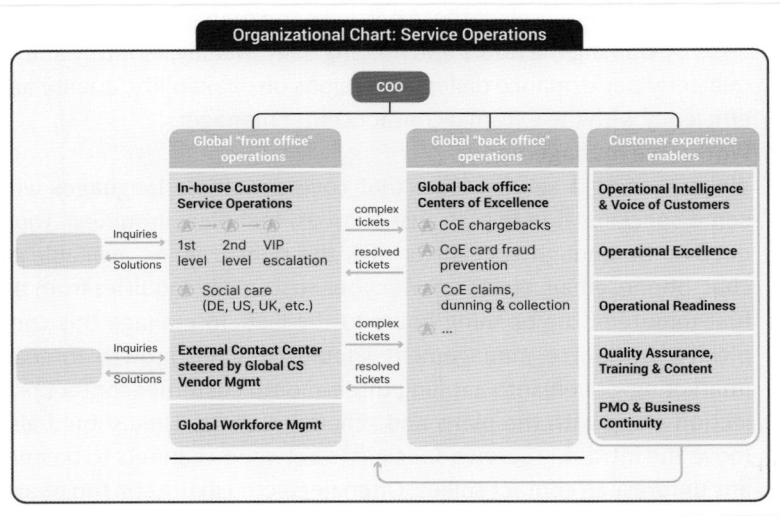

Figure 74: Organizational Chart: Service Operations

Let's dig deeper into what each of these functions does:

- **In-house customer service operations**

  This unit directly handles customer inquiries and is typically divided into teams of 12–15 service specialists with one team lead. Depending on the size of a customer base, a company may have one or more teams per language or market. It is essential to cover multiple levels of complexity and escalation. At the minimum, a company needs a "second-level" team that assists with more complex inquiries (e.g., a technical team). A complaints/VIP team may cover those contacts when the "second level" cannot handle any more. This is usually required for very important customers (like journalists or investors) and those with highly complex or emotional problems that are posted publicly. Social media community managers who are responsible for replying to public posts on Facebook, Instagram or Twitter are often part of this unit, too.

- **Vendor management**

  In a fast-growing scale-up, keeping costs competitive is feasible only if you turn to external contact centers or specialized back offices. Near-shore or off-shore locations can be affordable sources of extra staff and provide flexibility. The in-house centers can be used to set quality standards and your external partners to ensure efficiency and flexibility while driving down costs. The vendor management team will select these partners and manage them on a daily basis by walking the floors and holding daily, weekly, monthly and/or quarterly performance dialogue sessions on availability, quality and efficiency with the external contact center managers.

- **Workforce management**

  When running a service team that covers multiple languages with some specialization (e.g., transaction vs. technical inquiries), there need to be enough specialists with the right training available on chat, phone, email, etc. to answer your customers' inquiries from the first minute of the opening hours to the last. To manage this complexity, workforce management should turn the growth forecast (marketing-driven) into a rolling three-month customer contact projection along with the plans and schedules shifts. They should also move the intra-day service specialists between channels to balance any unforeseen contact spikes. Often neglected in the startup phase, this team may be the difference between delivering a best-in-class cost per contact of USD 3–5 and a cost that is twice as much.

- **Back-office**

  Not all inquiries can be solved in real-time with the customer. Your back-office should specialize in tasks that take longer and require more in-depth knowledge. For example, checking chargeback requests, solving credit card fraud requests and requesting unpaid fees from customers are common inquiries for a back-office in Fin-Techs. Ideally, this team should be structured around Centers of Excellence that focus on key customer journeys (see Practices 11, 83). It can be beneficial to have the front-end and back-end teams share one (virtual) room, as this provides consistent customer communication and avoids friction when handing over cases.

- **Operational Intelligence (OI) & voice of the customer**

  These are a company's data devotees. This small team (2–3 FTEs) creates real-time performance dashboards per market and per customer journey by often monitoring availability, quality interactions, productivity, customer satisfaction and employee happiness. The OI team should work with a company-wide central data team and a business analyst from each operations department. OI should be performing quantitative analyses of top contact reasons as part of the customer feedback routine between customer service and the product teams. They should also put a daily contact spike analysis in place as an early warning system for operational risks. If an overseen spike in contacts is happening (e.g., ATM issue in Spain), this system alerts key leaders to enable a fast resolution.

- **Operational excellence**

  This team keeps processes optimized, well documented and following the standard. While they are often introduced too late in scale-ups, this team is critical for improving customer satisfaction and efficiency metrics. They are usually experts in Lean Six Sigma–style process optimization and can handle ISO 9001 certification, as well as oversee maps of key processes (see Practice 80).

- **Operational readiness**

  Ongoing product launches in new markets call for a small team (2–3 FTEs) to coordinate as "vanguards" of operational readiness between operations, product and marketing. Is this company trying to launch FinTech services in France? The operational readiness colleagues will be the ones making sure all the French service specialists are well trained, the FAQs on your website are updated and internal communications to all relevant teams are accurate and issued on time, etc. They usually organize daily or weekly meetings with all relevant stakeholders and support operations in a new country or for a new product in the first 8–12 weeks after launch. After that, they will hand it over to the "business as usual" teams, so they can focus on the next launch.

- **Content, quality, training and coaching**
  These colleagues update a company's knowledge base, customer-facing wording, text modules for written communication, FAQs/support center, video tutorials, chatbot and in-app communication on an ongoing basis. They are also the ones who set quality standards (e.g., for customer verification, adherence to processes), organize onboarding and refresher training for new products and prepare regular knowledge quizzes. The coaching team should deploy one coach per service team and deliver one to five coaching sessions per service specialist per month (depending on performance levels).
- **Project management office (PMO) & business continuity**
  Is a company trying to onboard a new contact center, relaunch an internal knowledge base or launch a messenger channel? They will need to set up a PMO with 2–3 FTEs. This point of contact can help coordinate key initiatives, facilitate decision-making and make sure that they are carried out as part of weekly meetings.

Note: Procurement teams often also collaborate closely with Operations and are often overseen by the COO.

Practice 75: Scaling the right service operations roles at the right time

While a startup phase will be overseen by a small team of operations generalists, the early growth phase calls for the operations teams to specialize.

- First, specific markets and languages should be covered by **specialized customer service teams**. This includes 2nd-level escalation teams, with a VIP team for complex cases, and service colleagues who specialize in working with customer journey groups of varying complexity (e.g., in a FinTech this could be onboarding, payment and new products).

- Second, a **readiness team** will need to be assembled to coordinate the operations surrounding a product and market launch. This is the operational backbone for market expansion.
- Third, a **workforce management team** that plans and schedules your front-office will need to be created. They also will be in charge of regularly adding new languages and specializations.
- Fourth, an **operational intelligence** team should be fully staffed at the latest in the early growth phase. They will deliver real-time performance dashboards and help to track key metrics continuously.
- Fifth, during later growth stages, investment in the service capacity at scale can occur by expanding the pool of external contact centers and back-office providers. This is the task of the **vendor management team**, which should work with the quality assurance team to build up a network of external partners.
- Sixth, the later growth stages are also the latest point in time to invest in **operational excellence** in order to streamline all processes (see Practice 80) and establish a **project management office** to coordinate any upgrade initiatives (e.g., integrating new tools, ramping up partners) in order to take the weight off of the specialist teams.

Now that the organizational structure is in place, it's time to look at the service operations practices. In the scale-up phase, three types of practices have become particularly relevant: **preventing (transactional) contacts**, **deflecting customer requests** to self-service and enabling the live service team to **resolve customer inquiries** while creating moments of service delight (see Figure 75).

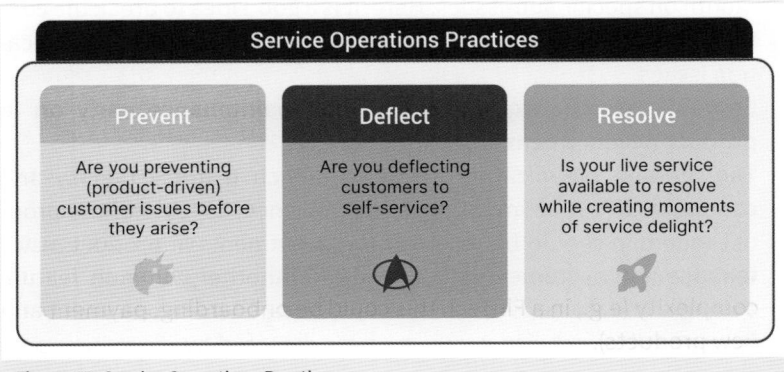

Figure 75: Service Operations Practices

Preventing contacts

Practice 76: Preventing unnecessary contacts in the first place

How often have you called Netflix, Amazon or Google? Great customer experience is driven by a product that works intuitively and does not require the customers to contact the company. Hence, eliminating issues before they even occur is a cornerstone to an industry-leading customer experience. The more often a customer needs to contact a company, the lower its Net Promoter Score will be. Around 80% of contacts stem from outside the service organization. They are usually based on a mix of these three different issues: **product issues** (e.g., a cloud service pro-vider is down and an app goes offline), **process issues** (e.g., a customer has trouble changing their address online), **communication issues** (e.g., the marketing team issues a confusing email or the operations teams communicate inconsistently). Working together across departments to prevent these issues reduces the churn rate and improves the NPS. It also saves on costs, with a company typically paying between USD 3–8 per customer contact.

Measures to put in place to work toward having as few unnecessary con-tacts as possible:
- **Regular and precise reporting on contact reasons**
This includes the top 10 contact reasons overall, the top 10 per country, their frequency in each case, top quotes from satisfied and dissatisfied customers and ideally a "qualitative" deep dive every month on specific sub-issues. Here, it is a good idea to break the con-tacts down into those driven by process, product and communica-tion issues.
- **Embed customer experience/product maintenance early on in product development**
The product organization needs to launch features quickly and continuously WHILE investing in maintenance; 10–20% of the prod-uct roadmap should be reserved for investments in product main-tenance and customer issue resolution. Another common feature among some startups isa "bug duty quarter", where one tech team is responsible for&xing product issues detected by customers on a rolling basis.

- **Follow the "polluter pays principle"**
  Contacts should be allocated to the owner within the executive team (e.g., a rise in delivery-related contacts would be addressed by the COO or VP Delivery). Product-driven contacts should be allocated to the product profit and loss statements owned by the specific product owners. This encourages stakeholders to promptly resolve the issue and avoid future cases.
- **Monitor technical incidents in real-time**
  This includes monitoring of the core "uptime" KPIs, which refer to the time your website or app is available to the customers with no technical issues. If a customer cannot log into their online bank account due to a traceable technical error, these minutes will not count toward "uptime," which is usually expressed in the form of many "9s" (e.g., 99.99999%). An incident management framework (incident detection, investigation, priority classification & escalation) is also helpful here.

Deflecting contacts

Practice 77: Deflecting transactional contacts to an automated self-help

Investment in automation or self-service options while having "breakout" options for live assistance can vastly reduce the contact volume for routine cases. For example, the communication startup Doodle invested heavily in automation and self-service in 2018 by integrating a machine learning (ML) based answer bot for editing tickets automatically, improving their ML-based and self-help guide for key customer journeys and focusing on automated one-touch tickets (i.e., queries that can be clarified with a single contact). This dramatically improved the response time from 17 hours in 2018 to 6.5, while also boosting CSAT from 90 to 95. Another example: the fintech Revolut deployed the chatbot Rita to solve transactional tasks such as downloading bank statements or reordering debit cards, thereby cutting a substantial share of unnecessary contacts. When the fintech N26 observed that many customers asked to have their money transferred back to them, for instance due to an unauthorised transaction, they developed an in-app feature enabling customers to request chargebacks with one click.

These types of self-service features boost customer experience while-cutting costs. In fast-growing companies, self-service channels should be the starting point for customers when it comes to providing a strong customer experience and keeping costs manageable. Web FAQs, self-service videos and interactive voice recognition (IVR) are good practices that have the potential to solve 3–7% of incoming contacts. Structuring these channels according to key customer episodes, enabling them to be found online easily and including visible routing options to live channels is one way to do this. A company that primarily receives simple transactional requests can use chatbots and website or in-app self-service features to potentially resolve up to 60% of (routine) contacts. If a company believes the chatbot could be a competitive advantage and drives customer delight, it can be an advantage to develop it in-house, potentially by relying on open-source software (e.g., RASA). If the number of user intents (i.e., different types of customer requests) are above 50, a machine-learning-based chatbot is of the essence. Refraining from choosing purely rule-based chatbots is often helpful, as the underlying decision trees will keep needing to be adjusted as the product portfolio grows. Voicebots are becoming increasingly popular, especially those that speak in English. Major banks such as Bank of America (Erica) and Capital One (Alexa) already rely on them.

Resolving contacts

Practice 78: Investing in a hybrid operating model and specialization to ensure availability at all times

Customers expect to be able to reach a helpful service colleague whenever they need it. To be able to provide this, it is often helpful to put in place two elements:

- **Establishing hybrid operating models to ensure availability efficiently**
  This combines in-house and external contact centers under a hybrid operating model to handle peaks. While the in-house center acts as a quality benchmark and takes on more complex cases, the external partners provide cost-efficiency and flexibility. Nearshoring or offshoring contact centers to countries in Eastern Europe, South America or Asia often provides a good balance between lower labor

costs and a well-educated workforce. For a 1000-person operation, three partners are a good benchmark (one leaves you too dependent, while five may be too complex to manage). Opting for a mix of global contact centers (e.g., Concentrix, Sykes, Majorel, Webhelp) and having some that specialize in your specific industry is often helpful.

- **Establishing specialization with a focus on market, skill and escalation**
  Having several contact center teams could improve customer satisfaction and first contact resolution by 3–5% through specialization. For a basic international setup, specialization should be considered along target markets, languages and specific tasks (e.g., technically complex queries). Say a UK customer has an onboarding issue: they should be served by a different specialist than a UK customer who has a technical problem. An 80/20 split is a good rule of thumb, with a company's reps applying their specialization 80% of the time while handling all other customer inquiries for the remaining 20%. With this split, they will remain flexible on all types of contacts as required, but they will also become experts in "their" specialization. Specialized escalation teams are also important when dealing with "edge cases" or customers who fall outside the established digital paths (e.g., a UK customer with an Indian passport loses her phone in the US). Such customers have the potential to create long "contact chains," which can be publicly embarrassing for rapidly growing companies and is why specialist teams – consisting of second-level and VIP customer teams at the minimum – should quickly take care of such cases. Some scale-ups have additional "SWAT teams" in reserve, too, which customers can contact directly via a dedicated email address while taking advantage of a return-to-rep policy.

Practice 79: Resolving customer inquiries with autonomous teams and close-knit performance management

A live service team's quality is measured by its customer experience scores and the degree to which it can resolve cases during the first contact. Boosting these quality scores calls for maximum team autonomy while following a strict performance management regime and includes the following two features:

- **Harnessing the power of self-organized teams**
  When service teams combine the right expertise, information, processes and authority, they will serve "their" customers exceptionally well without the need for intervention. Under the Team of Experts model (TEX), T-Mobile was able to cut service costs by 13%, boost its NPS by 50% and reduce attrition and absenteeism by 50% in three years. Its self-organized teams of ~50 colleagues served customers in a specific region, with a focus on loyalty and reinforcing relationships rather than contact handling time. These teams are run as mini-companies, co-located in one spot, and are encouraged to collaborate and resolve customer issues as they see fit. The cross-functional teams include reps, a team lead, dedicated coaches, technology specialists for more complex inquiries and a resource manager responsible for workforce planning.[302]
- **Pursuing close-knit performance management**
  This enables the early detection of teams that aren't living up to customer expectations. Key metrics here include volume (e.g., tickets per customer journey), stability (e.g., incidents), availability (e.g., average speed of answer), quality interactions (e.g., FCR, CSAT, NPS), productivity (e.g., AHT, utilization, cost/contact), back-end performance (e.g., backlogs) and employee happiness (e.g., sickness, attrition). All data should be viewed per market and customer journey. Weekly performance reviews by the service operations management should be complemented by monthly performance reviews at C-level. The Operational Intelligence team can be in the driver's seat to set this up.

Practice 80: Investing in Lean Six Sigma processes while giving teams enough room to create moments of service delight

An outstanding service experience rests on process rigor *and* enough room for service colleagues to break rules and delight customers.

As the first element, becoming **proficient in Lean Six Sigma processes** is often a good starting point. Lean Six Sigma is about defining and delivering processes, so customers consistently receive quality answers with minimum deviation regardless of the service rep. To embrace Lean Six Sigma, a map of customer-facing processes should first be kept updated (some companies rely on ISO 9001 certification for proper documentation). In a second step, "process owners" from the management team should be assigned. They should also be supported by junior "process champions" and together are responsible to keep key processes up to date. Has the company launched a new customer verification method? Process owners and champions would then check all new possibilities to verify customers and would develop verification options for "edge cases" (e.g., a customer with a UK passport living in the US). They would also turn these new processes into knowledge base articles so that the front-office colleagues can handle all types of verification issues with ease. The operational excellence team performs and coaches to teach process owners and champions how to map, optimize and refine processes. Lastly, this team should deploy a simple workflow tool, ideally decision-tree-based, to guide the front- and back-office colleagues as they resolve customer cases.

While "process proficiency" with Lean Six Sigma is necessary for a great service experience, a company needs to allow their front- and back-office colleagues to **occasionally break the rules to create moments of service delight**. The Brazilian FinTech Nubank relies on its customer service reps – or Xpeers, as they are known – to go off-script, whether by sending customers handwritten notes, gift boxes or even a snapback cap. The scale-up Dollar Shave Club has a budget for customer service agents to go off-script and wow the customer: when a new customer joked to the service team about the Dollar Shave Club being like a family, the team sent them a Godfather DVD set. In a similar vein, when seven-year-old Luka Apps lost his Ninjago toys in a supermarket and wrote a letter to the Lego Group in Denmark, the company responded by sending him Ninjago figures and a story from the Ninjajo universe. Allocating extra budgets and the time to allow customer service reps to go off-script for these experiences is essential. Doing this at scale is prohibitive in terms of cost, but measuring the number of occasional experiences that go viral on social media will boost a startup's reputation for excellent customer experience.

Practice 81: Investing in a loosely coupled, yet highly integrated suite of service tools

Letting a company's service colleagues work without proper tools is like traveling to the moon in a ski suit. Most companies face the following choice when it comes to service tools: they can either buy a platform already equipped with tools (the "big bang" approach), or they can actively choose tools and integrate them into a micro-service architecture. The latter is usually the better choice for scale-ups, as it enables a start-up to cherry-pick from the market without being reliant on one supplier. There are tools that help to route contacts from customers through multiple channels to the service colleagues (e.g., Genesys, Glia) – see 01 and 02 in Figure 76. And there are at least six "agent support tools" that enable fast and reliable issue resolution: a customer relationship management software connected to internal databases (e.g., Salesforce, Zendesk, Pegasystems); a rule-based routing tool that redirects contacts from different channels to specialized queues – sometimes part of a CRM (e.g., Twilio, Sinch, Plivo); an internal knowledge base facilitating consistent external communication (e.g., LucidCX, Unimyra); a workforce management tool for scheduling, shift planning and intra-day management (e.g., erint, NICE, Aspect, and Teleopti); a learning management system that facilitates regular training and quizzes (e.g., SAP Success factors, Tovuti, Cornerstone OnDemand); and a real-time recommendation engine that proposes the next best action (NBA) to take (e.g., Pega, Algonomy). For an overview, see 03 in Figure 76.

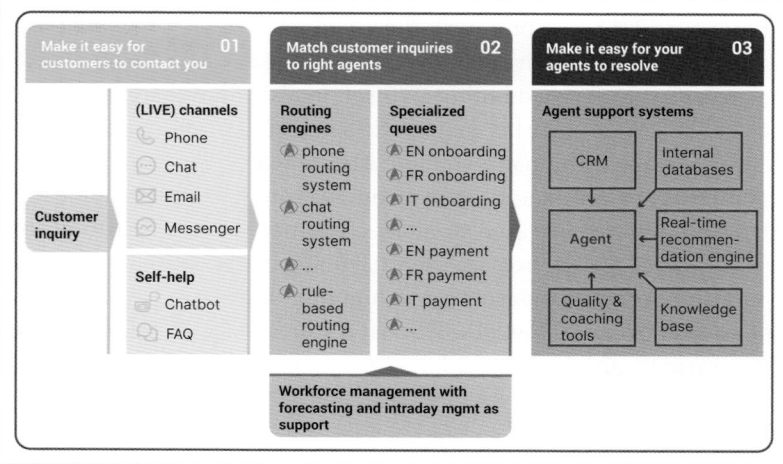

Figure 76: Service Tools Overview

Practice 82: Steering external partners to jointly drive business goals

Scaling up services quickly is often only possible with support from external partners – in addition to the in-house team. The reason? If a startup is in growth mode, often they won't be able to find enough customer service colleagues in one location. For this issue, external contact centers can provide one solution. Managing these partners effectively is its own science and calls for the following:

- **Being clearly visible on the partner's radar**
  A smaller partner will prioritize a startup's needs, but they may face supply issues and lack a global network. A larger partner will be able to get a startup up to scale quickly, but they may also not always have the startup be in their top priority. It is best to aim to deliver 15–25% of the external partner's revenue in the respective region, as this will make the company relevant but not dependent. Multiple partners will improve a startup's negotiating position and will not jeopardize its services in case they need to replace partners quickly. As a rule of thumb for scale-ups: the partner organization should be at least twice the startup's age. If they are not substantially older than the startup, the startup probably won't be able to learn from them.
- **Aligning KPIs to meet overarching business goals**
  Delivering successfully on an ultimate business goal should be the driver of the partner's performance payments. Say a startup hires an external partner for video-based digital customer verification, where the goal is to ensure a high conversion rate (besides fraud protection). The partner will push to be incentivized for rapid answer times, a metric they can directly affect. But by paying a bonus for conversion – the startup's ultimate business goal – the partner will be encouraged to work on improving this metric (e.g., by delivering ideas). Agreeing on performance payment for KPIs that do not serve the startup's overall goal(s) directly is often not a good idea.
- **Interacting with the partner daily**
  Fire and forget is not a good approach to creating a high-performing partner network. External partners can interact with the partner daily at an operational level via a jointly shared real-time performance dashboard, and check-ins with senior management should occur at least once a month if performance is at risk.

Practice 83: Boosting back-office throughput with performance management, automation and centers of excellence

A strong front-end customer experience calls for a well-oiled back-office to build the stage on which the customer service team can perform its magic. A high-performing back-office is often based on the following building blocks:

- **Organizing your back-office in Centers of Excellence (CoE) that are built around customer journeys**
  Repetition of processes by the same staff can lead to higher efficiency and fewer errors. Performance can be further enhanced by having customer service and the back-office function as a joint unit, with responsibilities such as autonomously optimizing the knowledge base, correcting faulty subprocesses and ensuring shift capacity in the event of unforeseen volume peaks. We have seen scale-ups with an accountability-based CoE setup for entire customer journeys improve their first-resolution time and customer experience scores by at least 20%. It is important to remember a CoE's focus should be on optimizing customer journey KPIs (e.g., resolution rates, Net Promoter Scores, etc.) and not just efficiency targets, such as tickets per FTE solved.
- **Ensuring performance transparency for ticket flows and corresponding capacity**
  Having a dashboard with an overview of open tickets per process by age (1–6, 7–14, 14+ days) is an effective way to measure back-office efficiency. Other KPIs here include first response time and resolution time per ticket. Scale-ups need to keep ticket handling capacity in line with a startup's needs. For instance, a startup ideally re-forecasts ticket volume each month and aligns the demands for new FTEs with their in-house recruitment teams. Outsourcing simple tasks that are relatively difficult to automate and therefore time-consuming (e.g., digitizing and classifying mail) can further help to alleviate capacity constraints.
- **Driving down ticket inflow with self-service and end-to-end process automation**
  There are two types of processes that lend themselves to automation: self-service features that increase customer satisfaction while cutting costs (e.g., in-app chargeback for a FinTech) and automating

"purely" internal processes (e.g., dunning and invoice collection services). Investing in both prevents back-end operation costs from ballooning when scaling up a customer base. How does a company know which back-end operation processes to focus on? Processes can be ranked according to time spent (or FTE-saving potential), (direct) financial savings and (if applicable) regulatory necessities as demanded by public authorities. It may not be possible to initiate full automation from the outset, such as upgrading a Google spreadsheet approach for managing unpaid customer bills to a fully automated "dunning cycle." However, even "throwaway" solutions, like enabling the back-office to send out batch emails in one click before implementing a fully automated solution, can cut the average response time of a process from two weeks to two days. This may already be enough as the first step. Finally, the pressure should be kept off operations by automating and refining processes in the back-office and at the customer interface (e.g., using optical character recognition to extract critical data from customer correspondence).

Practice 84: Investing in resilience to quickly recover from demand and supply shocks

In the early growth phase, the FinTech N26 like many startups was growing faster than it was able to build up service processes and capacity. Unexpected incidents such as contact spikes due to bugs in the app or very successful marketing campaigns occasionally overwhelmed the operations team and led to hours of waiting time for video verification or on the customer service phone lines. One solution? A massive investment in resilience. One way to do this is to quickly build the following three pillars of resilience in a startup's operations.

- **Designing for variety**
  This can be done by spreading the risk through the establishment of systems that work together but can function independently if one fails (e.g., video calls, photo-based ID and Postident options to complement each other). It is beneficial to think of a startup's operations as a game of roulette – it is not ideal to bet everything on black. In operations, if one system temporarily goes down, the customer needs to still be able to rely on the other two.

- **Building in redundancy**
  This means building a surplus that you can rely on in times of crisis, such as multi-skilled employees who can be assigned to different areas or external vendors who can ramp up additional staff quickly when needed. Generally, when working toward resilience, a startup needs to plan for higher volumes than recorded and anticipate longer implementation times. A good rule of thumb is to have 20% more resources than what is actually needed at any one time. As a bonus, redundancy in an external partner network (e.g., contact centers) creates competition and keeps prices low.
- **Including a recruiting buffer in hiring plans**
  It easily takes a few months to get a new employee up to speed. This is a time that startups don't have when scaling up rapidly. Therefore, the recruiting buffer should amount to around 10–20% to ensure a constant people inflow based on customer demand projections. As most scale-ups are well-financed, you can usually afford the inefficiency that goes along with this in order to secure a resilient and reliable customer experience.

Recommended publications:
- Matt Dixon (2013). *The Effortless Experience: Conquering the New Battleground for Customer Loyalty.*
- Nick Mehta and Dan Steinman (2016). *Customer Success: How Innovative Companies Are Reducing Churn and Growing Recurring Revenue.*
- Bill Price and David Jaffe (2014). *Your Customer Rules!: Delivering the Me2B Experiences That Today's Customers Demand.*
- Thales S. Teixeira (2019). *Unlocking the Customer Value Chain: How Decoupling Drives Consumer Disruption.*
- Some good podcasts include: *The Modern Customer Podcast* (Blake Morgan), *Relate* (Zendesk), *Experience This!* (Joey Coleman and Dan Gingiss).

Watch our video on the six key pitfalls to avoid in your service operations function by scanning the QR code or following this link: https://youtube/MpPXDLCmzDE.

How to set up a service operations team that can scale? Watch our video by scanning the QR code or following this link: https://youtube/Eek9eMk0ZBk.

Definitions

- **ASA (Average Speed to Answer)**: a measure of the amount of time it takes for a customer support team to pick up and respond to a customer contact.
- **Backlog**: the buildup of work exceeding the current capacity that still needs to be resolved. In customer support, the backlog describes those customer support tickets (requests) that remain unresolved within a certain time frame.
- **Contacts (or "tickets")**: interactions between customers and customer service reps; a low number of contacts per customer is often considered a positive since it indicates that customers are not encountering issues or are able to solve them with the resources available to them.
- **Customer journeys**: all the key interactions a customer can have with a company, product or service – usually framed in statements like "I want to close an account."
- **First contact resolution rate**: the percentage of contacts or tickets solved in the first contact (i.e., one phone call, one email, one live chat session), thereby eliminating the need for further interaction with the customer.

- **ISO 9001 certificate**: a seal of approval demonstrating that a company has met the statutory and regulatory requirements relating to the quality of their products or services.
- **Lean Six Sigma**: a data-led and team-based approach to management that aims to maximize customer satisfaction by removing any processes or use of resources that do not contribute to the creation of value for the customer.
- **Live service**: the provision of real-time customer service, usually via phone, chat or messenger.
- **Net Promoter Score**: a measure of customer satisfaction and loyalty, ranging from −100 to +100, assessed by asking customers how likely they are to recommend a product/service/business to another person.
- **Occupancy rate**: the percentage of the "logged-in time" during which a customer support team member is either directly supporting a customer or is available to do so. Ideal levels are often around 80%, and more can lead to burnout and attrition of the team, while less can become inefficient. Occupancy does not factor into training times, meetings, etc.
- **SLA (Service Level Agreement)**: a contract between a company and a customer that defines the minimum levels of service a customer can expect to receive, as well as any penalties should those levels not be met; for example, an agreement to provide a support team response in 24 hours or less.
- **Tickets**: a system for recording the interactions that take place between customers and customer support teams. Tickets document the communication that takes place between each party and allows support teams to monitor the progress of a customer's contact.
- **Utilization rate**: the percentage of all available time that a customer support team member spends on contact-related activities. If there are a lot of training sessions, meetings and other non-customer-facing activities, the utilization is reduced.
- **Vendor management**: the processes for organizing external service providers in order to ensure cost efficiency, high levels of service and risk mitigation.

10　Supply Chain Excellence

Shipping customer happiness consistently

With Matthias Wilrich

Key pitfalls to avoid for scale-up builders　**!**

- **Optimizing the supply chain in silos rather than seeing it as a product.**
  Contrary to popular belief, the total outcome cannot simply be maximized by optimizing the individual parts. Improvements on one dimension can hurt another; a supply chain is about balance. There should always be support and a focus on the weakest link while performing a continuous balancing act on the chain as a whole. It is important to not think in terms of silos, while also working toward creating an awareness of "supply chain as product" and then finding the optimal balance between its various multipliers.
- **Not taking a granular approach to optimize order economics.**
  Supply chain leaders who do not take savings seriously enough by counting down to each cent will not reach best-in-class levels in cost efficiency. Real-time tracking, analytics and the right benchmarks count here. Most B2C companies will find the biggest share of costs to lie in delivery operations (whether parcel, drivers or service staff – the "last mile") and should focus on optimizing costs in that block instead of opening quality, speed or reliability issues due to early optimization of smaller blocks, e.g., picking, inventory keeping, packing (see Practice 85).
- **Hiring supply chain specialists too late.**
  This describes a failure to complement intelligent generalists from the early days with specialists in supplier and vendor management that have seen scaling and know the "tricks" that can help to scale up fast. This might include procurement experts that know favorable contract clauses and price benchmarks or senior warehouse managers that understand warehouse operations and people management in depth (see Practices 86, 87 and 88).
- **Investing in supply chain resilience too late.**
  Failing to do so makes recovery from demand and supply shocks costly and slow. Key components include: investments in supplier network resilience (e.g., multiple locations, switching abilities, low supplier concentration), transport resilience (e.g., multiple transport modes), delivery network resilience (e.g., multiple carriers) and healthy buffer stocks in inventory (see Practice 89).

- **Insufficiently anchoring flexibility in contracts.**
  Some scale-ups do not negotiate enough flexibility into their supplier and logistic partners' contracts. This might include early cut-off times, small forecasting precision corridors, maximum volume commitments instead of peak surcharges, lack of space expansion options or long ramp-up announcement timings. Flexibility when scaling a supply chain is of the essence and needs to be negotiated without yielding to high commitments or costs.
- **Insufficiently anchoring performance clauses in contracts.**
  Some scale-ups do not incentivize performance enough in supplier and logistic partners' contracts. This might include extra revenues or malus, depending on the performance levels (e.g., estimated time of delivery, production lead time, production capacity, inventory accuracy, picking accuracy, delivery accuracy, product quality standards) (see Practice 90).
- **Underinvesting in supply chain technology.**
  In the scale-up phase, some companies do not invest enough in deep customization or in-house development of supply chain technologies. This might include aggregated ERPs, warehouse management systems (WMS), order management systems (OMS), route planning and optimization tools, transportation management systems (TMS) or category management tools. One key principle for these "make or buy" decisions is if customers can be delighted and a startup can create a true competitive advantage with technology developing in-house. If these are possible, then there is a strong argument for in-house development. If this can't be done, an adopted off-the-shelf solution might be better.

We may be living in the digital age, but moving atoms, not only electrons, still matters for many scale-ups. From meal-kit companies such as HelloFresh and Blue Apron to eCommerce scale-ups like Drizly and LoveCrafts, businesses that ship physical goods understand that getting the supply chain right counts – especially when a startup is on the road to building a unicorn company.

What can a strong supply chain operations division optimize for? Given the resources available to maximize delivery, these optimizations focus on net promoter scores with a low cost per order. This requires a focus on at least three key areas: delivery experience, low cost per order and cash efficiency. A startup should try to excel in all four, but when they have to make trade-offs, providing a world-class delivery experience at an average-only cost-per-order is almost always better than becoming a world champion in cost management too early in the scale-up journey. It is also important to keep in mind that while cash efficiency and supply chain resilience often do not seem to matter too much in the startup and the early growth phase, they do matter in later growth phases, as the value of the goods and the capital tied to a warehouse and risk imposed by a potential supply chain disruption increases (Figure 77).

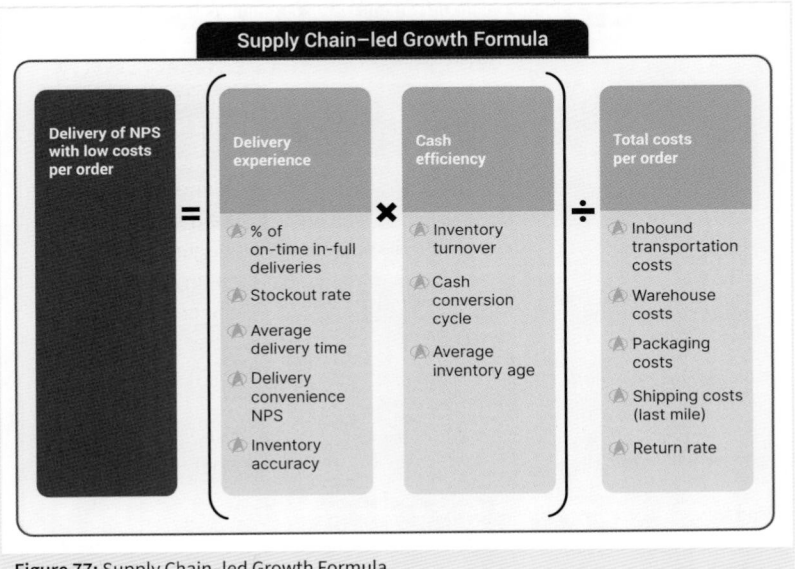

Figure 77: Supply Chain–led Growth Formula

This formula can be turned into a set of OKRs, which will vary depending on the type of scale-up under consideration such as full-range providers (e.g., Amazon, Otto, Allegro) or companies with a focus on one eCommerce vertical (e.g., Vivere, Warby Parker, Wayfair). In the following practice, there are some examples of OKRs for inspiration (Figure 78).

OKRs

Practice 85: Establishing the right supply chain OKRs

Typical Annual Supply Chain Objectives and Key Results for *eCommerce* Scale-ups

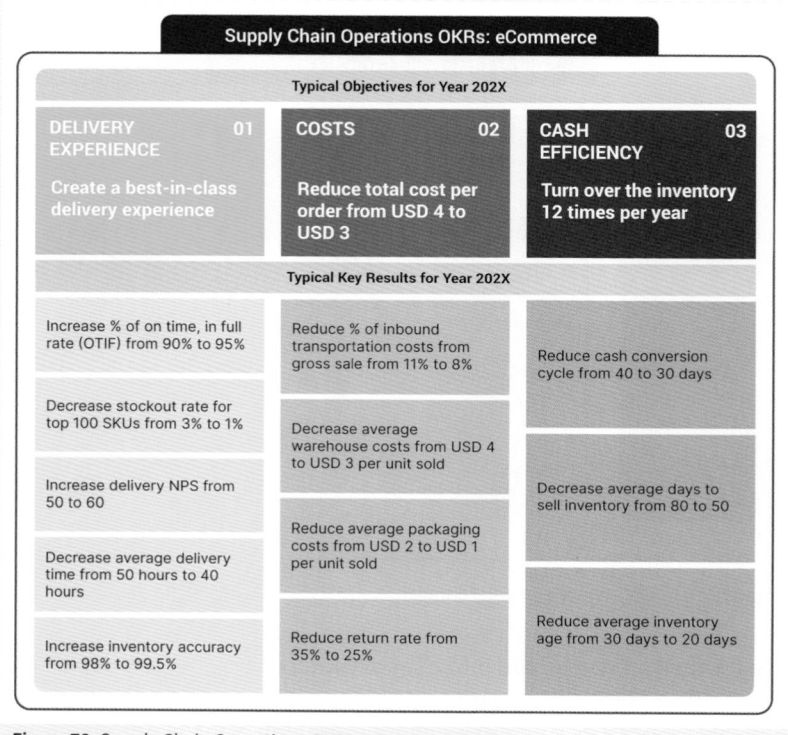

Figure 78: Supply Chain Operations OKRs: eCommerce

To build a truly resilient supply chain, a startup should begin by asking themselves the questions below for each of their objectives and adapt their operations accordingly.

O1. Delivery experience: Is your delivery experience fueling growth?
The premium iPad screen protector brand Paperlike has followed Steve Jobs' prominent focus on a marvelous unboxing experience. The product

arrives in a sleek envelope that features a custom postcard with a thank-you note by the founder and an illustration by a Paperlike customer. Despite the product's simplicity, this company has nailed it to make the customer feel enchanted when they unpack their Paperlike. Other delivery best practices can be found in grocery delivery startups like Gorillas, Flink or Fancy. Gorillas, for example, promises delivery times as low as 10 minutes, which are made possible by the fact that each of their own warehouses only serves a radius of ten e-bike minutes. This hyper-quick delivery adds a "wow-effect" to the delivery experience, which makes a huge difference with customers, as well as investors. Delivery can be thought of as the tip of the iceberg. It's the part the customer sees, but there's a lot more going on underneath it, too.

Factors that shape an excellent delivery experience can be divided into three categories: **reliability, convenience** and **experience**. First, the central key result for reliability is the on-time and in-full rate (OTIF). A broken delivery promise, no matter where it was set, is evidently the worst that can happen to your delivery NPS. Second, when optimizing convenience, you can implement different modes of delivery (e.g., include the possibility to pick up and drop off ("PUDO") a parcel from a fixed location) – ideally 24/7. Furthermore, for convenience, the flexibility for the delivery process matters as well. For example, this includes the possibility to reschedule a shipment "in-flight," allow delivery to a neighbor, or offer a second delivery attempt when no one is at home the first time or the opportunity for customers to set tighter delivery windows (e.g., 2–4 o'clock) to receive their package. Finally, in order to improve the delivery experience, delivery staff attire, a wowing speed of delivery (see the food delivery examples above) and great packaging pays off.

Typical key results: Making deliveries "on-time and in-full" (OTIF) is the top priority here. Your OTIF is the share of expected products in the quantity ordered that arrive within the designated time window (95%+ is good; more than that often leads costs to skyrocket). Other key metrics include the customers' delivery NPS, the average and median absolute delivery time, % demand fill rate and inventory accuracy. The latter measures if the stock you display to customers online matches your warehouse inventory.

O2. Costs: Are you driving down your total costs per order continuously?
Reducing the total costs per order (CPO) is often one contribution to improve "unit economics" in a scale-up. The CPO is usually driven by direct costs, such as inbound and outbound logistics costs, warehouse costs, packaging costs and return ratio. An eye should be kept on indirect costs, too. A cheaper logistics partner might seem attractive, but a startup could end up losing repeat buyers due to a lower delivery NPS, get more customer service requests due to fewer on-time deliveries and have higher return rates due to higher defects upon delivery. Likewise, it may be tempting to optimize unit economics through hard cost reduction and a reduced delivery experience, but a world-class delivery experience with average delivery costs is a better goal for most growth companies. The supply chain masterclass can be implemented to reduce costs without worsening the customer experience, and sometimes it can even improve it (e.g., by more direct shipping setups). Many of the levers that can be pulled to adjust this are already in the network design, while others are in process improvements. There is also potential in scaling of volumes due to partner contract renegotiations.

Typical key results: Inbound and outbound costs should be factored in as a percentage of gross sales, warehouse costs per unit and packaging costs per order. Also, it is important to pay attention to the return rates, as these can cause a company to lose cash for up to 30 days at a time.

O3. Capital efficiency: Are you saving cash across your supply chain?
When it comes to capital efficiency, eCommerce icon Amazon is a shining example. The company's excellent capital efficiency delivers *negative* cash conversion cycles, meaning it is paid by customers before it has to pay the vendors.[303] Amazon has sufficient negotiating power, with a negative CCC (Cash Conversion Cycle) of −33 in the year 2020.[304] This was a key driver in Amazon's phenomenal growth, as it has allowed the company to invest strongly in services using its own cash without the need to take out expensive loans or issue stock. For scale-ups, there is often enough capital available to finance growth in the early growth phase. While speed is what counts here, achieving capital efficiency can be an effective way to save cash and continue the growth story once a startup begins to grow.

Typical key results here include a cash conversion cycle (also called a "cash-to-cash cycle"), which measures the days between when a business pays its suppliers and when it receives a payment from customers. To receive money from customers as quickly as possible, it may be advisable to explore invoice factoring options (i.e., services that allow you to sell invoices to a third party), which can advance 85–90% of the amount of the invoice and settle the rest of the invoice (minus a fee of 0.5% to 5% of the invoice total) when the client makes their payment. This can be especially useful for B2B and B2C scale-ups, where customers take a long time (15 to max. 90 days) to pay. Other key results include the inventory turnover ratio. A ratio of 5 to 10 is ideal for scale-ups in most industries. Sellers of high-end goods (e.g., many vertical brands) will need a lower ratio in order to minimize any product that is out-of-stock. On the other hand, merchants of spoilable goods will typically aim for a higher ratio. Companies can also keep order cycle times and/or production cycle times in mind as relevant KPIs.

Organizational chart and roles

Practice 86: Defining the roles & responsibilities for a supply chain operations function

When scaling up, the supply chain teams are responsible for keeping the processes and systems working together seamlessly to ensure the flow of products and services from the company to the customer base. A typical supply chain operation usually consists of:

- A **procurement team** to negotiate contracts and to manage suppliers.
- A **transport logistics team** to manage inbound (freight forwarding) logistics via air, ship, road and rail and an outbound logistics team for last-mile delivery to the customers.
- A **fulfillment team** to manage warehouses.
- Several **enabler teams**, such as a category and inventory management team, a readiness team and/or an operational excellence team, as well as a business intelligence team.

These units are supported by customer service teams (see the Service Operations section for details). Figure 79 is the organizational structure of a typical supply chain operations division.

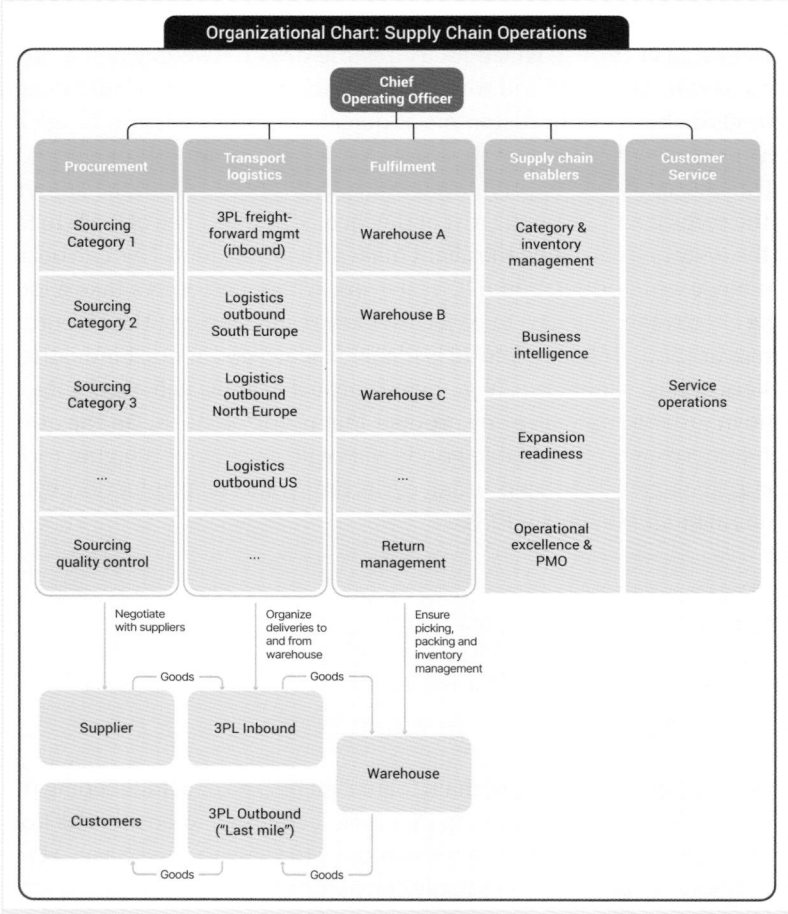

Figure 79: Organizational Chart – Supply Chain Operations

Now let's take a closer look at what each of these functions does. It is important to note that this structure is typical of an early growth eCommerce company managing an outsourced supply chain. The exact setup depends on the growth stage and the breadth of the product range (e.g., full-range eCommerce provider, eCommerce with a focus on one vertical such as fashion).

- **Procurement**

  Top responsibility: negotiating contracts and sourcing goods. This includes identifying suppliers, conducting negotiations, competitive bidding and contract management. They need to communicate constantly between suppliers and internal stakeholders, implement evaluation methods for supplier performance and manage supplier risk and the fluctuating costs of products, materials and transportation. When successful, they can improve cost management, reduce risk and stimulate supplier innovation to gain a competitive advantage. Procurement teams are usually organized according to categories they source (e.g., electronics, food, fashion) or supplier key accounts. If the scale-up is larger, the startup can have a geographical specialization within the category team (e.g., electronics from South China, electronics from India). It is good practice to have a separate quality control team that makes sure that the company's product standards are met. This should not be done by the category purchasing teams, as they sometimes "fall in love" with the products they buy. By a similar line of argument, the decision regarding which products to buy, in what quantities and at what time can be delegated to the category and inventory management team.

- **Transport logistics**

  Top responsibility: inbound and outbound transportation. Inbound logistics includes selecting and managing freight forwarders, with a focus on pallet shipping via air, ship, road and rail. Outbound logistics focus on 3PL management for last-mile deliveries, including track & trace for parcels and pallets. The transport logistics team also ensures the inventory stocks remain as balanced as possible between a company's warehouses.

- **Fulfillment**

  Top responsibility: warehouse center management. This unit is often organized according to different warehouses, with several heads of warehouse management (for each warehouse), order picking teams for different product types (e.g., large, small) and a team of return managers. Inside the warehouse, a typical process starts with documentation (gate entry/goods receipt note), inbound quality check (IQC) and put-away and inventory control, before moving on to product order fulfillment. The full sequence includes product inquiry, order confirmation, order accounting to order changes, picking, sorting, pre-consolidation (weighting, labeling and packing) and consolidation (loading and bill of lading). A round of final optical quality control is performed before handing the delivery off to Transport Logistics. Having a unit of "problem solvers" for each section (inbound and outbound) at hand to tackle challenging problems right away can take the stress off of the regular crew and improve warehouse efficiency.

- **Supply chain enablers**
  Top responsibility: make other supply chain teams successful. A company will usually need at least four enabler teams. The first team is a category and inventory management team. How much of a particular SKU will the company sell each week over the next few months? This planning question lies at the heart of this team's task. A demand forecast accuracy of 70% is a good benchmark to aim for. As part of inventory management, they identify stocks that do not sell fast enough and ensure new orders are placed early enough. The second team is a business intelligence team with 2–3 FTEs that works hand in hand with a central data team to establish supply chain dashboards and makes sure the supply chain KPIs are available in real-time. The third team is the expansion readiness team. They focus on getting new products and market launches ready in time. They coordinate with other divisions and project management (e.g., when establishing a new supply chain in a new country). The fourth team is a combined operational excellence and project management office. This can run process improvement initiatives outside the parameters of "business as usual."

- **Customer service**
  Customer service teams are often part of a typical supply chain operations division. For further details, see the section on service operations.

Practice 87: Scaling the right supply chain roles at the right time

When startups are focused on getting the products out the door by any means necessary, each successive growth stage calls for added resilience and excellence in a supply chain. Here's how the sequence can typically go:

- **Startup stage**: Here relying on in-house order fulfillment as the cheapest and most efficient option is often one way to go. At this stage, a startup has full control over its brand (i.e., Jeff Bezos, founder of Amazon, storing and packing books in his garage and delivering them by car when he started the company). Another option is to choose a fast-moving, small 3PL close to the HQ to learn the basics of fulfillment.
- **Early growth stage**: Outsourcing some or all of the order fulfillment is often a worthwhile pursuit. External fulfillment gives a level of flexibility needed to grow a business and learn process excellence from a startup's logistics partners.
- **Later growth stage:** Moving elements of the order fulfillment process back in-house often gives extra control over customer data while saving costs.

Now that the organizational structure is in place, let's turn to supply chain practices to build supply chain excellence.

Supply Chain

Practice 88: Hiring supply chain specialists early on

Negotiating with suppliers and carriers and building up a scale-up's supply chain is often greatly accelerated by industry experts. Hiring them in the early growth phase often pays off. How can delivery issues be avoided in peak times? What expectations should a startup have in terms of supplier service levels? What performance and price benchmarks should be negotiated effectively? What KPIs can be used to track performance? To speed up learning curves, industry experts can provide a strong support network.

Typical specialists to look out for include:
- A **procurement and negotiations expert** if you have broad or tight-margin product portfolios,

- A **China-sourcing expert** who speaks Mandarin if your supplier concentration in China is high,
- A **last-mile specialist** if last-mile customer demand is high,
- A **specialist for driver management and route planning** if the startup is running its own fleet,
- A **contract freight & transportation guru** if the company's cargo is
  traveling long distances.

Some entrepreneurial endeavors seemingly call for a generalist
approach (e.g., a mono-product setup with normal parcel delivery). It
is important to be aware that there is almost always at least one area in
a supply chain where a new standard can be set to "wow" customers.
Making sure the generalists can identify that aspect is key, instead of
merely establishing a plain-vanilla supply chain.

Practice 89: Investing in supply chain resilience to quickly recover from demand and supply shocks

Fitbakes, a UK-based snack company, ran into supply chain issues
during the Covid-19 lockdown in 2020. One of its major 3PLs became
overwhelmed by the number of orders it was receiving, and several of
Fitbakes' essential suppliers were unable to import goods. By changing
to smaller and local alternatives, at least temporarily, it was able to re-
vamp production and distribute its products again to customers.[305] It is
not just black swan events like Covid-19 but also internal causes that can
make a shock-resistant supply chain very valuable. These shocks can include everything from an advertising campaign whose impact is greater
than expected, to a bug in the warehouse management software, to an
unreliable 3PL partner. A strong scale-up operations team will anticipate
this by considering one or more of the following levers:

- **Supplier network resilience**
  The gold standard here is to have a high number of suppliers in geographically dispersed regions. A low supplier concentration helps the
  supply chain to recover from shocks faster but can increase costs. A
  typical KPI that can be minimized here is the procurement cost share
  of the top 5 suppliers.

- **Transport resilience**
  Here, the number of transportation modes a company has in place matters (e.g., air, ship, ground), as well as having multiple routes and locations.
- **Delivery network resilience**
  It is key here to have multiple last-mile carriers which can quickly replace one another for each market.
- **Inventory buffers**
  This provides extra leeway. A clever way to build this up is through retention of title (i.e., goods in your storage facility still belong to suppliers until they are sold).

Other levers include **real-time logistics visibility** and **managing cash and networking capital** by reducing the finished-goods inventory and running regular **supply chain stress tests** on major suppliers' balance sheets.

Practice 90: Boosting partner and supplier relationships with smart and scalable contracts

It is essential to have all key contract issues that still need to be negotiated on the radar. The following contract issues can guide discussions with external vendors:

Carriers:
- **Delivery charges**
  What is the price per delivery per volume band?
- **Delivery service level**
  What % has to be delivered the next day (one-day delivery), and what % next day +1 (two-day delivery)?
- **Cut-off time**
  By when do goods need to be dropped into a carrier's injection hub for it to count as fulfilled?
- **Forecasting precision**
  - How many weeks in advance do you need to commit your forecast? (3–4 weeks is a good rule of thumb)
  - How far is it possible to deviate from the forecast (in %) before the supplier's SLA commitments are no longer valid? (>15% is good)

- Do any minimum parameters need to be applied in regard to pick-up volumes? Ideally, this should be 0.
- **Surcharges**
  Are there any peak surcharges or other surcharges (e.g., fuel)? Ideally, there should be no surcharges.
- **Injection hub**
  What injection hub can be used and is there a fallback option if it is congested during peak time?
- **Billing time**
  How many days may elapse before the bill needs to be settled? 30–90 days is the industry standard for Europe.

Suppliers:
- **Base price**
  What is the price paid per product delivered? What are discounts per volume band?
- **Minimum order quantity**
  What is the minimum amount of goods that need to be procured per batch?
- **Lead times**
  How many days may the supplier take to deliver the goods at the maximum?
- **First-mile process**
  What times, locations and costs are involved here?
- **Transport logistics modes**
  Who pays for transport logistics? Is the agreement e.g. based on ex-works (buyer pays for shipping) or "delivery all paid" (the supplier bears all risks and costs involved in transporting goods)?
- **Procurement type**
  Are you settling on a classic inventory model? Examples include cross-docking (no storage during transport, which means it is usually slower for the customer), dropshipping (supplier ships the product directly to the customer, resulting in lower supply chain complexity against a higher quality risk), consignment (ownership is retained by the supplier, with payment kept on hold until the product is sold) or "quasi-consignment" (billing time of 90 days with a return option by buyer)?
- **Billing time**
  How many days may elapse before you need to pay the bill? 30–90 days is the industry standard for Europe.

Fulfillment/Warehouse:

- **Base price**
  What price do you need to pay for storing/delivering/picking one item?
- **Performance bonus**
  Which service or quality levels (e.g., OTIF, errors/incidents per million) lead to which bonuses? A fulfillment partner should only be able to make profit based on a strong performance.
- **Fulfillment time guarantees**
  What levels of fulfillment are guaranteed (e.g., within 24 hours for up to X parcels or items)?
- **Performance improvement shares**
  To what extent (in %) are savings shared if the fulfillment partner invests?
- **Setup time for new workstations**
  After how many days does the fulfillment partner need to be able to ramp up new workstations?
- **Forecast accuracy and capacity planning**
  Generally, the more flexibility for a startup, the better. The partner's pain is that when they provide a startup capacity for the peak, it might go un- or underutilized in the slack. A healthy compromise must be found, and they need to allow for continuous reforecasts based on the company's scaling. However, a company also needs to be prepared to put their money where their mouth is. If they forecast 40,000 parcels a month and then only achieve 10,000, they need to pay for excess capacity. Fair agreements usually require a minimum of 60–75% of forecasted volumes to be achieved by you as the customer.
- **Inventory accuracy**
  What is the guaranteed level of accuracy all year round (not just during the annual stock take; >99% is good for a young company)?

Incentivizing customer satisfaction and growth is key when concluding contracts with supply chain partners. Whether in contracts with partners or in employees' KPIs, a company needs to prioritize customer satisfaction and growth in terms of the goals to be achieved. Typical pitfalls here include:

- **One-sided optimization goals**
  It is important to align your partner's agenda with yours. For example, an agreement to fix the process costs without having any performance KPIs in place will lead a partner to save costs at the expense of performance.

- **One-step-too-short incentives**
  A company should incentivize for outcome, not output. For example, they should avoid not incentivizing for orders fulfilled, and instead incentivize for orders fulfilled on time.
- **Bonus malus schemes that lead to insufficient or excessive margins on the part of a partner**
  Ideally, a company should model its business case and estimate its margin. For example, a very good margin in warehousing in Central Europe is 10%. Third-party logistics partners should only be able to achieve this if they overperform in terms of time or volume handled per day, not by minimizing input costs.
- **Insufficiently measuring and communicating customer KPIs**
  Employees will not remain motivated about repetitive or difficult tasks simply because their boss is breathing down their neck. Companies can implement team KPIs in warehouses (gamification) and show positive customer feedback and KPIs (appraisal) on screens or wallpapers. This is essential for showing the relevance of customer happiness to supply chain teams.

Practice 91: Becoming proficient in supply chain operational excellence and maintaining a hands-on attitude

Operations, supply chains and logistics: whatever the team, this is a primarily hands-on and physical domain. While optimizing, it might seem like moving Lego pieces, but minor tweaks can make all the difference – and that makes it important to understand the following:

- **Build a lean coordinating team**
  If ten people are needed to manage transportation, either there is a *lot* of cargo to transport or there isn't a supportive IT system at work. This can also be a sign that a company is reliant on Excel sheets. Both should be avoided. While it is important to work hard, success comes from working smart.
- **Make DILOs (Days In the Life Of) part of the onboarding**
  New joiners should spend a day, or even a week, getting a grip on their assigned domain and/or other critical areas. This allows junior hires to learn about what they are working to optimize, while senior

hires are encouraged to break with their traditional beliefs (after all, every supply chain is different) and earn the respect of their colleagues in the warehouse or in the field. Regardless of status, both should return to their position with ideas on how to make processes smoother, faster and cheaper, or more effective. If they have no such ideas, this is a sign that the wrong people may have been hired.

- **The supply chain needs to become increasingly analytical when scaling**
The "get stuff done squad" is ideally complemented by smart analytical thinkers that love data early on, because together they can work miracles and implement more and more optimization levers, such as smart pick algorithms, inventory order matching, replenishment algorithms, storage on-shelf logics (short routes start with inbound), etc.

- **Avoid too much process specialization**
Increasing the number of packaging sizes from six to eight is the type of micro-optimization that may save on shipment costs, but it also comes at the expense of flexibility as processes become more complex (e.g., a workbench needs to be restocked with packages more often or a packer makes more mistakes). Overspecialization can get in the way of scaling the supply chain while at the same time preventing a company from yielding economies of scale in the cost per order.

- **It is a people business**
Scaling a supply chain – whether outsourced or in-house – can lead to an increase in operational staff. These are the people who are making sure the machine keeps running. They may have indirect (picking, packing) or direct (delivery) touchpoints with customers, which is something a digital business can lack. If the operational staff is happy and motivated, a business will flourish. It is best for a company to keep its operational people close, even if they are not on the direct payroll (e.g., by involving them in optimization exercises and rewarding them for improvement suggestions). They can also celebrate blue-collar staff on social media to give them public recognition and contribute to building a sense of employee loyalty and an employer brand. Last but not least, a company can work on ensuring that they get the positive feedback they deserve: from supervisors, from the HQ team (even from the analytics colleagues) and from happy customers.

Recommended publications:

- Lora M. Cecere (2014). *Supply Chain Metrics that Matter.*
- Ramon Abalo Costa (2019). *eLogistics – Logistic for eCommerce.*
- Eliyahu M. Goldratt (2014). *The Goal: A Process of Ongoing Improvement.*

Watch our video on the essential OKRs and trade-offs in a supply chain function by scanning the QR code or following this link: https://youtube/op2ebta_vmc.

How to set up a supply chain team that can scale? Watch our video by scanning the QR code or following this link: https://youtube/vsFqtxXCzRc.

Definitions

- **Cash-conversion cycle**: a metric that tracks the efficiency of turning inventory spending into cash; the lower the metric, the more efficient the company is at investing working capital in its inventory of products/services and selling those products/services for cash.

- **Consignment**: a business arrangement in which one company (the consignor) sells products on behalf of another company (the consignee) for which the consignor receives a percentage of the sale price.
- **Cross-docking**: the technique of receiving products into a distribution center and immediately loading them onto outbound transportation (i.e., removing the need for storage during the distribution process).
- **Cut-off time**: the latest time in a business day by which an order must be received so that it can be processed and transferred to the carrier (for delivery) on the same day.
- **DILO (Day In the Life Of)**: an observation technique for assessing the efficiency with which work is carried out. It can help to elevate the quality of the work by identifying and eliminating unnecessary tasks.
- **Dropshipping**: a retail fulfillment model in which a company does not handle goods directly but instead takes orders from customers and fulfills them via third parties that produce and ship the goods to the customer. This model reduces the level of complexity in the supply chain but does constitute a higher risk in terms of product quality assurance.
- **Inventory turnover**: the number of days until the whole inventory is sold completely (i.e., "turned") – it is a measure of how well a company is turning inventory into sales.
- **Inventory accuracy**: any discrepancies between the inventory on records and the actual inventory in stock.
- **Net Promoter Score (NPS)**: a measure of customer satisfaction and loyalty, ranging from −100 to +100, which is assessed by asking customers how likely they are to recommend a product/service/business to another person.
- **OTIF (On-Time, In-Full)**: a measure of supply chain efficiency. OTIF calculates delivery performance with respect to the quantities, timings and destination of delivery as set out in a customer order.
- **Picking**: the process of picking individual items from a distribution center to fulfill customers' orders.
- **Packing**: the process of sending the order to a packing station to securely pack, seal it and equip it with a label for shipping.

- **Return rate**: a metric measuring how often items are returned by customers (i.e., the percentage of shipped items that are returned).
- **SKU (Stock Keeping Unit)**: a system for managing and tracking inventory. SKUs contain numbers and letters which together make up a code that denotes the important characteristics of a product.
- **Stockout**: when the customer orders for a product exceed the amount of inventory kept in the warehouse.
- **Supply chain**: the network of organizations, resources, information, activities and people through which raw materials and components are transformed into finished products and services and are in turn delivered to the end consumer.
- **Total fulfillment cost per order (CPO)**: a metric for the average warehouse cost (incl. picking, packing, shipping, storage and returns logistics) per sale.

GROWTH CAPITAL

11 Six Questions Every Growth Stage Investor Asks

With Vanessa Pinter

Key pitfalls to avoid for scale-up builders:

- **Selecting VC partners based on brand only, not on added value**.
  A typical pitfall when it comes to selecting venture capital firms is to
  have a bias toward the glamorous option. While having several top VCs
  investing in the company helps to attract talent and other investors, it
  also pays to have venture capital partners on board who are operationally effective in areas like executive recruiting, sales introductions and
  strategic advising based on a relevant network.
- **Failing to rally around investors for the next funding round
  early enough.**
  Some entrepreneurs start fundraising too late, which results in them
  being pressured to close a funding round – and being at a disadvantage
  during negotiations. Establishing an inbound investor relationship process to build up a pool of potential investors and start raising funds at
  least six months before the money runs out is often helpful here (see
  Practice 93).
- **Lacking clarity of thought when pitching to investors.**
  Long-winded and ill-structured pitch decks are a recipe for failure when
  it comes to funding goals. When pitching for growth capital, clarity
  of thought on the serviceable available market, category leadership
  and the path of becoming profitable in the long term are all key (see
  Practice 92).
- **Agreeing to term sheet clauses in the early rounds that make negotiations in the later rounds difficult.**
  Conceding special terms to early-stage venture capital companies often
  fires back in the later rounds. Later-stage investors will, at the minimum,
  ask for the same terms that were agreed upon with early-stage investors. Typical topics not to concede early on include: liquidation multiples
  of more than 1x, free investor sales rights for shares and below-industry-
  standard approval thresholds by the board for salaries or investment
  decisions. Getting a "plain-vanilla" term sheet early on and sticking to it
  is the best advice here.

- **Agreeing on overly aggressive valuations.**
  Entrepreneurs are sometimes offered and accept valuations "which you
  have to grow into." This increases the probability of a down round later
  on. A major pitfall in term sheet negotiations comes from conceding for
  a higher valuation on issues that will have a negative impact if expectations are met (e.g., investor-friendly anti-dilution protection or warrants
  with overly ambitious milestones).

Sourcing growth capital for a scale-up is a true study of contrasts. While
the company may have found investors in the startup stage thanks to a
strong vision and an outstanding team, this is no longer enough when
setting a scale-up on the path to unicorn status.

For later-stage investors, there are six essential areas that a scale-up
has to provide answers for: future vision, rockstar team, venture-scale
market, category-leading product, business model and fund fit. While
a compelling story is still relevant, it is now important to show that the
scale-up is ready to become a category leader, that the business metrics
show a path to a profitable business and that the executive team can
scale. This section is designed to help sharpen pitches to growth investors in particular – you will find various elements helpful for the earlier
fundraising stages as well.

What growth capital sources are available?
Growth capital refers to Series B/C/D/E round sizes of more than USD
20 million awarded to companies that are usually valued at more than
USD 100 million. There are four types of investors that can be approached
to lead investments in a growth stage funding round:
- growth-stage-focused venture capital (e.g., HV Capital, Atomico,
  Lakestar, Sequoia, Accel),
- "growth equity" companies (e.g., General Atlantic, Vitruvian
  Partners),
- private equity firms (e.g., KKR, The Carlyle Group),
- and corporate VCs (e.g., Allianz X, Google Ventures, Unilever Ventures).

Private equity companies are usually only interested in investing if the business has healthy earnings before interest and taxes (EBIT). Venture capital and growth equity firms will invest in companies even if they are currently unable to show a profit.

A company's overall value will grow with the company. As this happens, the founders' and employees' ownership stakes will be gradually reduced (or "diluted"). Retaining sufficient founders' and employees' shares helps to maintain a collective sense of ownership and drive. To incentivize the workforce, investors will usually make sure that the unallocated employee stock option pool hovers between 8% and 15%.[306] The founders' shares should not be diluted too fast – as a rule of thumb, founders should give up roughly 20% of their shares per round before allocating ESOP to employees. This varies greatly based on the industry and initial founding dynamics, but as a guideline founders should still hold 80% of shares pre-seed, ~65% after the seed round, and ~50% after Series A; however, they should allocate the ESOP pool from these shares. The median IPO founder share size of a tech company is 15% with an average of 21%, and higher values for companies that generate cash early (e.g. eCommerce).[307]

On what basis do growth stage investors decide to invest?
Six of the most important questions to address in the growth stage are depicted in Figure 80.

Six Growth Stage Investment Criteria

FUND FIT   01

Does your company fit the investor's fund in terms of industry, size and funding needs?

- Right region? (e.g. Europe)
- Right maturity stage? (e.g. growth stage)
- Right industry / business model? (e.g. SaaS)?
- Enough unallocated money in the fund?

TIMING   02

Why now?

- Business part of a "blue ocean" with market, customer behavior, technology, capital and regulation trends facilitating the company's growth?

MARKETING POTENTIAL   03

Is your serviceable available market worth more than USD 1 billion and not overcrowded with competition?

- Serviceable available market (SAM) > USD 1 billion?
- Not in a market with well financed, larger attackers with a similar value proposition?

CATEGORY LEADERSHIP   04

Have you created a defensible solution 10x better than any other in that market?

- Products and services in place that solve customers' problems 10x better than existing solutions?
- Defensible position leveraging proprietary data and technology, patents, trademarks, networks, unique insights or skills?

BUSINESS MODEL   05

Does your company's performance to date show a path toward becoming profitable in the long term?

- Revenue growth rate percentage + EBITDA profit margin > 40 ("Rule of 40")
- Net revenue retention > 120%
- Customer Lifetime Value / average customer acquisition costs > 3
- Average B2B sales cycles < 12 months

TEAM   06

Have you assembled a great team that can scale?

- Clarity of thought on direction?
- Scale-up mindset to step up from do-it-yourself executives into chief company builders?
- Diverse in thinking and complementary in skills?
- Resilient and determined to make its mark on the world or deliver a step function of better customer experience?

Figure 80: Six Growth Stage Investment Criteria

NEW VERSION:

1. **FUTURE VISION: Do you capitalize on the next inflection points?**
   - Clear outlook on an inspiring 10-year future to which the company contributes?
   - Why now? Business part of a "blue ocean", with market, customer behavior, technology, capital and regulation trends facilitating the company's growth?
2. **ROCKSTAR TEAM: Have you assembled a great team that can scale?**
   - Scale-up experience with clear roles?
   - Enough ambition?
   - Resilience and determination?
   - Collaborative founding team dynamics?
3. **BUSINESS MODEL: Does your company's performance to date show a path toward becoming profitable in the long term?**
   - Growth: e.g. revenue growth rate percentage + EBITDA profit margin > 40 ("Rule of 40")
   - Unit economics: e.g. customer lifetime value / average customer acquisition costs > 3 or strong contribution margin?
   - Go-to-market: e.g. clarity on customer acquisition and new markets?
   - Churn prevention: e.g. net revenue retention > 120%?
   - Sales cycles: e.g. average B2B sales cycles < 12 months?
4. **VENTURE-SCALE MARKET: Can you achieve USD 100 million in annual revenue within 7-10 years?**
   - Ability to create USD 100 million in annual (recurring) revenue within 7-10 years without capturing more than 10% of the respective market?
   - Serviceable available market (SAM) > USD 1 billion?
   - Not in a market with well financed competitors in regional proximity with a similar customer value proposition?
5. **CATEGORY-LEADING PRODUCT: Have you created a unique customer value proposition which is 10x better than any other in that market?**
   - Unique customer value proposition compared to top competitors?
   - Defensible position leveraging proprietary data and technology, patents, trademarks, networks, unique insights and/or skills?

6. **FUND FIT: Does your company fit the investor's fund in terms of industry, size and funding needs?**
    *   Right region (e.g. Europe)?
    *   Right maturity stage (e.g. growth stage)?
    *   Right industry / business model? (e.g. SaaS)?
    *   Enough unallocated money in the fund?

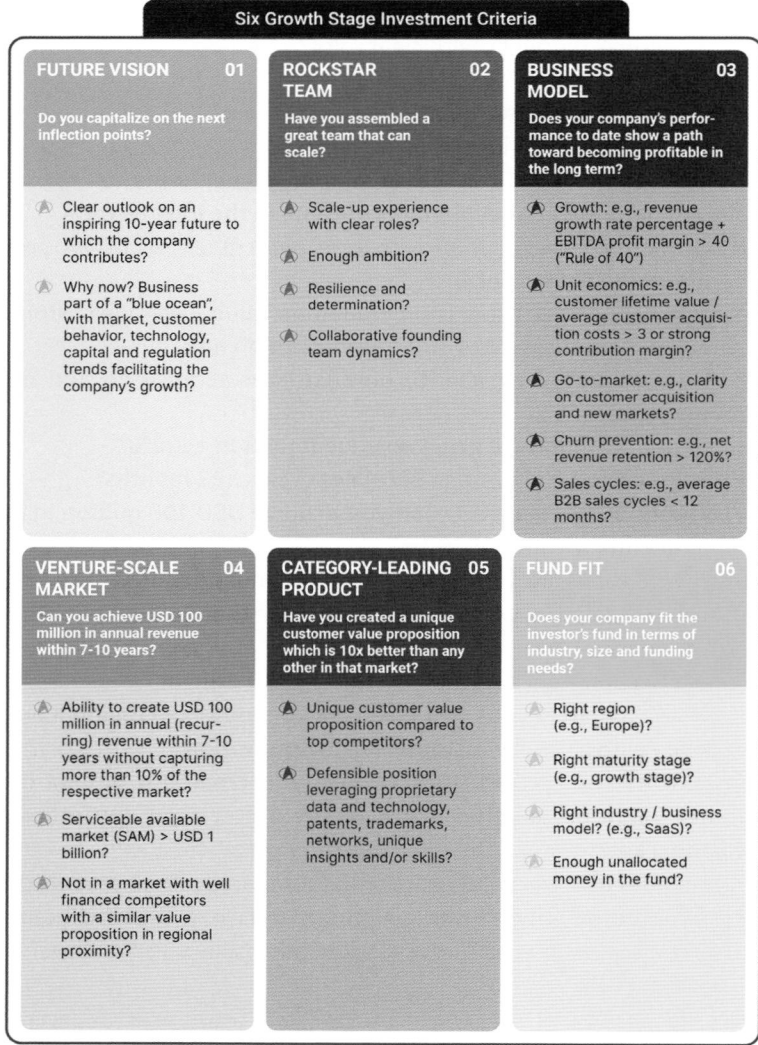

Let's look at each one in more detail.

Future vision

Practice 92: Do you capitalize on the next inflection point?

What future do you aspire to see 20 years from now – and how do you think your company can help make it a reality? When raising capital, entrepreneurs should ideally set out their next inflection point with maximum clarity while demonstrating how their business model will benefit from it. Think of it like a story's starting point in a pitch deck.

One prime example of an inflection point is humanity's need to move toward a net-zero-emission economy. Against this backdrop, a scale-up could present the case that over the next few years, every customer who leaves a supermarket or restaurant will want to offset their carbon footprint before checkout. To this end their product will enable the consumer to see the carbon emissions of every product they buy and give them the chance to offset it with an app.

Web 3.0 constitutes another likely inflection point. As Pete Townsend, Managing Director of the Launchpool Techstars Web3 Accelerator, notes: Two decades from now we could have reached the point where more people exchange value via crypto than those who do not.[308] How will we know we have reached this tipping point? Because people will no longer be talking about crypto. A strong vision in this field comes from the foundation behind Ethereum, one of the largest cryptocurrencies, that aims to create a fairer financial system. In their words: "Today, billions of people can't open bank accounts, others have their payments blocked. Ethereum's decentralized finance (DeFi) system never sleeps or discriminates. With just an internet connection, you can send, receive, borrow, earn interest, and even stream funds anywhere in the world."

Or the idea that part of human interactions will occur in interoperable virtual worlds, VR-based social metaverses as depicted in the sci-fi novel Snow Crash. Here, the investment story could be to create an immersive virtual world that will unleash a new wave of creativity and economic activity from its users. Or imagine a future where everyone owns their own data and can decide if they want to sell it to advertising companies for profit. This is an idea that is running behind the Brave Browser, where advertisers need to buy their native currency, Basic Attention Token

(BAT), to show ads to users, which then receive the BAT when they see or watch the ad (which a cut going to Brave).

Investors that are looking for the next inflection points often ask "Why now?". The question is whether now is the right time for this particular business model. This is how US venture capitalist Marc Andreessen frames discussions on investments with his teams. Making it clear to investors why building a company now is certain to pay off. If market, customer behavior, technology, capital and regulation trends are facilitating a company's growth, this means it is riding the wave early – so the timing is perfect. Investors want a business that moves in a "blue ocean" market (i.e., where new demand is created), rather than one that has to fight with competitors in a shrinking profit pool.[309]

One example of a firm getting the timing wrong was when IBM launched the world's first smartphone, the Simon, back in 1994. This was a full thirteen years before Apple changed telecommunications forever with the iPhone. The lack of ubiquitous mobile broadband technology likely played a big role here. An even greater disparity can be seen with the unveiling of videoconferencing technology at the 1964 World's Fair, which didn't come to prominence until the 2010s. Another example is when NASA used fiber optics in the television cameras that recorded the 1969 Moon Landing – it took until the 1990s for fiber optic networks to be introduced on a wider scale.

Rockstar team

Practice 93: Have you assembled a great team that can scale?

It's all about the team: great companies are built by AAA players (see the chapter on People Excellence). Nowhere is this more apparent than in the book *Super Founders* by Ali Tamaseb, which looks in detail about the founders of billion-dollar companies. The founders' age, for example, does not strongly correlate with success of building a billion-dollar company, with half over the age of thirty-four at the time of founding. Neither does industry experience: approximately 70% of CXOs of billion-dollar companies have less than one year of relevant work experience, if they don't build biotech or healthcare tech companies. And 40% of founders of billion dollar companies have only a bachelor or are university drop-outs. So if age, industry experience and education do not count a lot, what does?

When assessing leadership teams at scale-ups, investors often use the following criteria:

- **Scale-up experience and clarity of roles:** More than 60% of founders of billion-dollar companies have scaled up a startup before. A moderately successful exit of > USD 10 million makes them three times more likely to found a billion-dollar company than a random comparison group.[310] This is why investors check to see if key executive team roles comprise people with scale-up experience – not as part of an Amazon or a Google, but as a co-builder (founder or early employee). Complementing skills and clarity of roles count here: Is the CEO smart, driven and able to sell the vision? Is there a CTO that has scaled a technology organization before? Can the Chief Product Officer formulate an attractive, feasible product vision? Can the Chief Marketing Officer manage customer acquisition costs and orchestrate the go-to-market? Is there a Chief People Officer to build a talent acquisition machine at scale? Can the COO create outstanding customer experiences while maintaining a competitive cost-to-serve? Is the executive team diverse enough in terms of gender, age and ethnical backgrounds?

- **Ambition:** The company aims to become the globally leading company in crypto staking and trading for B2B customers? The ambition of the team is to enable every shopper in Europe to off-set carbon emissions after all ecommerce transactions? This is the kind of ambition level investors want to see. Being very bold on the 10 year ambition, but realistic on the 1-2 year horizon, is often good advice here.

- **Resilience and determination:** Does the team have a track record of ambitious career achievements demonstrating that it can overcome all obstacles? Are they driven to make their mark on the world or look for a 10x improvement in customer experience? Having a clear purpose and business ambition is useful in "near-death situations" for the company (e.g., when insolvency looms or a major crisis needs to be resolved). A typical red flag here is if the founders have a clear personal backup plan when asked what they would do if the company was to fail.

- **Collaborative founding team dynamics:** Are the founders a great team with a stable relationship? Do they know each other from school, university or a previous company? Most investors only invest in founding teams that know each other for many years. Personal ties, like husband & wife, brothers, mother and daughter, etc. are no obstacles, but should be stable for many years. There is some evidence that prior professional relationships (e.g. working as colleagues) lead to less co-founder departures as prior social relationships (e.g. friends or family).[311] A very unequal split of shares in the founding team can be a red flag, too.

Business model

Practice 94: Does your company's performance to date show a path toward becoming profitable in the long term?

Growth investors want to see a path toward becoming profitable in the long run and they assess this based on a scale-up's performance to date. Growth investors will want to see that a company can deliver in at least five areas:

- **Rapid growth**
  In Series A and B financing, startups are expected to grow their revenue metrics by at least 2x per year. For later rounds, investors will often apply the "Rule of 40": adding the annual recurring revenue growth rate percentage and the EBITDA profit margin percentage should enable the 40% mark to be reached. In other words, growing annual revenue by 40% without profit is okay, as is growing annual revenue by 20% while delivering a 20% EBITDA profit margin. Growth KPIs vary according to the business model. For example, enterprise sales companies would do this by focusing on bookings, total customers and revenue, while SaaS enterprises would look at recurring monthly and annual revenue and eCommerce businesses would have their sights set on the monthly revenue and compound monthly growth rate.[312]
- **Strong unit economics**
  Growth investors want to see a path to strong "unit economics", i.e., the ability to scale up the lifetime value of customers without scaling up customer acquisition costs to the same proportion. Many VCs aim

to invest in companies with customer lifetime values of at least 3x the average customer acquisition costs (CAC). Example: To acquire a new customer, a neobank invests USD 100 in online marketing, brand campaigns and the salaries of its marketing & sales team. The customer lifetime value should then exceed USD 300 at the minimum. In a venture context, investors will tend to use a five-year period (at most) for a financial model driven by the Net Present Value (NPV). An alternative would be to measure the months required to pay back the CAC, which should ideally be fewer than 12.[313] Note that gross margins feed into a customer's lifetime value, which is why many growth investors seek out high gross margins driven by a business model light on assets and people. Good gross margins for public SaaS businesses range between 50% and 75%, with the higher end applying to SaaS companies on the market for more than 10 years (see Tom Tunguz's analysis here).

- **Clear Go-to-market**
Scaling up usually only works with expansion along geographies, customer segments or channels (see Practice 24). Investors, therefore, often assess go-to-market capabilities along dimensions such as launch plans for different markets, and operational capabilities based on visa, tax, banking, marketing and branding capabilities in new markets. Index Ventures has published several playbooks for internationalization which outline these capabilities in depth.[314]

- **Churn prevention ("No leaks")**
Growth stage investors are not fond of businesses that use their money to acquire customers and then lose them. This is why it is essential to pay attention to the net retention rate (NRR) on a cohort basis. In a nutshell, NRR is the percentage of revenue earned by a company from retained customers in comparison to a previous period (usually 12 months prior) after accounting for upselling, downgrades and churn. NRR of 120+% is healthy, as this implies earning 20% more than the previous year through the existing customer base.

- **Short sales cycles**
Sales cycles matter to B2B companies. They refer to the average time needed to obtain a signed contract and ideally stay below 6 months.[315] Companies aspiring to become unicorns should avoid focusing exclusively on major corporate clients with high contract volumes and sales cycles that can take up to a year to complete. A high-velocity sales model is more attractive to many growth

investors, as it is inherently less risky. However, these contract volumes are smaller, there are more available and less time is required to close the cycle. Overall, striking a 50/50 balance between elephants and smaller "deer" clients is often a favorable approach.

Venture-scale market

Practice 95: Can you achieve USD 100 million in annual revenue within 7-10 years?

Growth investors look for companies in "venture-scale markets". Attractive for investors are companies that either have a disruptive approach to a large, stable market that will enable rapid capturing of market share or markets that are growing rapidly. You ideally prove that you are working in a venture-scale market both with a bottom-up and a top-down approach:

Can you build a business generating USD 100 million in annual (recurring) revenue within 7-10 years without having to take more than 10% of the respective market? Many growth investors ask this question. Often this means creating a **"bottom-up" model** that shows the number of new customers you aim to acquire per year, modeling the number of customers you lose per year (i.e. churn) and the revenue you estimate that each customer generates per year. Why is this a key question relevant for many growth investors? Because they aim to invest in the next unicorn, companies that are valued more than USD 1 billion. This valuation is often calculated by multiplying annual revenues with a factor between 3 to 10. Assuming a factor of 10, you need to obtain USD 100 million in annual revenue. While capturing 50% of your market to achieve this is often hard to believe, you become very credible if you need less than 10%.

It is often a good idea to complement this "bottom-up" approach with a **top-down assessment** of market potential. TAM, SAM, SOM are the magic words here. TAM refers to the total addressable market – often globally. Say a FinTech offers bank accounts and bookkeeping services specifically for SMEs: the TAM would be the total global revenue currently paid by all SMEs for this type of service, e.g. USD 5 billion. The SAM is the share of the total addressable market a startup realistically can capture based on its business model in the next few years, something which is often limited to a geographical region. To calculate this, multiply the projected average revenue per user (ARPU) by the number of potential customers in the relevant markets. If our FinTech is in France, the SAM might refer to the European market, e.g. USD 1 billion. Finally, the serviceable obtainable market (SOM) expresses the percentage of SAM that the startup realistically can capture – often at or below 10%. In our case this would result in USD 100 million serviceable obtainable market – 10% of 1 USD billion SAM. As a rule of thumb, the SAM for a startup should (usually) be valued at more than USD 1 billion. Hence, aiming for markets with a TAM of USD 5+ billion is usually good advice, depending on how tricky it is to acquire a sizable market share. Ideally, both the top-down and the bottom-up approach should result in broadly similar numbers.

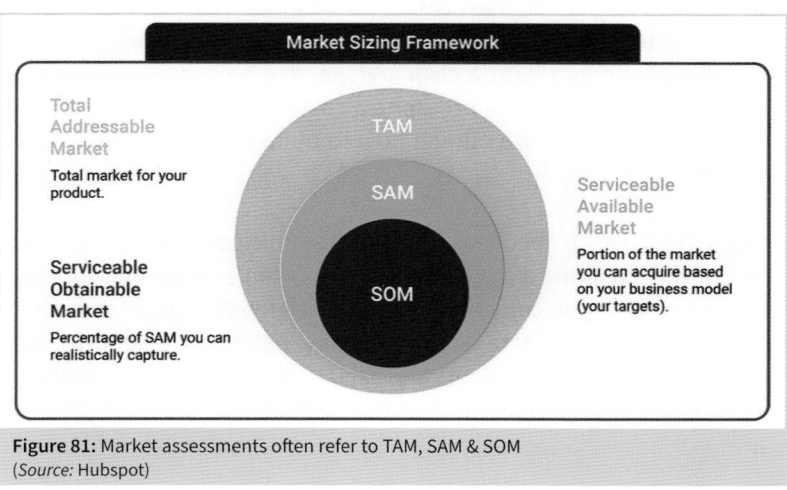

Figure 81: Market assessments often refer to TAM, SAM & SOM
(*Source:* Hubspot)

If the market potential is there, the market should not be a crowded red ocean. An early warning sign for this is a market-driven rise in customer acquisition costs. If it is costing more to attract new users, the profit pool is shrinking. While it is common to have at least a few competitors around the world, investors tend to be reluctant to fund startups in close proximity to well financed, fast-growing competitors with a similar customer value proposition.

Category-leading product

Practice 96: Have you created a unique customer value proposition which is 10x better than any other in that market?

Growth investors are not interested in financing yet another mid-market company. They want to get on board with the next category leader. Typical category leaders ("price setters") include Apple with the iPhone, Salesforce for its CRM systems, and AWS for cloud services. A scale-up will have to demonstrate two things to be considered as a category leader. First, it needs to demonstrate that its products and services have the potential to solve customers' problems 10x more effectively than existing solutions. The benchmark here is an industry-leading Net Promoter Score (NPS) that increases over customer "cohorts." This is important, as companies with the highest NPS grow by more than 2x on average in comparison to competitors with an industry-standard score. Typically this is complemented with a clear perspective on a unique customer value proposition – the main reasons a customer should buy from the company. In Practice 5 we outline how to build such a customer value proposition in depth.

Second, the scale-up needs to create a defensible position. Preventing a competitor from hiring a great team, tweaking an existing value proposition and catching up comes from having a defensible position built by leveraging proprietary data and technology, patents, trademarks, networks, suppliers, unique insights and skills – all of this will put a scale-up in a good position to maintain its competitive edge in the future.

Fund fit

Practice 97: Does your company fit the investor's fund in terms of industry, size, and funding needs?

This is the simplest question of all. Growth investors will only invest if the scale-up reaches a minimum annual revenue (e.g., USD 50 million) and if it accepts large cheques (e.g., USD >10 million). Finding these thresholds out straight away helps both sides. The geography, industry, business model and growth stage need to match, too. Public sources, such as Crunchbase, will list all the completed deals of a particular investor, which can be a good way of finding out if they are a good fit – there's no need to look back any further than two years, as the focus of many funds is constantly in flux.

Many growth investors aim for a 3x to 5x return for growth rates and are willing to participate in subsequent financing rounds. If the fund has already spent more than 60% of its allocation, it may not have the resources to commit to major new investments, so it is important to seek information on this as soon as possible. Also, it is crucial to be aware that most funds have a maximum exposure to a single company of 10-15% of the total fund size.

Recommended publications:
- Brad Feld and Jason Mendelson, *Venture Deals - Be Smarter Than Your Lawyer and Venture Capitalist,* 2019
- Scott Kupot, *Secrets of Sand Hill Road,* 2019
- Mahendra Ramsinghani, *The Business of Venture Capital, Insights from Leading Practitioners on the Art of Raising a Fund, Deal Structuring, Value Creation and Exit Strategies,* 2014
- Andrew Romans, *The Entrepreneurial Bible to Venture Capital - Inside Secrets From The Leaders In The Startup Game,* 2013
- Ali Tamaseb, *Super founders: What data reveals about billion-dollar startups,* 2021

Watch our video on the six questions every growth stage investor asks by scanning the QR code or following this link: https://youtu.be/jH-49Q1a9KA.

Definitions:

- **Customer lifetime value (LTV):** a metric that evaluates what a customer is worth to a company across the length of their entire relationship with the company.
- **EBITDA (Earnings Before Interest, Taxes, Depreciation, and Amortization):** a measure of a company's financial performance, often used as an alternative to other financial metrics (e.g., revenue, net income).
- **Growth capital:** a kind of investment in companies valued at more than USD 100 million, usually as the Series B/C/D/E investment of more than USD 20 million.
- **Net Revenue Retention (NRR):** a metric measuring the total change in recurring revenue over a period of time, including expansion as well as cancelations, downgrades and expirations.
- **RO40 (Rule of 40):** a metric for gauging software companies' performance. RO40 states that a company's revenue growth rate combined with its profit margin should exceed 40% if it is to balance growth ambitions with profitability.
- **Sales cycle:** the steps of the sales process required to convert someone into a paying customer.
- **SAM (Serviceable Addressable Market):** as a more refined version of TAM, SAM reflects the share of the total addressable market a startup realistically can capture based on the current business model – often limited to a geography (e.g., total vegan fast-food sales in the US).
- **SOM (Serviceable Obtainable Market):** this expresses the percentage of SAM that the startup realistically can capture – often at or below 10%.
- **TAM (Total Addressable Market):** as a key metric in market size analysis, TAM assesses the total size of a market and is calculated by adding up or estimating total sales for a product/service often globally (e.g., total global fast-food sales).

12 Fifteen Key Issues in Growth Term Sheets

With Vanessa Pinter

Key pitfalls to avoid for scale-up builders   **!**

- **Not taking the best lawyer you can possibly find**
  Missing out on experienced lawyers when it comes to term sheet negotiations is saving at the wrong end. To have sound legal advice and help
  in negotiations, a company ideally chooses specialized lawyers with
  several years of experience in negotiating VC-funded deals for startups.
  The best lawyers will refrain from telling a company that something is
  impossible and will instead provide their recommendation of the steps
  that need to be taken. Selecting large firms can also be well worth it here
  since they have the resources and clout to serve a company as it grows.
- **Ignoring key negotiation guidelines for acquiring growth stage capital**
  Pitfalls can include publishing any internal valuation targets and easily
  conceding to points in the term sheet that will put off later-stage investors. Likewise, agreeing to over-optimistic valuations can pose problems
  for the future. Generally, negotiations with VC partners should not run
  under high time pressure and should instead be based on relationships
  of trust that are planned and established early on (see Practice 98).
- **Failing to understand the 15 term sheet issues for growth capital in depth**
  Setting unfavorable conditions can have costly consequences in both
  the short and long term. Understanding the principal terms and options
  of a term sheet is a must for founders to ensure the fair growth of the
  company. This includes knowing about investor rights, employee stock
  options, dividends, vesting, anti-dilution clauses and board composition, as well as being aware of what is typically desired by investors and
  founders (see Practice 99).

A startup may be poised to enter the scale-up stratosphere, but they will still need the fuel to propel themselves there. The following is a guide on how to fill the tank by effectively negotiating term sheets and convertible notes in growth-stage funding rounds. While the content here is not legal, tax or financial advice, it is of paramount importance for a startup to understand all key term sheets and convertible debt options to craft deals that can set them on the track to becoming a unicorn.

Both the guidelines for term sheet negotiations (Practice 98) and the perspectives on the 15 most important term sheet issues (Practice 99) are a reflection of our best knowledge of the current market standards, as validated by over ten VC experts and lawyers. It is also always worthwhile to ask for additional perspectives from specialized lawyers for specific regions and industries.

Negotiating guidelines

Practice 98: Following major guidelines for term sheet negotiations

Helpful guidelines to get the most out of a term sheet negotiation usually include:
- **Finding the best lawyer possible.** These lawyers should present several VC-financed startup deals (preferably in the same industry) and ideally have experience working at a top corporate legal firm (e.g., Osborne Clarke, SMP, V14).[316] The feedback about them from other entrepreneurs should be excellent, too. The hourly rate is often in the range of EUR 300–450 for partners in Central Europe and a cap of the fees can be asked for (e.g., you pay EUR 30,000 at maximum).
- **Feeding the competitive edge.** The more term sheets obtained, the better a company's competitive position will be. When looking for a new lead investor, a company ideally aims to have 3–4 VC offers to choose from.

- **Optimizing for brand AND added value.** Would you trust a future board member to take care of your children while you are busy? This is the degree of trust needed when it comes to selecting board members. While having several top VCs investing in a company (e.g., Sequoia, Accel, Lakestar, Atomico, HV Capital) helps to attract talent and other investors, having a senior partner on board who is effective at executive recruiting, sales introductions and strategic advice and driven by an excellent network can be extremely beneficial. The board can be a mixture of big names and smaller ones, but operationally helpful VCs will pay off in the long run.
- **Getting a "vanilla" term sheet early on and sticking to it.** It is important to remember that later-stage investors will, at the minimum, ask for the same terms agreed upon with early-stage investors. Typical topics that a startup may not want to concede in its early days include liquidation multiples of more than 1x, free investor sales rights for shares and approval thresholds by the board that are below market standard. This is particularly true for salaries of new hires and investments. Point Nine has published a vanilla early-stage term sheet <u>here</u>, which provides a good starting point.
- **Avoiding overly aggressive valuations and overly investor-friendly terms.** A valuation "which you have to grow into" increases the probability of a down round later on. A company may want to be extremely careful when conceding for a higher valuation on issues that impact them negatively in the event that they don't meet these expectations (e.g., investor-friendly anti-dilution protection or warrants with overly ambitious milestones; details below). Avoiding very investor-friendly terms, such as a "double dip" in the liquidation preference (see Term 03) or interest on the equity of an investor, is also important.
- **Avoiding time pressure when closing a deal.** An inbound investor relationship process is typically established to build up a pool of potential investors (e.g., dedicated contact person for potential investors, continuously updated investment materials, criteria to filter investment proposals before reaching founder level) and to start raising funds at least six months before a company is due to run out of money.

- **Communicating funding or valuation targets in writing.** If a company is aiming for a USD 30 million round size and USD 200 million valuation, and they receive 90% of both, this can still be a highly favorable result. If they have communicated their intentions beforehand, there is a chance that this can be construed as a failure.
- **Getting on the radar of growth investors early.** The best entrepreneurs will compile a list of preferred growth investors directly after Series A and will start reaching out. Growth investors prefer developing a relationship long before the relevant due diligence for the funding round starts. Even if they do not yet invest, they can be often willing to support in making introductions to potential candidates, customers, etc.
- **Making "investment prospecting" as efficient as possible.** When investors approach a company, the company can ask for three things: minimum annual revenue, minimum growth rate and required minimum ticket size. If the company can't match it, they need to tell this to the investors. It is helpful if investors can communicate in the first contact the thresholds to invest.

Figure 81 lists the 15 most important term sheet issues to be negotiated during a growth round.

Key term sheet issues

Practice 99: Negotiating the 15 most important term sheet issues during a growth round

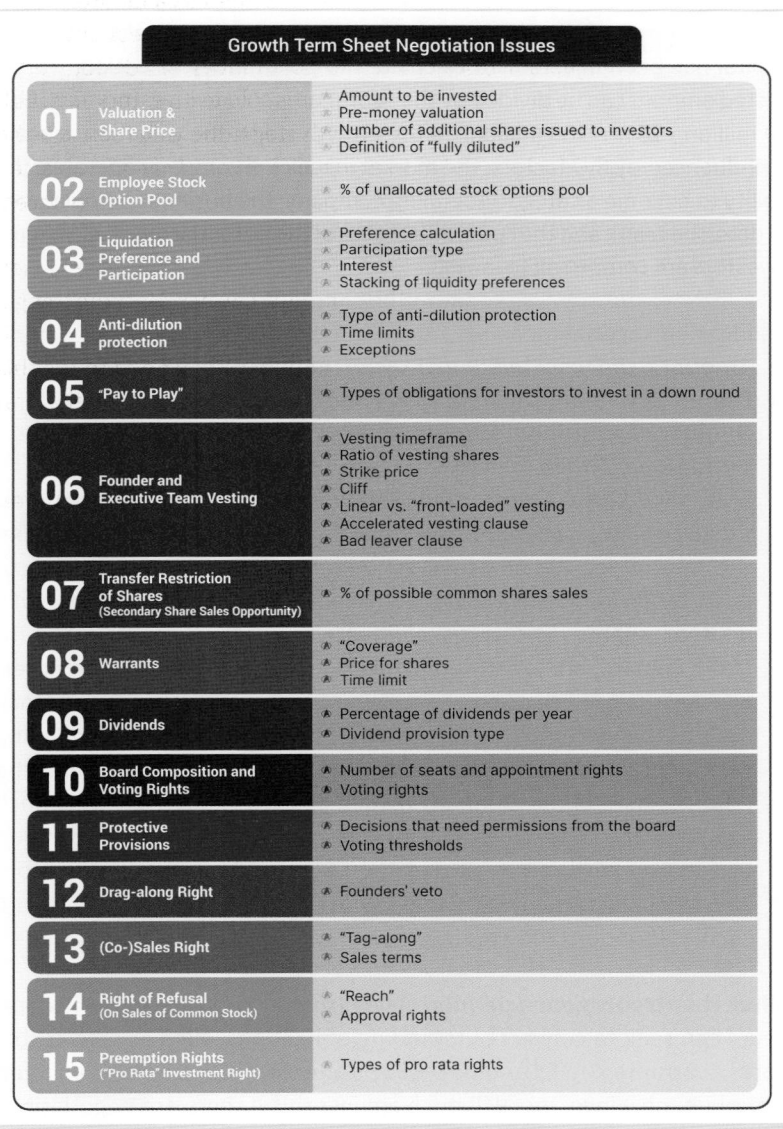

Figure 82: Growth Term Sheet Negotiation Issues

Let's look at each of them in-depth.

1. Valuation

This is the value of the company expressed in terms of the "pre-money" and "post-money" valuation. Pre-money refers to how much a company is worth before new investments come in; post-money is the value after new capital has been injected. To calculate the post-money valuation, the invested amount can be divided by the % of shares sold to investors (e.g., EUR 40 million / 25% = 160 million). In the growth stage, the valuation is heavily influenced by five factors: the market in which a company operates; the ability to become a category-defining company; the business performance to date; the team; and the competitiveness of the potential deal (i.e., if many investors are competing to invest).

Issues to be negotiated:
- **Amount to be invested (e.g., EUR 10 million)**
- **Pre-money valuation (e.g., EUR 40 million)**
- **Number of additional shares issued to investors**
- **Definition of "fully diluted"**
  This is the second most influential driver of ownership stakes after the pre-money valuation. The broader the definition is, the smaller the share price the new investor will pay. The share price is calculated by dividing the pre-money valuation by the number of "fully diluted" shares. The three elements commonly counted toward "fully diluted" are: outstanding obligations (e.g., convertible notes, warrants or SAFEs), existing employee stock option shares and stock options for new employees. Including these options prior to injecting new capital reduces the share price for the new investors, and the relative share of the company owned by the existing investors (incl. founders and employees) will also drop a little bit more. A common factor in growth rounds is that the ESOP pool is carved out before any new investors come in, thereby "diluting" existing shareholders, such as founders and employees.

What is entrepreneur-friendly? Aside from a fair valuation, entrepreneurs can seek to convert outstanding obligations, such as convertible notes, warrants, SAFEs and new ESOPs after the new capital is injected (although, new investors will push against this if there are negotiations with a high valuation).

2. Employee Stock Option Pool (ESOP)

Investors will insist (and rightly so) on reserving a certain percentage of a company's shares as unallocated stock options for future employees (i.e., non-founders and non-investors).

Issue to be negotiated: The number of shares reserved for employees. It is common for early-stage companies that this is around 10–20%. However, while in a growth round, they should allocate 8–15% if the unallocated ESOP pool becomes too small.[317]

What is entrepreneur-friendly? A company can attract an AAA team only if they have the room to reward ESOP properly. Therefore, agreeing on a more generous ESOP pool is often the right thing to do.

3. Liquidation preference and participation

This consists of the investor's right to receive a return prior to – and in preference to – other investors, founders and employees in the event that the company is sold. Typically, it represents "downside" protection for investors and is relevant only if the price paid for the company at the exit is smaller than the sum of all liquidation preferences (i.e., if a company sells for EUR 300 million, but they were financed with EUR 400 million).

Issues to be negotiated:
- **Preference calculation**
  If assuming an investor injects USD 10 million into a company, the preference calculation refers to the number of times the investor receives back the investment before the "common shareholders" (i.e., founders and employees) in the event of an exit. A one-time multiple is the usual, meaning an investor would receive USD 10 million. For companies that are in a challenging business situation, investors might demand a multiple of up to 3x, which can result in them receiving up to USD 30 million. The investors will always have the choice of receiving their liquidation multiple or selling their stock in the company exit if doing so returns a higher valuation.
- **Participation type**
  If investors receive a multiple of the invested capital AND can participate proportionately ("pro rata") in the remaining sales proceeds, they have the right of "participation." A company can negotiate three options here: non-participating preference (the common option) – investors

will not participate in the remaining sales proceeds after they have exercised their liquidation preference; participating preference ("double dip") – the investor receives the liquidation multiple and can sell shares with all other shareholders; and participating preference with a cap – here, the investor can only sell shares up to a certain amount.

- **Interest**
  The amount of interest paid on investor capital in case of an exit (interests in so-called "priced investment" rounds are very uncommon).
- **Stacking of liquidity preferences**
  Investors are paid first, followed by all other shareholders (e.g., employees, founders). This is a very common term and all investors will demand it. However, there are two options available for negotiating the distribution of cash to investors in case of an exit: whoever invested last is paid first ("waterfall") or capital can be paid out in a blended ("pari passu") manner, which means all investors are paid on a "pro rata" basis independent of when they made their investment.

What is entrepreneur-friendly? One ideal outcome is a combination of a one-time liquidation preference, non-participating preference with no interest and blended liquidation preferences. If a company has to accept a participation preference, a cap can be put in place, so if the liquidation preference option is pulled, the investor will only participate up to a certain amount.

4. Anti-dilution protection

In case a company needs to accept venture money to a share price less than the last valuation round ("down round"), the overall value of the company will drop. In this case, anti-dilution protection terms entitle the existing investors to receive more shares (retroactively) at the expense of founders and employees.

Issues to be negotiated:
- **Type of anti-dilution protection**
  There are four options to choose from: the first is *full ratchet down round protection*. This creates full investor protection in a down round and puts investors in a position that is similar to if they had invested based on the down round valuation (i.e., they will eventually

hold as many shares as if they had invested at the valuation of the down round). The second is the *narrow-based weighted average*. Here, only the new shares from the most recent round are used as a basis for calculation (excluding common shares, ESOP and warrants). The stake of founders and employees in the company drops in the event of a down round, albeit less than in a full ratchet scenario. The third is the *broad-based weighted average*. The new shares from the most recent round are used as the basis for calculation, with all options and warrants included. This means even less dilution for founders and employees. The fourth is *no dilution protection*. With this option, no investor protection is provided, and the dilution effect of the down round is borne equally by all investors, founders and employees.

- **Time limits**
  This allows for limits on anti-dilution protection for a certain number of months or until the next funding round.
- **Exceptions**
  Companies can exclude internal rounds for anti-dilution protection and include convertibles with a discount only.

What is entrepreneur-friendly? No dilution protection is the best option for the entrepreneur and their teams. However, this is not a common arrangement. Settling on a broad-based average with a time limit of one year and exceptions for internal rounds is one way to go.

5. "Pay to play" (P2P)
This refers to the obligation for investors to make investments that are proportional to their share value ("pro rata") in a down round. If they fail to do so, they will lose some of their special rights.

Issues to be negotiated:
- **No pay to play**
  Investors do not have to invest in a down round (common).
- **Conversion of preferred shares into "shadow preferred" shares**
  Investors who do not invest in a down round proportionally lose their anti-dilution protections.
- **Forced conversion of preferred stock into common stock**
  Shares of investors who do not invest in a down round "pro rata" are converted into common stock.

What is entrepreneur-friendly? A good outcome is to have a shadow preferred option in place if there is an agreement on anti-dilution protection for the investors. However, while this is more common in the United States, in Europe it is rather rare.

6. Founder and executive team vesting

The logic of share vesting: the longer someone works for a company, the greater the number of "active" shares. This arrangement is designed to prevent founders or executives from exiting the company early with many shares and leaving other founders and executives to improve the value of their shares without contributing.

Issues to be negotiated:

- **Vesting timeframe**
  The number of years until all shares carry the full economic value ("vested"). A common time frame is 4 years, although this is sometimes possible within 2–3 years if the founder or employee has a strong track record or experience.
- **Strike price**
  If an executive team member joins a startup in its early days, the reward should be worth more than the one belonging to someone who climbs aboard later on. This is why a strike price exists. It prevents latecomers from being rewarded for the value others have created. Say when signing a contract each share is priced at USD 1,000. If the company is bought four years later and the price has risen to USD 20,000 per share, the value this employee has co-created is USD 19,000 (i.e., the current share price – USD 20,000 – minus the strike price – USD 1,000). In the case of an exit event, the payout will be USD 19,000 for each share. Having this logic in place is both normal and fair.
- **Ratio of vesting shares**
  It is common to vest over a fixed period of time. However, there are occasions when someone can argue for a small percentage to be allocated to them straight away without vesting (e.g., the founder is very experienced, the company was "bootstrapped" – built without venture capital).
- **Cliff**
  It is an industry-standard for founders and managers to need to stay for at least a year before the vesting of any shares ("One year cliff"). Leaving before the cliff usually means that they will lose all their shares.

- **Linear vs. "front-loaded" or "back-loaded" vesting**
  If the vesting time frame is long, a larger volume of shares can be allocated earlier (e.g., 75% of shares vested in the first two years, with 25% in the final two years). However, schemes that let more shares vest in later years are sometimes used to incentivize the team to stay as long as possible (e.g., 10% vest in the first year, 20% in the second, 30% in the third, and 40% in the fourth).
- **Accelerated vesting clause**
  In case of an exit or change in ownership, all "unvested" shares become vested at once.
- **Bad leaver clause**
  It is common to have to transfer back all vested and unvested shares if a founder or employee breaks the law (i.e., fraud). In cases of owners of the shares leaving the company voluntarily within the vesting period, it is common that they will need to transfer back their unvested shares. In cases when someone is asked to leave for non-legal issues, they should be able to keep their vested shares – occasionally they might negotiate to keep the unvested shares.

What is entrepreneur-friendly? One good outcome for an entrepreneur would be: a vesting scheme of three years, one year cliff, front-loaded vesting, an acceleration clause and a bad leaver clause that allows them to keep their shares if they are asked to leave.

7. **Transfer restriction of shares (secondary share sales opportunity)**
Generally, one cannot sell shares prior to an exit. However, there are cases in which founders or senior employees can perform "secondaries" with a small percentage of shares before an exit.

Issue to be negotiated: The percentage of the shares excluded from "lock-up" that could be sold to other investors.

What is entrepreneur-friendly? This is uncommon during an early phase but is achievable during growth rounds if your business performs well.

8. **Warrants**
This is the option for investors to invest more capital usually for favorable prices within a certain time window.

Issues to be negotiated:
- **"Coverage"**
  The number of shares available for purchase by the investor.
- **Price for shares**
  Usually, this is the price of the current investment round or a future round.
- **Time limit**
  The number of months the warrant is valid.

What is entrepreneur-friendly? If one has to concede to an investor, this is one option to give. However, investing later on the price of the current round will reduce the share value for all the other investors, so it is of note to be cautious in granting this option.

9. Dividends
This is the percentage amount paid on an investor's money in case of an exit. In VC deals, no dividends are paid out prior to the exit.

Issues to be negotiated:
- **Percentage of dividends per year (e.g., 4–8%)**
- **Dividend provision type**
  There are three options here: dividends payable on the investors' shares (this is usually zero and common); non-cumulative dividends paid out in case of an exit; and cumulative dividends that "accrue" on investors' stock (i.e., dividends are paid out at the end of Year 1 and added to the invested amount, dividends in Year 2 are paid based on the increased investment).

What is entrepreneur-friendly? Avoiding agreement on dividends is often good advice, as the venture deal should be driven by an increase in company valuation alone. If one has to concede, it is best to always agree on a supermajority that needs to be sought from the board before this is approved.

10. Board composition and voting rights
Investors will ask for control rights that they exercise through the board of directors.

Issues to be negotiated:

- **Number of seats and appointment rights**
  Common appointments are 3–5 members for Series A, 5–7 for Series B, and 7–9 for Series C. Trying to keep the board as lean as possible pays off, as larger boards tend to be less effective. If (smaller) investors demand to have board seats, offering them observer roles instead can be a solution. It is best to agree on who is responsible for selecting independent board members (if any): investors only or investors together with entrepreneurs.

- **Voting rights**
  These are the number of votes held by each board member. Founders are sometimes granted "supervoting" rights, where their votes count by a specific multiple. However, this is uncommon.

What is entrepreneur-friendly? A good outcome is if entrepreneurs receive a veto right for critical decisions. For example, in response to the removal of managing directors, they can co-appoint independent board members and have a small board with an odd number of board members to avoid voting ties.

11. Protective provisions

This term provides investors with the right to veto actions that may affect their investment. The rationale is to protect the minority stakeholders.

Issues to be negotiated:

- **Decisions for which you need permission from the board**
  Common decisions on which the board usually has a vote include: changes of rights, numbers, preferences or privileges of investor stocks; raising additional capital; the sale of the company; the creation of new share classes; changes to the size of the board of directors; and payments or declarations of dividends. Decisions that might not need the board's approval include: hiring or firing executive officers or changing their compensation; pushing spending limits beyond the agreed budget; changing the business focus or launching new business lines; and purchasing another entity's assets.

- **Voting thresholds**
  It is essential to negotiate if growth stage investors have a separate voting right and what the percentage necessary of investor votes is for certain decisions (e.g., 60%).

What is entrepreneur-friendly? The requisite percentage for all decisions is ideally below 66%, as a higher threshold runs the risk of giving minority shareholders a de facto veto right.

12. Drag-along right

This common term gives the majority of investors the right to force common shareholders (founders and employees) and minority investors to sell the startup and make an exit. It is well justified, as it prevents minority shareholders from gaining unfair bargaining power in case of an exit.

What is entrepreneur-friendly? In this case, the negotiation of a minimum exit valuation is a good result.

13. (Co-)sales right

This term defines the parameters for shareholders to sell shares in the company, as long as it is still privately held and not publicly traded.

Issues to be negotiated:
- "Tag-along"

  If a majority shareholder wants to sell stock without making a full exit, this term gives minority shareholders the right to sell shares under the same conditions. There are at least three versions: tag-along rights for investors only (the common option); tag-along rights for both investors and founders with a cap; and tag-along rights for both investors and founders without a cap for founders (e.g., they can sell up to 2% of the stock held). A total sales option is sometimes common as well: it enables founders and all shareholders to sell all their shares in case of change-of-control or sale of shares to competitors. This aims to prevent selling shares to competitors.
- **Sales terms**

  Options: investors can sell stock freely or they need majority approval of the board for a sale (the common term).

What is entrepreneur-friendly? Aiming to secure a tag-along right can be of the essence, as this might provide leverage over investors in case some want to leave the company prematurely. Also, investors should always require permission from the board for approval to sell their share.

14. Right of first refusal (on sales of common or preferred stock).

Investors can buy in proportion to their share value ("pro rata") shares from shareholders who want to sell.

Issues to be negotiated:

- **Reach**

  Only investors or both the investors and founders can buy stocks. Both options are common and occur frequently.

- **Approval rights**

  There are two variants here: "right-of-first-offer," meaning existing investors can decide if they wish to buy shares before common shareholders approach outside investors; or "right-of-last-look" – in this case, existing investors need to approve these sales after negotiating with the growth-stage investor and can jump on the deal instead of the new investor.

What is entrepreneur-friendly? Trying to avoid a "right-of-last-look" is helpful. Early investors may insist on it, but it can present an obstacle for starting negotiations with a growth-stage investor (as due diligence at this stage is expensive and there is an increased risk of not getting a deal).

15. Preemption rights ("pro rata" investment right)

Preemption rights permit an investor to maintain their percentage ownership in subsequent financing rounds. For example, if they have a 10% equity stake in a startup after Series A, they will be entitled to purchase 10% of the shares for the preferred stock issued in Series B to the agreed-upon price of the current round.

What is entrepreneur-friendly? This is a common, well-justified term. However, one should never agree to "super" pro rata rights, as they allow existing investors to increase their shares in the company in the next round, which can inhibit growth stage investors from joining a startup.

Further term sheet issues:

There are other term issues that need to be under control, but a top-shelf lawyer will handle these. These include: conversion of preferred in-common stock in case of an IPO; redemption rights; pooling options; registration rights and duties; reporting and information rights; non-compete clause; non-solicitation obligation; "pari passu"; no shop agreement; proprietary information & inventions agreement; indemnification; and assignment & redemption.

Companies that are not yet in a strong negotiating position for the next funding round often use **convertible notes** to source intermediate, or "bridge," financing. In essence, this is when a company receives a loan from an investor with the obligation to pay it back or (more commonly) convert the debt into equity (e.g., in the next funding round). Convertible notes can delay attributing a new price to shares ("priced round"), giving time to achieve major milestones and driving up valuation in the meantime. Convertible notes are often employed by existing investors, are quick to close and come with limited legal fees.

Issues to be negotiated:
- **Note amount ("face value")**
  The amount the company receives. This can range from less than USD 100,000 to several millions.
- **Interest rate**
  The annual interest to be paid on the note. A common figure is 6–8%, as this is often the minimum interest paid by VCs to their investors. Usually, the interest accrues and is converted into equity.
- **Maturity date**
  This is the time frame after the debt converts into equity or has to be paid back. A common time frame is 9–18 months with the agreement that the note converts into equity if the founding round is closed earlier.
- **Conversion and payback options**
  What happens when the maturity date is reached? Typically, either the note and interest are converted into equity, or the investor receives the money and interest back. The obligation to pay back the convertible debt to existing investors is uncommon, as it indicates distrust in the company's performance. This can dissuade new investors.
- **Discount on the share price**
  As the investor in the convertible note is financing additional time, which is used to increase the company's valuation, it is fair to offer a discount when the debt is converted into equity. A discount of 10–30% is the market standard with 20% most often seen. In some cases, the average share price is seen between the last and the next

funding round. Increasing the level of the discount is common, too. If, for example, the conversion is performed within 8–10 weeks, the discount is 10%, beyond that 20%.[318]

- **Valuation Cap**

  It is common to agree on a maximum price to be paid by the investor in the next round when converting the debt. For example, a discount of 20% on the new share price would equate to no higher than USD 100, even if the valuation minus the discount is higher. It is important to be extremely careful with agreeing on relatively low caps, as they can be viewed as anchor points for the share price in the next funding round by new investors.

What is entrepreneur-friendly? A good outcome is a convertible note with 6% interest, a maturity of 12 months, an agreement that the note amount plus interest converts into equity and a discount of 10–20%. Ideally, one shouldn't agree on a cap at all to avoid creating share price ceilings for the next funding round – at the minimum these should be ambitiously high. There are more issues a lawyer can help with, such as conversion triggers and conversion securities, especially during the growth stage.

Watch our video on the eight pitfalls to avoid when negotiating growth term sheets by scanning the QR code or following this link: https://youtube/9bCSJaswwxw.

Definitions

- **ESOP (Employee Stock Ownership Plan)**: a kind of employee benefit plan that gives employees the ability to acquire a portion of a company's shares at a discounted rate to encourage ownership and improve employee performance and commitment. This may come in many different shades (e.g., phantom stock, virtual options, restricted shares, options).
- **Term sheets**: a non-legally binding document that sets out the terms and conditions of an investment in a company and commonly contains information relating to the company's valuation and share structure.
- **Priced investment round**: equity investments based on a negotiated valuation of a startup. To delay this, startups sometimes use convertible notes, which set back the pricing of the shares to the next round.
- **Valuation**: the analytical process by which the current value of a company is assessed; usually achieved through analysis of the company's management, assets, capital structure and future earnings potential – the startup operators' negotiation skills and the amount of venture capital firms competing to invest are also major influence factors.

Contact Us

We hope you enjoyed reading *The Builder's Guide*. Visit our website www.
builderguide.org for additional resources and updates about our work. If
you have suggestions for improving our work and would like to contribute to *The Builder's Guide*, please message us on info@buildersguide.org.

We'd love to hear from you!
Martin, Thomas & The Builder's Guide Team

Notes

1   BCG, How to Harness the Power of Purpose | Purpose Driven Business, 2019; McKinsey, McKinsey Organizational Health Index. Using "Organizational Health" to build and sustain performance, 2011.

2   11 Reasons Why We Didn't Invest in Your Company, TechCrunch.

3   Global Marketing Trends, Deloitte 2020.

4   BCG, How To Harness The Power Of Purpose | Purpose Driven Business, 2019; Mckinsey, Mckinsey Organizational Health Index. Using "Organizational Health" To Build And Sustain Performance, 2011.

5   Edelman, Edelman Trust Barometer, 2018.

6   US Association for National Advertisers, Harris Poll and Carol Cone ON PURPOSE, "The B2B Purpose Paradox," 2020.

7   About Square, 2021.

8   https://www.salesforce.com/company/stakeholder-capitalism/, 2021.

9   Brian Chesky, Don't Fuck Up the Culture, 2014.

10 McKinsey, McKinsey Organizational Health Index. Using "Organizational Health" to build and sustain performance, 2011.

11 First Round Review, Draw The Owl and Other Company Values You Didn't Know You Should Have, 2015.

12 Barrett Values Center, The Evolution of the Barret Model, 2020; Hendrik Backerra Consulting, Corporate culture can make or break your organization, 2019.

13 Evernote, Product Page, 2021.

14 Several studies of Bain & Company describe these "elements of value" in depth.

15 Daily Business, Blow for flotation, 2021.

16 USA today, Airbnb launches initiative with Color of Change to root out racial discrimination on its platform, 2021.

17 S&P Global, What is the "G" in ESG?, 2020; UBS, What is the "G" in ESG?, 2018.

18 QTRADE, The G in ESG, 2021.

19 EconStor, ESG considerations in venture capital and business angel investment decisions: Evidence from two pan-European surveys, 2020.

20 CNBC, Some of Europe's top tech investors are adding "sustainability clause" to start-up deal terms, 2020.

21 Financial Times, Majority of ESG funds outperform wider market over 10 years; Morningstar, How does European sustainable funds' performance measure up?, 2020.

22 McKinsey, Five ways that ESG creates value, 2019.

23 Deloitte, The Deloitte global millennial survey, 2019.

24 Glassdoor, What job seekers really think about your diversity and inclusion stats, 2014.

25 Financial Times, Green Gold: How sustainability became big business for consumer brands.

26 FastCompany, How Patagonia grows every time it amplifies its social mission, 2018; and the opposite has also been demonstrated (a lack of ESG consideration leads to users witching), REF: Insider Intelligence, Sustainability is factoring into 2019 holiday purchases, 2019.

27   McKinsey, Five ways that ESG creates value, 2019.

28   EconStor, ESG considerations in venture capital and business angel investment decisions, 2020.

29   BlackRock, Larry Fink's 2021 CEO Letter, 2021.

30   Morningstar, Sustainable funds' Record-breaking year, 2020; Financial Times, ESG demand prompts more than 250 European funds to change tack, 2021.

31   US Securities and Exchange Commission, An honest conversation about ESG regulation, 2021; Government Commercial Function, Guide to using the social value model, 2020; FT Adviser, What advisers should know about the EU's ESG disclosure rules, 2021.

32   Apple, Apple commits to be 100 percent carbon neutral for its supply chain and products by 2030, 2020.

33   Microsoft, Microsoft will be carbon negative by 2030, 2020.

34   Edie, Net-zero by 2030: Lime becomes first micro-mobility firm to pledge to science-based targets, 2020; Future NetZero, Lime pledges to become "carbon-negative" business by 2025, 2020.

35   Ideas by WeTransfer, Breaking the climate-neutral barrier, 2021.

36   Radius, Rebooting the Earth, 2017; Fierce Telecom, VMware unveils Carbon Avoidance Meter to monitor data center energy usage, 2019.

37   Sifted, What does a head of sustainability actually do?

38   Mashable, Average US officer works 10.00 sheets of paper per year, 2014; Federal Electronics Challenge, The benefits of automatic Duplexing, 2013; Restore, Paperless office?, 2019; Geerings, The real figures of paper usage in the UK, 2021.

39   Center for corporate Climate Leadership, Instructions: Questionnaire for Suppliers on Energy & Greenhouse Gas Emissions, 2021.

40   Walmart, Sustainable Packaging Playbook, 2021.

41   StartUS, Top 5 Sustainable Packaging Startups out of 1.000, 2021.

42   McKinsey, The state of internal carbon pricing, 2021.

43   C2ES, Internal Carbon Pricing, 2021; I4CE, Internal carbon pricing: A growing corporate practice, 2021.

44   EDF, How companies set internal prices on carbon, 2016.

45   United Nations, Microsoft Global Carbon Fee, 2021.

46   Shopifiy, Carbon Offsets, 2021; Shopify Appstore, Offset, 2021.

47   Stripe, Wachstum als Klimapartner, 2021.

48   McKinsey, Diversity wins, 2020.

49   Triangle DEI, The Deloitte Diversity and Inclusion Model, 2020.

50   Gusto, Diversity and Inclusion, 2016.

51   Culture Amp, 5 Diversity and Inclusion Questions to use at your company, 2021.

52   FastCompany, How Etsy attracted 500 percent more female engineers, 2013.

53   The Verge, Spotify to let employees keep working remotely and now choose what country they work from, 2021.

54   Facebook, Personio post, 2020.

55   Yahoo finance, WeWork is a corporate governance nightmare, 2019.

56   CNBC, WeWork fiasco may have startups rethinking their governance structures before heading for public markets, 2019.

57 Wiley Online Library, The throne vs. the kingdom: Founder control and value creation in startups, 2015.

58 Harvard Business Review, When and Why Diversity Improves Your Board's Performance, 2019.

59 The Guardian, Revealed: Google's "two-tier" workforce training document, 2018.

60 Independent, Amazon prime day hit by huge strike, 2018; The Guardian, "I'm not a robot" Amazon workers condemn unsafe, grueling conditions at warehouse, 2020.

61 Zalando, Employee Participation and Representation at Zalando, 2021.

62 Notion Capital, The Unicorn Trajectory: Who Unicorns Hire and When They Hire Them, 2019.

63 Hyperight, Using data in hyper-growth recruiting mode, 2020.

64 Workable, Job offer acceptance rate metrics FAQ, 2021.

65 Lever, 2019 Talent Benchmarks Report, 2019.

66 TLNT, Lessons from Google and Netflix on how to onboard employees, 2020; ERE, Google's Simple Just-in-time Checklist improves onboarding results by 25%, 2015; Process.st, Why Google's onboarding process works 25% better than everyone else's, 2018.

67 ERE, Google's Simple Just-in-time Checklist improves onboarding results by 25%, 2015.

68 LinkedIn, How to wow your new hires rather than numb them, 2015.

69 Sales Hacker, If you are chumming more than 10% of your Salespeople they aren't the problem, 2016.

70 Isl Recruitment, Triple threat: the three reasons your tech employees leave, 2019; Medium, 7 key employee turnover statistics, 2019.

71 Forbes, Salespeople are burning out faster than ever, 2016.

72 People matters, Should we measure attrition in terms of regret?

73 Glassdoor, SAP promises employees "Become everything you want," 2018; SAP, Job Sharing and Co-Management at SAP, 2018.

74 LinkedIn, LinkedIn Data proves the Impact of a strong talent brand, 2015.

75 Very good culture decks of HubSpot here and of Netflix here, 2021.

76 LinkedIn, Active vs. passive candidates, 2014.

77 Stanley Milgram, The Small World Problem, 1967; Wikipedia, The Small World Experiment, 2021.

78 HR Dive, Applicant quality continues to plague employers, 2016.

79 LinkedIn, The ultimate list of Hiring Statistics, 2014.

80 Undercover Recruiter, Why Employee referrals are the best source of Hire, 2021.

81 Lever, "The Little Grey Book of Recruiting Benchmarks," 2016.

82 LinkedIn, 2015 Talent Trends, 2015.

83 Burton Advisers, 5 tips for "Reining in" talkative candidates, 2019.

84 Amazon, What is a "Bar Raiser" at amazon, 2019.

85 Careerbuilder, Candidate Experience Study, 2017.

86 See for example Deloitte 2019 Global Millennial Survey; LinkedIn 2020 Global Talent Trend Report .

87 Holloway, Formalizing Levels, 2021.

88 Radford, As Market Realities Change, Radford's Global Job Leveling Model Rises to the Challenge, 2018; Lattice, What is Job Leveling and How Does It Work?, 2020.

89 University of Wisconsin, Job Families Handout; Gradar, Job Families, 2021.

90 Gradar, Overview of job families, 2021.

91 PayScale, Leveling Guide, 2021.

92 Proton Engineering Blog, Careers, 2021; Indiana University, IU Classification Career Level Guide, 2021.

93 HBR, How You Promote People Can Make or Break Company Culture, 2018.

94 Indeed, Samples of Self Assessments: Templates for Your Business, 2021.

95 IBM, The Real Story Behind Millennials in the Workplace, 2015.

96 Amazon, Upskilling 2025, 2020; Career minds, CHROs: Here are the top 5 companies investing in upskilling in 2020, 2020.

97 Poensgen Digital, HR in the digital age, 2021.

98 re:Work, The five keys to a successful Google team, 2015.

99 Netflix, Culture, 2009.

100 Netflix, Culture, 2009.

101 Laura Delizonna, High-Performing Teams Need Psychological Safety. Here's How to Create It, Harvard Business Review, August 2017.

102 Netflix, Netflix culture, 2021.

103 Workstarts, 11 Companies that have adopted unlimited holidays (and what they found), 2020.

104 First Round Review, How This Head of Engineering Boosted Transparency at Instagram, 2018.

105 Culture Amp, 10 Employee engagement initiatives used by top companies, 2021.

106 The balance careers, The Pros and Cons of working at Startup Company, 2019.

107 Index Ventures, Rewarding Talent: A Guide to Stock Options for European Entrepreneurs, 2021.

108 Index Ventures, OptionPlan, 2021.

109 Index Ventures, Rewarding Talent: A Guide to Stock Options for European Entrepreneurs, 2021.

110 Index Ventures, Rewarding Talent: A Guide to Stock Options for European Entrepreneurs, 2021.

111 AWS, An Insight look at the amazon culture, 2021; Amazon, Our leadership principles, 2021.

112 Bain & Company, Why Customer Loyalty Beats Quarterly Earnings, 2020; Bain & Company, Net Promoter System, 2021.

113 Internal study, Bain & Company.

114 Team SaaStr, How To: NPS 75 With 40K Customers with CEO and CXO of Gusto, 2021.

115 Jeff Toister, *The Service Culture Handbook: A Step-by-Step Guide to Getting Your Employees Obsessed with Customer Service*, 2017.

116 The Economist, The quantified serf, 2015, citing several dozen academic studies providing evidence that ambitious and specific goals lead to unparalleled performance.

117 First part of the quote is attributed to Muhammed Ali directly, the second part edited by the Adidas "Impossible Is Nothing" campaign 2004.

118 SRE Google, Postmortem Culture, 2017.

119 For a template for conducting postmortems, see here.

120 Re:Work, The five keys to a successful Google team, 2015.

121 Slack, Psychological safety first, 2019.

122 Andrew Chen, How do you find insights like facebooks "7 friends in 10 days" to grow your product faster, 2021; Mode blog, Facebook's Aha Moment is simpler than you think, 2015.

123 SlideShare, Unlocking Growth, 2014.

124 Boxrox, Know what matters most to your members, 2020.

125 The survey question Sean Ellis posed was: How would you feel if you could no longer use [Product Name]? Answers: very disappointed, somewhat disappointed, not disappointed, N/A – I no longer use [ProductName]; Growth Hackers, Using product market fit to drive sustainable growth, 2019.

126 Medium, AARRR Framework-Metrics, 2017.

127 The Verge, How Soundcloud's broken business model drove artists away, 2017.

128 Index, Expanding into Europe, 2011; Index, The US Expansion playbook for European founders, 2020.

129 Marty Cagan, *Inspired: How to Create Tech Products Customers Love*, 2018.

130 Marty Cagan, *Empowered: Ordinary People, Extraordinary Products*, 2020.

131 Medium, The three responsibilities of Product Leadership, 2020.

132 Melissa Perri, *Escaping the Build Trap: How Effective Product Management Creates Real Value*, 2018.

133 Tesla, The Secret Tesla Motors Master Plan, 2006.

134 Todd Lombardo, Evan Ryan, Michael Connors, *Product Roadmaps Relaunched: How to Set Direction while Embracing Uncertainty*, 2017.

135 Christian Strunk, How to define a product vision, 2021.

136 Harvard Business Review, It's Not Just Semantics: Managing Outcomes vs. Outputs, 2012.

137 Medium, Amazon Press Release: How to smartly create a different kind of business plan, 2018.

138 Melissa Perri, *Escaping the Build Trap: How Effective Product Management Creates Real Value*, 2018.

139 New Work Podcast, "Auftragsklärung."

140 Harvard Business Review, The Biggest Lie in Corporate America Is Phase 2, 2012.

141 Masters for Sale, Strategy Session 2, 2020.

142 Zalando, Mission zTypes, 2017; Zalando, Wie Zalando Media Solutions Kundensegmentierung neu erfindet, 2017.

143 Hotjar, How to create a simple, accurate user persona in 4 steps, 2018; One Zero, The long Road to Inventing Design Personas, 2020.

144 Dan Olson, *The Lean Product Playbook: How to Innovate with Minimum Viable Products and Rapid Customer Feedback*, 2015.

145 Zalando, Mission zTypes, 2017.

146 Dan Olson, *The Lean Product Playbook: How to Innovate with Minimum Viable Products and Rapid Customer Feedback*, 2015.

147 Kano Noriaki, Nobuhiku Seraku, Fumio Takahashi, Shinichi Tsuji, Journal of the Japanese Society for Quality Control (in Japanese), Attractive quality and must-be quality, 1984.

148 Todd Lombardo, Evan Ryan, Michael Connors, *Product Roadmaps Relaunched: How to Set Direction while Embracing Uncertainty*, 2017.

149 Medium, Story Point Alternatives, 2017.

150 Trello, Slack Platform Roadmap for Developers, 2016.

151 Medium, The Magician, 2016.

152 Medium, The Magician, 2016.

153 InVision, The New Design Frontier, 2019.

154 Invision, The new Design Frontier, 2019.

155 Brad Frost, Atomic Design, 2013.

156 UX Collected, 4 things you need to know about Atomic Design, 2020.

157 CB Insights, The Top 20 Reasons StartUps Fail, 2019.

158 Eric Migicovsky, How to Talk to Users, 2019.

159 GV Library, GV's Guide to UX Research for StartUps, 2019.

160 Marty Cagan, *Inspired: How to Create Tech Products Customers Love*, 2018.

161 Asana Guide, Sprint-Planung, 2021; The Product Manager, 10 Best Product Management Tools of 2021, 2021; Product School, A Curated List of Tools and Software for Product Managers in 2020, 2020.

162 Mark Andreesen, Product/market fit, 2007.

163 Chegg Study, Etsy uses DevOps for rapid Deployment, 2021; Tech Beacon, 10 Companies killing it at DevOps, 2015; HelpSystems, 6 Companies that are doing DevOps well, 2018.

164 Puppet, Stage of DevOps Report 2017, 2017.

165 The Register, Websites, Apps, Security cams, IoT gear knackered, 2017.

166 Think with Google, Find out how you stack up to new industry benchmarks for mobile page speed, 2018.

167 Increment, What broke the bank, 2019.

168 ITIC, Hourly Cost of Downtime Survey, 2020; Uptime, Unplanned Server Downtime costs for 2019, 2019.

169 Nicole Forsgren, Jez Humble, Gene Kim, *Accelerate – The Science of Lean Software and DevOps, Building and Scaling High Performing Technology Organizations*, 2018.

170 Doug Seven, Knightmare: A DevOps Cautionary Tale, 2014.

171 Nicole Forsgren, Jez Humble, Gene Kim, *Accelerate, The Science of Lean Software and DevOps, Building and Scaling High Performing Technology Organizations*, 2018.

172 StarUp Grind, Learn from 3 Cyber Security Fails, 2021.

173 IBM, Cost of Data Breach Report 2020, 2020.

174 Ponemon Institute, 2019 Global State of Cybersecurity in Small and Medium-Sized Businesses, 2019.

175 OWASP, Top 10 Web Application Security Risks, 2020.

176 Accenture, Accenture Cybersecurity Report, 2020.

177 Altexsoft, How to structure a Data Science Team, 2020.

178 DATAQUEST, Data Analyst Skills-8 Skills you need to get a Job, 2020.

179 Towards data science, Most In-Demand Tech Skills for Data Engineers, 2020.

180 Various setup models, such as centralization, consulting and centers of excellence, are outlined here: Altexsoft, How to structure a Data Science Team, 2020.

181 Matthew Skelton, Manuel Pais. *Team Topologies: Organizing Business and Technology Teams for Fast Flow*, 2019.

182 ENISA, How to set up CSIRT and SOC, 2020.

183 IBM, DevSecOps, 2020.

184 Marty Cagan, *Inspired, How to Create Tech Products Customers Love*, 2018.

185 Agile Manifesto, Principles behind the Agile Manifesto, 2021.

186 Eric Ries, *The Lean Startup, How Constant Innovation Creates Radically Successful Businesses*, 2011.

187 Agile Alliance, Subway Map to Agile Maps, 2021.

188 More details can be found here: www.agilealliance.org.

189 Patuka, Flavours of Agile, 2018.

190 Rackspace Technology, What is DevOps?, 2013.

191 Google Services, State of DevOps 2019, 2019.

192 Google Cloud, DORA's State of DevOps research program, 2021; Gene Kim, *Accelerate*, 2018.

193 Gene Kim, *Accelerate*, 2018.

193 Google Services, State of DevOps 2019, 2019.

194 Google Services, State of DevOps 2019, 2019.

195 Gene Kim, *Accelerate*, 2018; Belighted, Continuous Delivery: Faster Product-market Fit for Startups, 2018.

196 Medium, Continuous delivery tool landscape, 2017; Taptu, The Eight Phases of a DevOps Pipeline, 2019; Harness, The DevOps Tools Lifecycle Mash for 2021, 2021; Digital.ai, The Periodic Table of DevOps, 2020.

197 Guru99, Software Configuration Management in Software Engineering.

198 Jez Humble, *David Farley, Continuous Delivery, Reliable Software Releases Through Build, Test, and Deployment Automation*, 2010; Pluralsight, Role of Configuration Management in DevOps, 2019.

199 Pluralsight, Role of Configuration Management in DevOps, 2019.

200 Gene Kim, Jez Humble, Patrick Debois and John Willis, *The DevOps Handbook: How to Create World-Class Agility, Reliability, and Security in Technology Organizations*, 2016.

201 Inflectra, Software Testing Methodologies, 2020; Software Testing Fundamentals, Software Testing Definition; Lawrence Tan, Unit Tests, UI Tests, Integration Tests & End-To-End Tests, 2019.

202 Digital Ocean, An Introduction to Metrics, Monitoring and Alerting, 2017.

203 re:Work, The five keys to a successful Google Team, 2015.

204 Slack, Psychological Safety first, Building trust among teams, 2019.

205 Google, Accelerating SRE's to On-Call and Beyond, 2017.

206 Gene Kim, Jez Humble, Patrick Debois, *DevOPS Handbook – How to Create World-Class Agility, Reliability and Security in Technology Organizations*, 2016.

207 Martin Fowler, Microservices, 2014.

208 For more details, see Martin Fowler's Microservices Resource Guide.

209 A Cloud Guru, How to build a multi-region active-active architecture on AWS, 2018.

210 ScienceDirect, Platform Architecture, 2014.

211 Medium, Pattern for resilient Architecture, 2018.

212 AWS, Elastic Load Balancing, 2021.

213 O'Reilly, Chaos Engineering, 2017.

214 Principles of Chaos, Principles of Chaos Engineering, 2019; Medium, Chaos Engineering, 2019.

215 Owasp, Top 10 Web Application Security Risks, 2020.

216 Ponemon Institute, 2019 Global State of Cybersecurity in Small and Medium-Sized Businesses, 2019.

217 Usecure, The Complete Guide to Security Awareness Training 2021, 2021.

218 Imperva, Vulnerability Assessment, 2021.

219 The State of Security, What Type of Vulnerabilities Does a Penetration Test Look For?, 2018.

220 NIST, Integrating Cybersecurity and Enterprise Risk Management (ERM), 2020.

221 Venkatesan, Top 10 lessons from ISO 27001 Certification journey, 2019.

222 see Andreessen Horowitz.

223 Wp content, Interpreting the Architecture, 2021.

224 Oracle, Data Warehouse Defined, 2021.

225 AWS, What is a Data Lake?, 2021.

226 Databricks, What is a Lakehouse?, 2020; Snowflake, What is a Data Lakehouse, 2021.

227 AWS, Amazon Personalize, 2021; Medium, Product Recommendations with Machine Learning, 2018.

228 Brandwatch, Understanding Sentiment Analysis: What it is & Why It's Used, 2018.

229 Airbnb, Whitepaper How to create Loyalty beyond Reason, 2021.

230 Smart Insights, E-commerce conversion rates – how do yours compare?, 2021.

231 Smart Insights, E-commerce conversion rates – how do yours compare?, 2021; Shopify, E-Commerce benchmarks, 2019; Unbounce, The Unbounce Conversion Benchmark Report 2020, 2020.

232 Crunchbase, Net Dollar Retention, 2018.

233 The Seventh Sense, 11 data backed strategies to increase your average repeat purchase rate, 2018; Omnisend, 10 E-commerce benchmarks you need to know, 2017.

234 AirBnB/TBWA/Chiat/Day, How to create loyalty beyond reason, 2017.

235 Indi Samarajiva, How Uber discovered that 80% of its ads were useless, 2020.

236 Wordstream, Understanding Return on Ad Spend (ROAS), 2020; Searchscientists, ROAS For ECommerce Stores, 2019.

237 Brian Balfour, 5 Steps To Choose Your Customer Acquisition Channel, 2013.

238 Unbounce, The Unbounce Conversion Benchmark Report, 2020.

239 HubSpot, The Ultimate List of Email Marketing Stats for 2020, 2020.

240 smile.io, How Uber's Referral Program Drives Radical Growth, 2017.

241 Curata, The Content Marketing Pyramid: A Strategy For Generating More with Less, 2017.

242 Upworthy, The Sweet Science Of Virality, 2013.

243 Metrilo, 3 eCommerce Conversion Funnels: Practical Guide, 2017.

244 Wordstream, 10 Remarketing Facts that Will Make You Rethink PPC, 2019; Wishpond, 7 Incredible Retargeting Ad Stats, 2021.

245 Omar Mohout, *Lean pricing, pricing strategies for startups*, 2015.

246 Kevin Hale, Y Combinator, Pricing 101, 2019.

247 First round review, It's Price Before Product. Period., 2016.

248 First round review, It's Price Before Product. Period., 2016.

249 Madhavan Ramanujam, Georg Tacke, *Monetizing Innovation: How Smart Companies Design the Product Around the Price*, 2016.

250 See more questions in Sean Ellis and Morgan Brown's *Hacking Growth*.

251 Andrew Chen, How do you find insights like Facebooks "7 friends in 10 days" to grow your product faster, 2021; Mode blog, Facebook's Aha Moment is simpler than you think, 2015.

252 John Egan, "How we increased active Pinners with one simple trick," 2016.

253 Addy Dugdale, Zappos' Best Customers Are Also the Ones Who Return the Most Orders, 2021.

254 For Entrepreneurs, Inside Sales Best Practices, 2012.

255 Aaron Ross, Jason Lemkin, *From Impossible to Inevitable*, 2016.

256 HubSpot, Sales Close Rate Industry Benchmarks, 2021; Aaron Ross, Jason Lemkin, *From Impossible to Inevitable*, 2016.

257 Sam Thomas Davies, 7 simple but powerful ways to lower SaaS Customer Chum, 2021.

258 Tom Tunguz, Blog "SaaS Investors Dilemma," 2015; Point Nine Blog "SaaS Metrics: Benchmarking Your Churn Rates," 2015.

259 Crunchbase, Net Dollar Retention, 2018.

260 Salesforce, Building a Booming Market That Oracle Long Ignored, 2009.

261 Aaron Ross, Jason Lemkin, *From Impossible to Inevitable*, 2016.

262 Drift, Why Slack's Growth Strategy Led to Billions Without A Sales Team, 2016.

263 Harvard Business Review, Stop Email Overload, 2012.

264 CNN Business, Salesforce to buy Slack in $27.7 billion deal, 2020.

265 SaaSX, SaaS Sales Efficiency Calculator, 2018; Thomasz Tunguz, Sales Efficiency benchmarks for SaaS Startups, 2013.

266 Matt Dixon and Brent Adamson, *The Challenger Sale*, 2011.

267 For Entrepreneurs, An Argument for Specialized Sales Teams, 2012.

268 Aaron Ross, Marylou Tyler, workbook from the book Predictable Revenue, 2015.

269 For Entrepreneurs, An Argument for Specialized Sales Teams, 2012.

270 Harvard Business Review, Why Women Are the Future of B2B Sales, 2020.

271 Mark Roberge, *The Sales Acceleration Formula, Using Data, Technology, and Inbound Selling to go from $0 to $100 Million*, 2015.

272 HubSpot, Everything you need to know about Sales Commission in 2021, 2021; Mailshake Blog, 7 Sales Commission Structures, 2019.

273 Details on sales commission plans in: Jacco van der Kooij, Fernando Pizarro, *Blueprints for a SaaS Sales Organization*, 2018.

274 Nicolas De Kouchkovsky from Sales Hackers provides an excellent overview of the 950+ tool providers with a potential starting point to populate a tool provider longlist: Sales Hackers, The 2019 SalesTech Landscape, 2019.

275 Mark Roberge, *The Sales Acceleration Formula, Using Data, Technology, and Inbound Selling to go from $0 to $100 Million*, 2015; Mark Roberge; Sales Hiring.

276 Matt Dixon, *The Challenger Sale – Taking Control of the Customer Conversation*, 2013.

277 Gabriele Oettigen, *Rethinking Positive Thinking: Inside the New Science of Motivation*, 2015; Alexander Graham, *Excellence in coaching: The Industry Guide (2nd ed.)*, 2010.

278 Medium, The greatest Sales Deck I've ever seen, 2016; Medium, The greatest Sales Pitch I've seen all year, 2017; Medium, The (second) greatest Sales Deck and Pitch I've ever seen, 2017.

279 Drew Beechler has written a very good description on storytelling by Salesforce here, 2021.

280 A good overview is available here: Cropper Chronicles, A Breakdown of 5 Lead Qualifications Frameworks, 2019.

281 Mark Roberge, *The Sales Acceleration Formula – Using Data, Technology, and Inbound Selling to go from $0 to $100 Million*, 2015.

282 BCG, Three Steps to creating Value from B2B Discounts, 2015.

283 Gainsight, How to determine the best Customer Success Manager Ratio, 2015.

284 ToTango is one of the CSM tool providers and uses similar metrics: YouTube: Everything Customer Success, Measuring the Effectiveness of a Customer Health Model, 2017.

285 Net Promoter System, How the Net Promoter Score relates to Growth, 2021.

286 Matt Dixon, The Effortless Experience, 2013.

287 Matt Dixon, "Reinventing Customer Service," Harvard Business Review, 2018.

288 Medium, What Startups can learn from Amazon's cash machine, 2017.

289 Matt Rickard, The Negative Operating Cycle, 2020.

290 Raconteur, 5 companies that reset their supply chains, 2020.

291 Techcrunch, Deciding how much equity to give your key employees, 2020

292 Crunchbase, How to Maximize Founder Equity at Exit, 2018; Y Combinator, A Guide to Seed Fundraising: Fundraising, Seed Round, Investors, 2016

293 See the vision on Web3 and the crypto space of the Managing Director of the Launchpool Techstars Web3 Accelerator, Pete Townsend here: https://www.techstars.com/newsroom/ investment-thesis-1-0-launchpool-web3-techstars-accelerator

294 Chan Kim and Renée Mauborgne, *Blue Ocean Strategy*, 2015

295 Ali Tamaseb, *Super founders: What data reveals about billion-dollar startups*, 2021

296 Noam Wasserman, The Founder's Dilemmas - anticipating and avoiding the pitfalls that can sink a startup, 2012 (Chapter 4)

297 Anu Hariharan from Y Combinator provides a very thoughtful perspective on the business models mentioned below here.

298 Klipfolio, CAC Payback Period | MetricHQ, 2020

299 Index, Expanding into Europe, 2011; Index, The US Expansion playbook for European founders, 2020

300 Cody Slingerland, The Complete Guide to SaaS Sales | Software Sales Tactics and Strategy, 2020

301 A good list of VC lawyer firms is available here.

302 Lewis Hower, Deciding how much equity to give your key employees, Techcrunch, 2020.

303 TechCrunch, Convertible Note Seed Financings: Econ 101 for Founders, 2012.